Promiscuities

...er and
...ts for
...Music
...by

..ay With Me)"
..Music Co.,

..ce Springsteen.

..y Anne Cameron
..mission of the

..age 57 from *Sappho's Lyre:*
..Copyright © Regents of

..Naomi Wolf.

..dex.

..havior. 2. Women—
..ed States—Social

..p://www.randomhouse.com/

..on acid-free paper

..tein

Grateful acknowledgment is made to the following for permission to reprint previously published material:

BMG MUSIC PUBLISHERS: Excerpt from "Gypsys, Tramps and Thieves" by Robert Stone. Copyright © 1971 by Careers-BMG Music Publishing (BMI). All rights reserved. Reprinted by permission.

DUTTON SIGNET, A DIVISION OF PENGUIN BOOKS USA, INC. AND ASHGATE PUBLISHING LIMITED: Excerpts from *The Tao of Love and Sex* by Jolan Chang. Copyright © 1977 by Jolan Chang. Rights throughout Canada are controlled by Ashgate Publishing Limited. Reprinted by permission of Dutton Signet, a division of Penguin Books USA, Inc., and Ashgate Publishing Limited.

DWARF MUSIC AND BIG SKY MUSIC: Excerpt from "Just Like a Woman" by Bob Dylan. Copyright © 1966 by Dwarf Music. Excerpt from "Lay Lady, Lay" by Bob Dylan. Copyright © 1969 by Big Sky Music. Excerpt from "I Want You" by Bob Dylan. Copyright © 1966 by Dwarf Music. All rights reserved. International copyright secured. Reprinted by permission.

HAL LEONARD CORPORATION: Excerpt from "Hot Child in the City" by Nick Gild... James McCullogh. Copyright © 1978 by Beechwood Music of Canada. All rig... the world excluding Canada are controlled and administered by Beechwood M... Corporation. All rights reserved. International copyright secured. Reprinted... permission of Hal Leonard Corporation.

JOBETE MUSIC CO., INC.: Excerpt from "Just My Imagination (Running Aw... by Norman Whitfield and Barrett Strong. Copyright © 1970 by Jobete... Inc. Reprinted by permission.

JON LANDAU MANAGEMENT: Excerpt from "Because the Night" by Br... by Norman Whitfield and Barrett Strong. Reprinted with perm... Reprinted by permission of Jon Landau Management.

PRESS GANG PUBLISHERS: Excerpts from *Daughters of Copper Woman* ... (Vancouver: Press Gang Publishers, 1981). Reprinted with perm... publisher.

UNIVERSITY OF CALIFORNIA PRESS: Excerpt from Fragment 8, ... *Archaic Lyric and Women Poets of Ancient Greece* by Diane Rayo... the University of California.

Library of Congress Cataloging-in-Publication Data

Wolf, Naomi.
Promiscuities: the secret struggle for womanhood ...
  p.   cm.
Includes bibliographical references (p.   ) and ...
ISBN 0-679-41603-X (acid-free paper)
1. Teenage girls—United States—Sexual b...
United States—Sexual behavior. 3. Uni...
conditions—1960–1980. I. Title.
HQ27.5.W65   1997
306.708352—dc21   96-46724

Random House website address: htt...

Printed in the United States of America

98765432

FIRST EDITION

Book design by Carole Lowen...

Promiscuities

*For Fay Goleman
and her
great-granddaughters,
Yardena and Rosa*

Experience, though no authority . . . were
right enough to me. . . .
—CHAUCER, "The Wife of Bath's Tale,"
The Canterbury Tales

The happiest women, like the happiest nations,
have no history.
—GEORGE ELIOT, *The Mill on the Floss*

Acknowledgments

This project belongs to many people who have helped me on many levels. My parents, Deborah and Leonard Wolf, and my brother, Aaron Wolf, carefully read the manuscript in its several drafts. Ann Godoff and Alison Samuel, both of them editors of radiant intelligence, were instrumental in developing the vision of this book from the beginning. Both women strengthened it immeasurably with their different insights and with their shared care and patience. Lynn Anderson was a perceptive and meticulous copyeditor. John Brockman and Katinka Matson, my agents, always remind me, with their friendship, what is lastingly important in the life of the writer. I cannot imagine the process of having completed the book without the unflagging efficiency of Martha Norbeck, who ran my office, and without the dedicated, skillful, and thoughtful research assistance of Shona Sabnis. That both of these young women worked so very hard while simultaneously completing their educational requirements and fulfilling other professional commitments has been an inspiration to behold. Daniel Goleman, Dr. Thomas Laqueur, Judy Coyne, Claire Messud, Rhonda Garelick, and Dr. Pepper Schwartz kindly gave the manuscript readings based on their different fields of expertise, and made invaluable suggestions. To Frederica Mathewes-Green I owe the genesis of my discussion of the relation of "petting" in earlier sexual mores to current debate. Fay Goleman, my grandmother, to whom this book is dedicated, and who was a pioneer champion of sex education in a course she taught at the University of the Pacific for many years beginning in the 1950s, made her long-range perspective available to me, in addition to her extensive library of mid-century course materials on sexuality.

Like many working parents, I was able to finish this project only with the help of many hours of child-care support. It is difficult to express just how appreciative I am for the loving, creative care given to my daughter, over the course of two years, by my parents-in-law, Joan and John Shipley, by Ann and Thomas Shipley, Christine Goodwin, Rosario Vasconez, and by my own parents as well. I hope that all of these caregivers, who were so much part of the production team that they should see the final result as a testament to their many hours of affectionate work, know how aware I am that nothing here could have been imagined, let alone completed, without them.

David Shipley, my husband, was this book's most thoughtful reader, commenting upon the manuscript in many stages; he contributed the insights for which he is justly beloved by the many other writers who have been lucky enough to have had him as their editor.

Above all, I am grateful to the women who decided to narrate their experiences to me. They gave many hours of energy, thought, and emotion to "come down in time," as the Neil Young song puts it. Their reason for doing so is that they wanted the world for girls in the future to be a better one. I can think of no more generous motivation for the risks of honesty and self-reflection that they took in order to get these stories down, and into the hands of the girls and women to whom they might be of use.

Contents

Introduction:
First Person Sexual

Secrets

How do we turn girls into women?

This discussion, which has recently taken on new urgency, often seems to me to be full of euphemisms, with crucial parts of the story left out. As we who grew into womanhood during and after the sexual revolution know, in our culture girls are turned into women through what happens to them, and what they choose to do, sexually.

It has been difficult to discuss this aspect of girlhood because the years of female adolescence that so determine girls' confidence are now inscribed with scenes, events, and memories that are extremely explicit. What ordinary contemporary girls can choose to do, and what is done to them, is very different, a much more intense sexual drama, than it has ever been before.

I wanted to retrieve this secret struggle for womanhood that now characterizes female coming of age. I call it "secret" not, of course, because teenage girls' sexuality is invisible; nothing is further from being the case. From the Brooke Shields Calvin Klein ads of my own adolescence to today's talk shows (Ricki Lake: "You Slept Around, Mom; Why Can't I?") to infuriated debates on teen motherhood among middle-aged men on the Sunday morning political programs, girls' sexuality is everywhere on display. It is made use of for dissection, proscription, and, most frequently of all, titillation. But the question of what to make of girls' sexual experience is usually taken out of girls' own hands.

In important work, many caring adults have sought to give girls voice. But many of the accounts we have are based on the observations of adults who were born and raised before the sexual revolution brought about this vast shift in the environment. Mary Pipher, in her book *Reviving Ophelia*, for instance, notes the difference between her own relatively sheltered upbringing and the sexual, violent world girls grow up in today. Sociologists of this generation are sympathetically documenting a strange new tribe whom they must visit across a cultural fault line.

But my girlhood, and the girlhoods of my contemporaries, took place on the far side of this fault line. We were among the first members of this new tribe, whose mores, when we were growing up, were part of an isolated phenomenon, but which have now spread so widely as to inform, if not define, the very nature of adolescence in America.

As I looked around for the stories, familiar to me from my own experience, of girls' secret struggle for womanhood in the post–sexual revolution world, and as I listened to women ranging from their teens to their thirties narrate the virtually always "extreme," *normatively shocking* narrative of their sexual coming of age, and as I listened to the younger women cast about angrily for rules that made sense, for guidance in the chaotic sexual world they inhabit, I began to feel strongly that the story I needed to tell was as close to hand as my own girlhood and the girlhoods of my contemporaries.

So the following is not a polemic but a set of confessions, a subjective exploration based on a collection of real-life stories. The emotional information yielded by these events is of a different, more intimate nature than that produced by surveys or questionnaires. By telling my story and asking other women to tell theirs, I wanted to elucidate the emotional truths that emerge from a particular generation's erotic memory.

I also wanted to write this book in this way because the teenage girl, as she is beginning to emerge within our debates, is understood more clearly as a victim of culture and sexuality than as a sexual and cultural creator. There is good reason for this, which has to do with the perils of teenage self-reporting: my teenage friends and I would have endured tortures rather than reveal to an adult interviewer, no matter how compassionate, any number of the things we were actually thinking about, doing, and saying. It is still far, far more acceptable to tell tales of submissive personal confusion in the face of a toxic culture than it is to assert the many ways, still unspeakable, in which teenage girls—the same ones who are so often genuinely victimized—are also, at other times, sexual marauders and adventurers, cultural analysts and subversives, fantasists and sapphists, egoists and conquistadors.

This book's title is about just this tension between the said and the unsaid. "Promiscuous," a word generally applied only to women and to gay men, is one of the harsh epithets with which the culture condemns a woman who has any kind of sexual past. It is a word that holds within it the mixed messages girls today are given about sex: "You're promiscuous if you do anything, but you're a prude if you do nothing," as one young woman put it to me. "You're *betrayed*," she said, using stronger language and a more vehement tone than I had been prepared for, "either way." The fear of being labeled promiscuous accompanies contemporary girls on each stage of their erotic exploration. If this story of growing up has a leitmotiv, it is the recurrent discovery of what the (very vivid) idea of the "slut" means in the life of a contemporary girl or young woman, how it regulates her behavior and becomes a category that assigns a meaning she did not choose to life events that she did choose. I want to explore the shadow slut who walks alongside us as we grow up, sometimes jeopardizing us and sometimes presenting us with a new sense of authentic identity; sometimes doing both at once. In looking at how the shadow slut still qualifies girls' and women's sexual development, this book asks: What might women's sexual subjectivity be like in a world where female desire was not blurred and tainted by such epithets?

For "promiscuous" can also be a broader, gentler word. It derives from the Latin, and can simply mean "of various kinds mixed together." This definition could stand as the best description of the sexual experiences through which late-twentieth-century girls learn what it means to become women.

Another reason I felt the need to tell these stories has to do with history. Women my age and younger have inherited a sexual script, derived from both the feminist and the sexual revolutions, that is by now out-of-date—or, rather, that requires a new ending.

Many women of our mothers' generation wrote critically about having been female in the shadow of the repressive hypocrisy of the fifties, and of "finding themselves" by casting off that era's inhibitions. For a quarter century, their conclusions have shaped much of our discussion of sex, women, and freedom. But conclusions drawn by a frustrated virgin no longer apply to the harder-to-talk-about experiences of the ambivalent slut.

In much writing from the feminist and sexual revolutions, for instance, the aim of giving girls and women access to the technologies of freedom—contraception and legal abortion, information about female sexual anatomy—shines like an unambiguous prize of victory. Women my age and younger inherited this. But this book could stand as the cautionary chapter that history insisted on adding to the hopeful premature conclusions of both revolutions. While, growing up, we had access to the technologies of pleasure, we still did not inherit a culture that valued and respected female desire. In some ways, our easy access to these technologies, in the absence of a true change in consciousness about whether women's desire is even a good thing, simply shifted the characters and settings of the melodramas of young womanhood—from frustration at endless petting without intercourse to frustration at early intercourse without petting; from the scarring, punitive back-alley abortion to the scarring, normative, legal abortion. Safer access to physical ecstasy, in a world that was not yet ready to tell us that *what we felt was good*, did not do away with our own, very different, set of sexual penalties, double standards, and sorrows.

Finally, I was also taken with this approach because of how storytelling relates to the process of "becoming women." Bombarded as we are by scripts that we did not write about becoming women sexually, we struggle to create meaning out of our "becoming women" through a rich, active, raunchy, subversive, even slapstick inner process of storytelling. Happy, sad, or, most often, paradoxical, these thoroughly crafted sexual autobiographies are as familiar to our most private selves as are our favorite books or songs. As we grow, we maintain within ourselves this intimate, well-told history.

These private histories tend, by early adulthood, to become fixed into a coherent story line. The important signposts that pointed to what it meant to be a woman in the culture, the revelations about what it meant to become a woman in one's own eyes and the eyes of one's peers, stand out in our memories with heightened significance: "This is what that signified in my progression toward womanhood," we think when we go over these private histories. "This is what I learned from it."

In private, we tell ourselves and our women friends—and the men friends whom we trust with this information—these tales. Yet these narratives are rarely spoken outside that private space or after adolescence, because they include elements of sex and greed, danger and narcissism, insecurity and bad behavior.

For these stories are not, of course, fit for public consumption. The honest facts about female sexual development in adolescence—especially the facts of girls' desire—have sustained a long history of active censorship. This history has ranged from public censor Anthony Comstock's persecution of Margaret Sanger for her 1912 printed lecture, "What Every Girl Should Know," with its frank account of sexuality in childhood, adolescence, and womanhood, to the nationwide wave of censorship that got *Our Bodies, Ourselves* pushed off high school shelves in the 1970s, to the 1996 episode in which Peggy Orenstein's excellent *Schoolgirls* was, because of a few pages in which girls spoke honestly about desire, targeted by religious groups.

When adolescent narratives of desire are driven underground, harm is done to the psyche. The straightforward narrative of a girl's life up to that point—most of which she could probably reveal to others—is transformed into a sequence broken by hiatuses, and stitched around great areas of silence.

These ordinary secrets of female adolescence are the ones you will read about in this book: about how pride in one's body becomes illicit; about being in love with other girls; about improper fantasies; about the intensity of female desire in adolescence (which is so shocking to us to confront, even while we take for granted that a sixteen-year-old boy's desire is not so different from a twenty-six-year-old's); about being "loose"; about wanting sexual attention; about violations and the ambiguities that can surround them; about brushes with the sex industry; about older men.

As adult women, the blanked-out places can keep us in a tiring state of low-level dishonesty: "I've never done this before." "That wasn't like me." "I don't know what got into me." A whole set of scenes, memories, sensations are still there within us, but they have become unclaimable. We must not know what we know, acknowledge what we have wanted, recall the sensation of what we have touched. On the empty spaces, the culture then is free to project an everchanging, always demanding set of images that have little or nothing to do with the true texture of the self.

"Your past is supposed to begin," as one woman said to me, "the moment a man lays eyes upon you."

Women's literature also gives examples of how erotic coming-of-age stories in the biographies of women—fictive and actual—are often wiped out, even though this is one of the great watersheds of female consciousness. Lolita is created and re-created by men, but she rarely writes her own account of events.

The biographies and memoirs of women usually exclude this material. There are exceptions, of course: Mary McCarthy, in *Memories of a Catholic Girlhood*, concedes it, though the heroine's sexual initiation is described in a blanking-out that, we will see, is typical: the half memory of pleasure is erased by the girl's virtual lack of consciousness. But the coming-of-age writing of Elizabeth Barrett Browning, Simone de Beauvoir, Doris Lessing, Jill Ker Conway, and even Betty Smith, author of the twentieth-century female adolescent classic *A Tree Grows in Brooklyn*, moves elliptically over the young girl's sexual curiosity, discovery, and pleasure. In fact, when that teenage erotic passion is acknowledged—as it is in Margaret Mitchell's *Gone With the Wind*—it is such a rare concession that women by the millions cherish the tale.

This gap in women's culture is particularly notable considering what a staple of the genre the male version is. If one is hard-pressed to locate narratives of female sexual awakening, one can scarcely escape the male counterparts. The male sexual bildungsroman is such a set piece that it is almost a cliché: from Jean-Jacques Rousseau to D. H. Lawrence to Ernest Hemingway to Jack Kerouac to J. D. Salinger to Philip Roth to Tobias Wolff, it seems that just about every male writer wants to tell you how he or his young fictional stand-in first felt sexual, first or most memorably got laid.

Male writers recover this material more often in a mood of liberation than with forebodings of subjugation, and for good reason: men usually aren't punished for it. Male readers and writers appear to take for granted that an account of masculine development should recognize the hero's crossing the threshold of sexual initiation, that integrating these years of discovery into male identity is important.

From their comfort with the material relative to women, it seems that male writers know the cultural rule that men participate in the definition of their sexual experience, and generally define it positively.

Women—whether they are writing, fighting a custody battle, bringing a harassment charge, or just trying to do their jobs—rightly fear that they, in many more ways than men, will be defined by their sexual experience, and defined negatively.

This taboo against women's ownership of their sexual past is not just a matter of literary taste; in the real world, it is also really functional. In spite of the rhetoric of freedom that surrounds us, women's reclamation of the first person sexual is filled with the risk of personal disaster. The diary of female sexual experience has often enough met such a bad fate that it is not surprising that women are wary of any public record of this past. Sappho's poems were burned and burned again, both literally and in the censure directed by male commentators at her fragmentary, fragile accounts of female desire. Anne Frank's comments about her emerging sexual feelings were—necessarily, given the time, but unfortunately—deleted from the earliest published versions of her diary. Teenage murder victim Jennifer Levin's journal, which may have included descriptions of her sexual experiences, was dubbed "Jennifer's sex diary" in the tabloid press, and her murderer's attorney tried to subpoena it to use against the dead girl. JENNY KILLED IN WILD SEX screamed the tabloid headlines.

When someone's past does "catch up with her," the rest of us wait and watch. And after the furor subsides, we sometimes breathe a guilty sigh of relief: the bullet that time had someone else's name on it. The woman in question has been scapegoated and separated from the "good girls," as rape accuser Patricia Bowman was in *The New York Times* article that described her as having "a little wild streak." Women can still be "ruined" by having a sexual past to speak of, just as they were with different methods of punishment in the eighteenth and nineteenth centuries. When narratives of sexuality are attached to the lives of grown women, however tangentially, the associations undermine their authority, as when Judge Kimba Wood lost her claim to the post of attorney general partly because of adverse publicity over her having worked for five days as a waitress in a Playboy club twenty-seven years before. Women learn—still—that any sexual "past" can be read as promiscuity, and that the taint of promiscuity can lead to social or professional censure.

But the punishment aimed at the woman who has been sexualized in this way inhibits all of us and can keep us from actions ranging from charging a supervisor with sexual harassment to running for school board to fighting for custody of our children. And in the wake of the sexual revolution, with the line between "good" and "bad" girls always shifting, keeping us unsteady, as it is meant to do, it will not be safe for us to live comfortably in our skins until we say: You can no longer separate us out one from another. We are all bad girls.

Apart from the desire to get closer to girls' emotional truth, why go through the intermittent personal discomfort of writing in the first person sexual, that most unladylike of voices? Partly out of stubbornness: if you are a girl, that is something you are encouraged not to do. That voice turns you into a slut. The few times I have alluded in writing to a sexual past, the reaction in some quarters has been so sharp that it reminded me afresh: in that direction a hardworking taboo lies. We must write that way again and again, until the taboo loses its power.

For another result of the silencing of the female first person sexual voice is that public debate treats female sexual experience in a way that has little to do with the ambiguities of real female lives: it posits false dualisms of good and evil, villains and saints, and—most destructive of all—sexy women who have bought in to male pressure or are engaged in appeasement, and sexless women. Like many women, I am weary of such stereotypes. Because of these stereotypes, it becomes all too easy to dismiss, for instance, numbers about sexual assault; we lack girls' voices describing just how normative, how thoroughly interwoven into the rest of their experience such episodes are.

Paradoxically, we also have a very unclear sense of what female sexual consent actually looks like. Too little good information is available to boys growing into men that illuminates what female desire actually looks and feels like, how to recognize it, and how to respect it. Girls, too, get bad sexual information and inherit a culture that misleads them about their own desire.

Desire
This book is also an inquiry into the nature of female passion, into the ways our culture values and devalues it, and into how cultures other than our own have understood it.

The sexual revolution certainly brought about a heightening of physical fulfillment in women. But many women have also confided to me that this alone does not provide them with a satisfying erotic self-recognition, since the sexual revolution raised neither the value nor the understanding of female desire high enough. In some crucial ways, it actually lowered both. To these women, the current images they see of female sexuality seem at best superficial; at worst, they seem to derive from a culture that does not much like women's desire at all. Many women have told me that they sense in some hard-to-define way that their desire, purely sensed and not filtered through a toxic culture, might well feel more fierce and more clean and more precious. But they say that they do not know how to imagine their way beyond the cheap images and scripts of our own place and time. As one friend put it to me, referring to her desire, "I know that comes from a good place. But that place is so covered over with stuff like this"—we had just seen the movie 9½ Weeks— "that I can always get to the pleasure but I can't always get to the good place it comes from."

To see how we were made into women through these often-distorted messages, I sought to reconstruct the "libraries" of adolescence that my girlfriends and I plundered for sexual information and imagery. The ragbag selection included: *Seventeen* magazine ("Your Reputation: Is It On the Line?"); *Penthouse; The Happy Hooker;* the characters of Betty (virgin) and Veronica (nonvirgin) in the Archie comics; *The Sensuous Woman;* Nabokov's *Lolita;* R. Crumb comics; *The Rocky Horror Picture Show;* the dog-eared early 1960s guides to "personal hygiene," popularity, and "petting" that were the only texts in our junior high school library to address the subject of girls and sex directly; Kotex and Tambrands "sexual maturation" guides, produced to be used in gym class; older girls; our mothers and their friends; and, for those of us with enlightened moms, our copies of *Our Bodies, Ourselves*—pages of which we knew by heart.

I engaged in this reconstruction because one aim of this book is to look at just how the scripts and images we have of female sexuality came to be what they are and how we can change them to reclaim for women that sexual "good place." For while the female erotic *drive* has been a steady force, assumptions about female sexual pleasure— and hence women's experience of their own pleasure—have varied wildly from era to era.

Growing up at the height of the sexual revolution, we were deluged with information about female sexuality, as we still are; but the information was and is still selective and distorted. We did not know we were and still are laboring under some major myths about women and desire.

I discovered this when, using the tools of an adult, I investigated the libraries of adulthood. In diaries, academic surveys, anthropological accounts, and social and medical histories I found some of the information about women and their desire that my younger self and my girlfriends, laboring in an information-saturated age under many kinds of ignorance, did not have. Better kinds of information about women and desire than the kinds our culture offers were not available to us; nor, indeed, are they easily available to most adult or teenage women even today.

The anthropologist Margaret Mead concluded in 1948, after observing seven ethnic groups in the Pacific islands, that different cultures make different forms of female sexual experience seem normal and desirable. The capacity for orgasm in women, she found, is a learned response, which a given culture can help or can fail to help its women to develop. Mead believed that a woman's sexual fulfillment, and the positive meaning of her sexuality in her own mind, depend upon three factors:

1. She must live in a culture that recognizes female desire as being of value;
2. Her culture must allow her to understand her sexual anatomy;
3. And her culture must teach the various sexual skills that give women orgasms.

Well, we girls in the 1970s had access to cultural resources numbers two and three, but our access to the first resource was, to say the least, ambiguous. Yet one myth that defined our adolescence was that, when it came to women and sex, we lived in the world's best epoch.

The story of women's desire that I learned as a teenager from the newly liberal and liberated culture was a meliorist one that went something like this: "Once upon a time long ago, women were enslaved by Old Testament morality; then, their sexuality was reviled by St. Paul, whose misogyny was codified by the Catholic Church. For nineteen centuries the church and the state repressed women's desire relentlessly; this repression was completed during the Victorian Age, with its pruderies and hypocrisies. Then Freud released modernity from the straitjacket of Victorianism, but he got it wrong by dismissing the clitoris. The 1950s were particularly bad times. Finally, the combined forces of the Sexual Revolution of the 1960s and the second wave of feminism set women free. Masters and Johnson, Kinsey, and the subsequent wave of popularizers all 'revolutionized' sex by declaring that there was more to lovemaking than intercourse. And now, in the 1970s, we were in the midst of an unprecedented Golden Age for women. The End."

Hence, we as teenagers were meant to believe that the sexual pop culture we saw everywhere around us—from *Penthouse* and *Story of O* to rape fantasies, miniskirts, and the Pill, from *Playboy*'s subsidy of abortion-rights organizations to sex-toy parties for suburban homemakers—was all supposed to be the manifestation of women's sexual freedom. The female erotic millennium was said to be dawning.

We were not taught that there have been other places and times in which sexual ideologies valued female desire much more profoundly than our own culture does. In a few other cultures, women's sexual pleasure has been placed at lovemaking's very center. A few cultures—or, at least, cultural moments—in the past have revered the transcendent level of sexual feeling in women and organized some aspects of social life to honor rather than to degrade it. I will be glancing at some of these other cultures, ranging from the Han Dynasty of ancient China to pre-Conquest Mexico. I will also look briefly at how some other societies, especially tribal societies, have managed to mark the passage from girlhood to womanhood. I don't offer these glimpses as if they are a comprehensive history of female sexuality. Nor do I offer them as if they could demonstrate the existence of bygone sexual utopias for women; there has never, so far as we can know, been any such thing. Rather, I offer these glimpses as a reframing device. Perhaps they will help us dream differently, help us understand, for instance, that just because our own time and place teaches that sexualizing women (and, certainly, sexualizing women more than men) lowers their status, that conclusion, which so informed our thinking as girls, is by no means inevitable.

Another signal myth that prevailed when we were growing up, and can even prevail today, is that "men want it more." This view is one I still hear, passed on with confusion and discomfort, from young women. But anatomists and sex educators over the last thirty years have found more and more evidence that women are not only designed, anatomically, to be at least as sexually intense as men—but even that women's capacity for pleasure is extreme in a way we have yet to accept.

We did not know, growing up, that our prevailing notion—that the male gender is the one more driven by lust—is a fairly recent historical invention. For most of recorded history, women's status as the more carnal sex was pretty much taken for granted, so much so that women's presumed carnality was used to justify their persecution. The witch-hunter's bible charged that "All witchcraft comes from carnal lust, which is in women insatiable." Only in the nineteenth century did Europe and North America engage in what can be called the Great Forgetting of what had been everyday common sense in many other times and cultures. Our own prevailing notion—that boys and men are more driven by lust than are their more sexually passive female partners—would have made people in many traditional Taoist, Islamic, Hindu, and Native American cultures, as well as Westerners of times not too distant, roll their eyes.

As time went on, I found that my reading into the lesser-known history and anatomy of female sexual desire became, for me, a form of recovery and redemption of the past. I read, in a sense, to redeem the slut in me, the part that feels (as it does, perhaps, in many other women) vulnerable no matter how many external signs of respectability I acquire; to reframe, if I could, the simultaneously very good and very bad girls that we, growing up, knew we were.

Method

Some of these tales are drawn from memory. Others are drawn from conversations I had with the women, now in their twenties and thirties, whom I sought out in 1996 in my hometown. I asked them to help me remember what it was like to grow up sexually when we did and how we did, how their own erotic autobiographies composed themselves in their own minds, and what conclusions they drew from the sexual events that had mattered most to them.

The conversations took place informally: a few women talking late into the night in hotel rooms or sitting on the floor in someone's house, the mood shifting rapidly from nostalgia to anger to hilarity to sadness. Occasionally, if we were at someone's home, a woman would get up to grab an old Tubes album or check an entry in a worn diary. Often, as a memory resurfaced, and the meaning of it was reconsidered through the eyes of a woman rather than a teenager, a silence would fall. During the discussions, time sometimes seemed to play tricks—to lengthen, as an image, a joke, or a dance we had forgotten was re-created in the conversation, or to telescope as the impressions and words crowded each other out.

The lives that follow are not representative. All the women whose stories I recount are white and more or less middle class, and the sexual codes they were learning were mostly white, middle-class codes. White middle-class American girls are members of a tribe, just like any other subculture, with certain clothing, language patterns, and belief systems. This book is about one subset of that tribe. I write about this tribe because it is the one I know best.

These girls' experiences are in some ways not unique: all over the country, millions of middle-class girls were having experiences both more dramatic and more ordinary than ours. In other ways, they reveal a particular worldview and time, specific to our location, an unusually libertine medium-sized city situated on the extreme western edge of the American continent. Though materially many of these girls were better off than many of their contemporaries, their crises and confusions are not confined to their demographic.

Because of the subject matter, the identities of everyone in the book have been disguised. To protect their privacy I took pains to alter names, personal features, parents' professions, and locations while being as true as possible to the events themselves, the girls and boys involved, and to the general subculture that surrounded us. The issue of who "owns" a life—the living person or the writer—can be a vexing one. I believe that, especially when it comes to something as private as sexuality, the living person owns his or her life and the writer must respect that. I feel this especially strongly in relation to women, who so often feel that their sexual biographies are wrested out of their control. All of the women whom I interviewed as adults asked me to tell their tales without using their names or including details that might identify them or others involved, and in the case of each woman, I have done so. Some of the women wanted to speak so anonymously they declined even a pseudonym.

As for what we said to one another, I've done my very best to reconstruct conversations that took place twenty years ago. While I am sure of the mood and the substance of the subject, and I checked slang and phrasing with those who were around at the time, I am not certain of the exact words; and memory is always idiosyncratic. In addition, the demands of reportage directly conflict with the demands of ethnography: in the former, the events and people involved must be identifiable; in the latter, they must not be. I hope to offer the reader "real toads in imaginary gardens," to paraphrase Marianne Moore; and following Emily Dickinson's imperative that could be an epigram for the enduring inhibitions in women's speech about sexuality: to "tell all the truth—but tell it Slant—" for "Success in circuit lies."

This subject of growing up female in the recent past is one to which the time and place in which my friends and I grew up might bring some particular illumination. Not only did we grow up during the sexual revolution; we also grew up, in a sense, *inside* the sexual revolution. My house was just above the Haight-Ashbury neighborhood in San Francisco, the loose-knit community that became a symbol of the erotic and material liberation of an entire culture.

The years and the place are unique in the time line of female sexuality: after the Pill but before AIDS, female desire seemed, in our adolescence, hedged about with fewer penalties than ever before— or, as of this writing, since. As one of the women I spoke with commented with a rueful grin, "Those were rockin' years."

They were. And they were also years of some chaos in the lives of children, and, particularly, female children. The following accounts include drug and alcohol abuse, early sexual activity, sexual incursions, early abortions, and experiences involving parental abdication. I have taken pains not to overstate these pressures upon us. My friends and their families were not considered to be in any way unusual or deviant. As I was going over the interviews and seeing in black and white proof of what I had known only informally and anecdotally—episode after episode of adult distractedness and family breakdown—a wry private subtitle would come into my thoughts: "an ordinary American girlhood." For while readers of another generation might think that some of the more sensational events in this account are extreme, readers of my background, who are my age and younger, will probably recognize many of them as being fairly typical aspects of coming of age in late-twentieth-century America. My hometown wasn't mainstream America, but it was a place where winds were blowing that would eventually touch and then transform the rest of the country too.

Some of our struggles as girls about the boundaries between women and men were intensified by the breakdown of the boundaries between adults and children. For we grew up in a society that proclaimed a sexual revolution in the absence of a coherent new sexual ethic; adult libido was released in what often felt like an absence of either constructive or repressive adult boundaries. The experiments of the revolution, great fun for adults, were sometimes played out at the expense of children. My recounting of what it was like to be a female child and teenager in the center of the decade-long Summer of Love is an argument, both bitter and loving, with my historical parents, the values of the sixties. Volumes have been written from an adult point of view about the wide social consequences of that great upheaval. Far less is known about how those of us who were children at that time absorbed its blessings and curses. As our parents pursued their own trajectories, we children became closely acquainted with the fallout from their flight. The sixties were no fringe legacy to us children in San Francisco. Well into the seventies, they created the texture of our lives.

We would encounter the most harmful manifestations of the times in the shape of thirteen-year-olds wearing dominatrix costumes alongside the adults showing off their tattoos in the cold air outside *The Rocky Horror Picture Show* every Friday night, the affluent parents who would take their children out of school for a week at a time so as not to miss the good snow at Tahoe, and in the baggies of elephant-tranquilizer-laced Sensimillan that bearded men in their thirties sold with a joke and a mellow smile to fifteen-year-olds at Grateful Dead concerts.

Nonetheless, many of the gifts of the time counterbalanced the corruptions. In spite of racial tensions in our schools, in its most hopeful moments the city could envision racism as a ludicrous attitude of representatives of the past that was in the process of withering away. The hippie ethos gave us a city of murals and street theater, where creativity and play could expand the sensibility of the most jaded; and, perhaps most important of all, in the form of the gay liberation movement, we saw love—human, physical, sexual, romantic love—stand as a metaphor for the highest good and animate the idealism of an entire culture.

I have no feelings about this contradictory epoch that are not ambivalent; delight and mourning are so closely intertwined that they seem part of one another.

Though details have been changed, what I hope remains intact is the essence of a group of girls' sexual coming of age in a particular set of circumstances in late-twentieth-century urban America. This is how we grew. And this is how it felt.

Promiscuities

The Time and the Place: 1968–1971

O nce upon a time, a scattered group of girls undertook the passage from girlhood to womanhood in a city built around a bay.

These are the girls who set out on this journey. In my earliest adolescence I encountered Dodie, my first real girlfriend, who lived up the block; Michelle, her single mother's mainstay; Cath, my brooding, impatient playmate in middle school; Shari, our mutual love object, the golden girl who dominated the just-adolescent neighborhood's society and who lived with her mother in a small apartment emptied of furniture by her mother's divorce from her airline pilot father; and Genevieve, with her delicate frame and lullingly confident demeanor, who was as self-contained and stealthy as a little cat. By middle school, my friends included Tia, whom I would meet at camp, and Dinah, theatrical and vulnerable, who lived in the working-class Mission District. My high school peers would be Sandy, the shrewd social commentator from the small crew of elite girls of a neighboring high school, whose memories I drew on particularly heavily (when she was a teenager, her parents kept a catering business barely afloat); Trina, broad-shouldered and straight-talking, was rigorously raised by her realtor mother; and Pattie, a serene girl with cropped hair whose single mom was a college secretary. Two of the girls I interviewed were three or four years younger than the rest. Jeanne had multiple piercings in her ears and one in her navel. Her extended family is made up of middle-class journalists and realtors, but as a teenager she lived at subsistence level with her mother, a potter, in a hippie enclave, sometimes in substandard housing, in the agricultural flatland south of the city. Tonya was a buzz-cut protoslacker who grew up in the suburbs in a family of somewhat conservative professionals.

The girls whose stories I recount here are almost all white, of Protestant, Catholic, Protestant-atheist, Jewish, or Jewish-atheist background. The extended clan of kids our age who hung out together was slightly more diverse: a few girls were Filipina, one or two boys were Mexican, and several kids were of mixed African-American and white parentage or were white kids with a black step-parent. My background is white and ethnically Jewish. My family occupied that odd place in the class structure that you inhabit when your father is a professor at a small state college and your mother is a graduate student: when we were growing up our family was cultur-ally upper middle class but economically lower middle class, paying rent rather than a mortgage and often worried about monthly bills. While all the girls can be called "middle class" in the American tradi-tion of vagueness about that term, their parents' incomes ranged widely. Some of the parents were affluent—investors or owners of major downtown businesses. Some were professionals—lawyers, doctors, social workers. And some—not a few—were much worse off, experiencing the hidden stresses of middle-class downward mobility: these parents included married couples who lived in a house of their own but were always one disaster away from bank-ruptcy. Several of these parents were heads of single-mother house-holds reeling financially after a divorce, living on the fringes of the professions or the arts, paying the basic bills with sporadic alimony payments, salaries from ill-paid middle-class "women's" jobs, or, in two cases, a welfare check.

The elementary school in our neighborhood was an integrated public school just above the Haight, well cared for and small. The public junior high school most of us went to was huge, poor, and anonymous. It had been built in the fifties on the unfashionable southern side of town, and every fall, it seemed to us, it was the set-ting for delicately choreographed double racial conflicts: Filipino versus Chinese, white versus black. Locker raids would turn up chakka sticks and switchblades. At times during these fights police cars would appear, to escort our school buses. The school over-looked flat avenues whose small sandy gardens and identical stucco houses in pastel colors stretched out to the sea. Some of us went on to a magnet high school that drew students from all over the city but whose population, and dominant teenage culture, was mostly first- or second-generation Chinese.

My parents, my older brother, and I lived in a rickety pre-1906-earthquake house perched several streets above the Haight-Ashbury, beside a long staircase that cut into an overgrown hillside. The streets just below were poorer; the street above, which became the theater for the neighborhood kids' social life, was much richer. Our family was eccentric but more or less stable.

The tremors that shook the other households up and down our block as the 1960s unfolded shook ours, too. But one aspect of our family life that my brother and I felt increasingly separated us from our peers was that the parent-child lines of authority were somewhat more old-fashioned, perhaps because of my father's Eastern European and Orthodox Jewish immigrant background, and his age—fifteen years older than my mother. Though they would participate quite actively in the upheavals of the time, our parents would also drag us to synagogue and Hebrew school. As the Haight turned upside down, we were still expected to be home for dinner each night, no matter how haphazard or bizarre the meal that my exasperated young graduate-student mother flung onto the table.

As the sixties turned into the seventies, I could feel things in our neighborhood begin to change. The postdivorce, post–sexual revolution, post–moral relativism world of today was taking shape. It created the conditions of our childhood.

The Haight-Ashbury had begun as a modest, uneventful part of town where a perpetual grit blew and where, during the forties and fifties, working people, white and black, had raised their families. But as time went on, what I could expect to see while dawdling at my mother's side grew less and less predictable. I began to notice that the young women I saw seemed to be freer than the tightly tailored, smiling girls on the early-sixties TV of my earlier childhood. They also seemed to be increasingly confused. One morning, one of them, standing nearly motionless at a bus stop, offered me some orange juice. My mother snatched it away just as I was about to drink it. "Hey," the young woman said to her in slow motion, "lighten up." "You don't know what's in it," my mother explained later. At about the same time some acid had been placed in trick-or-treat candy one street away. Not long afterward, another dazed girl showed up on the steps in front of our front porch. Beautiful, pale, and unresponsive, she had drifted through the eucalyptus trees exactly, I thought, like a wood sprite. My parents took her indoors and managed to contact her solid midwestern parents, who asked us to hold on to her for a few days until they could pick her up. My brother recalls that, at one point, still high, she tried to jump off the low roof of our house. My mother, who had been watering the garden, warded the girl away from the edge with her hose.

For a while, the Haight still had its hardware store, its liquor store, its two Laundromats. It still had its drive-in diner with a sign of a cowboy hat with steer horns attached. ALWAYS OPEN read one side of the revolving sign. NEVER CLOSED read the other. It still had its bowling alley with foot-long hot dogs and scalloped paper napkins. But new and very different enterprises were opening daily: the Free Clinic, for example, where you could wander in and get aspirin or sleep off a bad drug trip. On the corner of Cole and Haight, a freshly painted mural showed a rainbow, each band of color representing a stage of evolution. Amoebas swarmed in the blue, amphibians marched in the green, and in the orange band was a captivating scene of mammals—deer and elk and field mice—all psychedelically dancing. The least popular development of all in the eyes of the hardworking local merchants, the Free Store, opened its doors for business. You just walked in, chose what you wanted, and walked out. Head shops opened, too. They sold all manner of drug paraphernalia. They also sold posters of Country Joe and the Fish, scenes of Mucha-like nude women surrounded by pulsating rays, and charts that showed all the possible sexual positions. The counters displayed candles shaped like enormous penises ("Where did you see that?" I remember my mother asking, trying to keep the alarm out of her voice, as I, at six or seven years, drew a picture of one of the very biggest ones—purple, as I recall—that was on the lowest glass shelf, at child's-eye height).

Eventually, the neighborhood was entirely taken over by an influx of new characters. In Golden Gate Park, the stately carousel and placid duck pond stood intact and elderly Irish ladies still fed the birds. But someone had painted the carousel pillars the colors of the rainbow. All day long, every Sunday, the rolling beat of bongos would echo through the valley. Grown-ups gathered on the green fields in the park wearing clown makeup or lying together in a heap, faces to the sky, giggling. Grown-ups blew bubbles, played dress-up, and danced. There were puppet shows on street corners. Children were everywhere, usually naked on warm days, but they were peripheral to the adults' playtime. Sometimes it seemed as though everyone was a child. When, as an adult, I saw a documentary on the Summer of Love that showed a naked four-year-old trying desperately to get his tripping, dancing mother's attention until he started to cry, I felt my heart contract. I had an emotional memory of similar gatherings where playmates of mine had tried and tried to remind their parents, who were having so much fun, that they were still there—and still small.

The fact that a revolution of the senses would take place in our town had something to do with the interaction between the physical place and the people who gave themselves over to it. For our town made it hard to have ultimate faith in any belief system that made claims beyond the pleasures of the senses. San Francisco is a city built for sensual mysticism. Under its white sky and the fog that sometimes lets you see no farther than a block in each direction, it is easy to feel drawn toward ecstatic experience; there is nothing to choose but God, oblivion, or the body. Many people have described the physical beauty of San Francisco, but not so many have considered the influence of its various kinds of seductiveness on the orientation of a developing mind. We were growing up in a city so alluring that our personalities took shape around the supremacy of the idea of pleasure.

In every direction you were hit in the face with beauty. The gorgeousness was so excessive, it was like slapstick: the city poured champagne over your head again and again. It conspired to turn you into a hedonist. The camp and squalor of a tourist town crowded up against the blue opera theater of the bay. If you were not being overcome visually, the food would overcome you: fat, greasy Chinese noodles with shreds of sweet-salt dried pork; hot-fudge sundaes at Ghirardelli Square, where the ice cream salon had a miraculous marble vat the size of an ancient bathtub in which, all day long, rollers swept a four-foot-long wave of hot, thick chocolate back and forth.

The culture and landscape asked you to yield to the goofy sweetness of the moment and to all the excitement you could absorb from the day. There were entire neighborhoods so saturated with sensuality—visual, tactile, olfactory—that the alleys from which the famous vistas dropped away seemed to run with a perpetual current of desire.

Part of the excitement, too, was the precariousness of life on a fault line. Because we were California girls, each point on the map in our heads was punctuated by natural disasters. Disaster was the landscape's memory. We did not feel as confident of being rooted in the environment as our peers back East did. We felt that the land had been empty very recently, except for the Native American tribes that had lived less heavily on it before us, and that it could shake us off easily enough, and be almost empty once again.

Our schoolbooks reinforced our sense of being at nature's mercy. We learned about Death Valley, just a day's drive past my grandmother's house in Stockton, where the pioneers had had to drink brackish water and had cast their belongings by the side of the road to lighten the load for their parched horses and oxen. Down the highway from my summer camp was Donner Pass; as small children, we had trouble forgetting the image of the families in the Donner party who, in October 1846, trapped by continuous snow, survived by eating bark, twigs, and mice, and, at last, the bodies of their dead companions. Statues in neighborhood parks commemorated Fra Junípero Serra, who founded the missions that wrenched native-born populations from their civilization. Here, farther north, our textbooks taught us, the Lewis and Clark expedition had ended. And here, following the coastline, Sir Francis Drake's *Golden Hind* came to anchor, close-hauled around the westernmost promontory of her exploration; here boomtown Seattle had burned and San Francisco had trembled.

Most of all, there was the earthquake—"the Big One." By third grade we had learned about the terrible morning of April 18, 1906, when the sleeping city had been shaken into rubble within two minutes. I became obsessed with that earthquake and with the image of a gaudy, magnificent, lawless city—a city, once nicknamed "the Barbary Coast," built around a core of drinking and wild spending, where prostitution thrived on streets with names like Maiden Lane reduced to ruins. I used to stare at daguerreotypes of kitchen maids, standing arms akimbo, on the crests of hills familiar to me, their backs to the photographer and their picture hats still on, facing the scene. Before them plumes of smoke reached to the sky, façades were stripped away like wallpaper, and each neighborhood was a heap of snapped matchsticks scattered down to the bay. Horses lay dead in piles on the streets; telegraph wires had exploded into flames. Nature was stronger than civilization.

We were earthquake literate: we knew that the earth does not swallow people whole (though there was a photograph in a grade school library book of a black-and-white cow standing patiently in a rift). We knew the danger was not from the quake itself so much as from the collapse of a building (stand under the door lintel) or from fires that started near open gas mains. We knew that water would be scarce and that after it was all over, we should go to meet our parents—as the survivors of the '06 quake had done—in Golden Gate Park. Often at night I would imagine making my way down the hill to the park after the quake had hit and picture the hours of waiting for my parents to find me there, not knowing whether they would ever arrive. It was my first encounter with the possibility of my parents' vulnerability.

Though there were only a handful of tremors as we were growing up, the threat of the Big One—always anticipated, like a primitive local deity who, daily, both threatened and spared us—determined some of our relationship to our own physical identities. Nature was so greedy and so strong that there was little argument from our part of the world when the theory was presented that our own libidinous nature was stronger than civilization. And since nature was potent, we should be ready: cataclysm is imminent, so party now, eat now, do it now. Either the ocean or the earth will devour you—so devour what you can.

As we grew up, the idea of earthquake excited us; as we came of age, we felt subliminally that it turned everybody on. It gave girls in the Bay Area the license that young women have in wartime: If today is your last day, do you really want to die a virgin?

Not us. The city made us feel that we were not alive if we were not being sexual. The city my girlfriends and I explored as we grew up was a series of different worlds, and each provoked a different kind of sensual response. Down on Fisherman's Wharf we could wander through a scene of garish excess for the senses. There were bakery stalls piled with sourdough bread; alleys heaped with crushed ice and barrels of oysters and bins of crabs that were still moving; lighthouse scenes and Japanese gardens made of shells that lit up from within; eighteen-foot-high plastic columns filled with gum balls in every color; piles of saltwater taffy of every hue and flavor. Even the smells and sounds of that part of the city were sensual: the wharf was jammed with boats and stank pleasantly of warm pitch, caramel, and brine, and the men who watched the stalls passed lewd shouts to one another over the heads of tourists and teenage hometown girls.

"Sexland" was another neighborhood. The earliest images of female sexuality that I remember seeing were in the straight men's Sexland—North Beach and the prostitutes' neighborhood alongside it known as the Tenderloin.

One early memory, from when I was about eight, is of my best friend, Dodie, and me trying to peer inside the heavy, dusty red velvet drapes in a street-level window of the Paris Massage Studio on Taylor Street. The drapes screened everything behind them; their opacity itself was exciting. In front of them stood various Venus de Milos crafted in plaster. The sign outside was shocking pink. From an early age, we understood that the color of female sexuality was hot pink—pink neon, like the sign, or Balenciaga pink, like lipstick. The sign had black French-style scrollwork and big round lights around the edges. It signified the forbidden—whatever it was that everyone wanted, the secret place of satiny femininity. This hint of "sex" was still an early-1960s Baton Rouge kind of sensibility. This was a place where, we imagined, handsome men wearing narrow ties and holding slim cigars would come to pay homage to the lush creatures in feathery boas whom we would someday grow up to be. Behind that curtain, we imagined, these women had these men entirely in their power. We wanted to go inside.

Later, when I asked the girls I grew up with about their earliest memories of images of female sexuality, this image came up again and again. Sandy said, "I remember that. There was a girl sitting in there one night. She wasn't moving. She looked like she was made of wax. I knew what it was, even though no one had told me."

At eight, Dodie and I found the scene enchanting. For a while we were so preoccupied with what went on behind that curtain that we would study the listings for massage parlors and "go-go dancers" in the back of the *Chronicle's* entertainment section. Those listings would be considered quaint now; at the time, their raciness lay in what they concealed as much as what they promised. The women were featured and applauded in the ads exactly the way new flavors were advertised at the Baskin-Robbins ice cream shop where we would be taken for a treat. "Brandi," "Lola," "Kiki": the ink drawings were demure cartoons showing girls with heavy lashes and bee-stung lips. We wanted so much to be part of that world that we phoned the numbers and hung up, dying of giggles. Little girls have larger-than-life egos but feel invisible much of the time. Sex, it seemed from the listings, was a magic that would make us visible. We wanted to be featured like that, our names in lights, our charms described on the page for all to see.

But "sex" was also coming out from behind the red curtain. Around the same time, my father was arrested because of a nude ballet. My father's college, San Francisco State, was the site of a good deal of student activism. He was one of the early educators to work with "the kids" in the counterculture, and he helped to found a halfway house, called "Happening House," where teenage runaways could get food, shelter, and counseling. The kids slept on foam-rubber pads, and one room was filled entirely with foam rubber: we were allowed to leap and roll on it. During his absence one day, and without his knowledge, a radical group, the Yippies, staged a "happening": a nude ballet. For hippie culture, of course, public nudity was a statement of rejection of "establishment" values. The police busted the dance: twenty-four armed men burst in, trying to round up a group of naked dancers. When my father came in, the police asked, "Who's in charge?" "I am," he replied. He was booked. I was very frightened that he would never come out of jail. When he was released, after his acquittal, there was a big party at our house, with popcorn and strawberries, to celebrate. A paper sign hung on the wall, to welcome him home. It had two cherubs on it, their genitals covered with real fig leaves. I understood that this was a joke. I understood, too, that some people's decision to dance naked had almost destroyed our lives, and that the people at the party considered my dad to be a champion of something, and the worldview of the police to be a bad joke. I think I even half understood that two interpretations of nakedness were at war and that the stakes were high.

The last neighborhood that mattered to me was unlike any of the others: the landscape of nature, in the form of the forest behind our house. Our old house perched on stilts halfway up the crest of Mount Sutro was on the edge of a eucalyptus forest that was often hidden by fog.

The forest was magical. The eucalyptus trees shed their skins as they grew; strips of bark hung in layers from every trunk. Their leaves, shaped like sickles, had a dusty sheen into which I could press a perfect fingerprint, and their fruit was a round hairy button marked with a perfect cross. When the wind blew, the trees tossed and glittered like mercury. The whole forest smelled of medicine.

The forest floor was thickly overspread with a mat of vines. The same covering hung from trees and rock faces, with sunlight angling through gaps. The vines gave the forest a look at once wild and civilized, like green-paneled, green-draped drawing rooms whose roofs had fallen in. In the darkest part of the eucalyptus forest was a rock landing overlooking a deep ravine, where, when I was still small, I knew the older kids went to get high and have sex.

Nature's impulses and habits were used by the world in which I grew up to redeem anything—and sometimes to justify anything. It was easy to make the connection between nature and license. That neighborhood was, sensually, the best place of all: you could lie on your back, look up at the strokes of the leaves, and feel perfect. "If it feels good, do it," we would learn. If we had a question about sex as we grew older, the response "It happens in nature" generally signified the end of the conversation. Nature was the final arbiter, taking over the role of organizing principle that Law and Custom, increasingly derided, slowly had to relinquish. In that forest I first learned to kiss, and later, almost, to make love. It seemed at once to be a place that was entirely sexual and a place where nothing impure could happen.

As my understanding of the kinds of scripts about sexuality available to women bore down on me, the forest would function the way that fantasies of wilderness functioned for the urbanized eighteenth-century European mind: I would find myself making a mental reference to the forest when I searched for a symbol for female lust that was not derided and caricatured by the images that populate our world.

The changing scripts about sexuality did not remain in their various neighborhoods. Pretty soon, they began to come up to our comfortable block tucked away above the Haight and almost surrounded by the forest. They began to transform what happened in the middle-class and upper-middle-class white families that lived on the street. They changed the clothes our teachers wore and the expectations we children had, and they radically challenged the sense of safety we had taken for granted in our earliest childhoods. In their final effect, these scripts would break down the idea of childhood altogether; we would become that cute, troubled, adulthood-coveting new species, "kids." I think that we who were small in the early sixties were perhaps the last generation of Americans who actually had a childhood, in the Victorian and post-Victorian sense of childhood as a space distinct in its roles and customs from the world of adults, oriented around children's own needs and culture rather than around the needs and culture of adults.

2

The Facts of Life

I t used to be that girls watched their mothers and learned how to be women that way. But by 1968, it seemed that our mothers were suddenly watching someone else—the media equivalent of Barbie, the James Bond girl, and the blond Carnaby Street dolly bird—and learning to be women all over again in a new way. We too were watching Barbies and learning what womanhood meant. This upended the natural progression of the generations and, at a critical moment in our development, would give some of us—those who would look more like Barbies than our mothers could—more power than they had.

Barbie was the first toy that taught us what was expected of us sexually. The fact that some of the moms were trying to become hip young Barbies made it that much more important for us to understand. The twelve-inch dolls held the key to it all. That is why girls, now as well as then, are obsessed with them.

Barbie taught us a lot—sometimes more than we wanted to know. Her posture showed us that being sexual meant being immobile. It meant: walk on your toes, bust out, limbs rigid. My friends and I would prance around trying to imitate her. The doll also raised several generations of girls whose first memory of being sexual and grown-up was walking on tiptoe. We learned from Barbie's feet that the most important activities for us would be those we would perform à pointe. We would have to learn to twirl, sashay down a runway, and someday stretch up to a tall man for a kiss. If there is any doubt that Barbie is designed to appeal to girls' fascination with what the culture considers to be appropriate female sexuality, think of the doll that came out when we were children that actually grew breasts when you twisted her arm.

When we were eight, we would still try to play real games with Barbie. Dodie had the whole Barbie ranch house set, the pink convertible, Barbie and Skipper, and the eunuch Ken. As we played, we would shake each doll in turn to indicate that it was speaking. But there was always something a little forced in play with Barbie.

"Dancing at the embassy tonight?" Dodie's Barbie would ask my Skipper in a not-bad British accent.

"Why, certainly," Skipper would mince, twisting her torso. "And first we'll have drinks at the club."

"What shall I wear?" Barbie always, always wailed. "And my hair is a mess."

"How about this?" The lower-caste Skipper would open the dollhouse closet and gesture to a glittering cocktail sheath, slit up the side.

"Oh, come on!" Dodie would boss in her normal voice. "Barbie can't wear that. This is a *ball*." I might shoot her a look, but they were her Barbies.

Finally the Barbies were dressed. We could choose from a pink charmeuse baby doll, a green sequined Motown gown, a fire-engine-red jumpsuit with a real zipper, a black Chanel-style bouclé suit, sueded bellbottoms with real fringes, and daisy-patterned halter dresses. Most of Barbie's clothes suggested a night in a speakeasy or an afternoon in a harem. But once we'd dressed the dolls, there was not much to do. That was it. They were adorned. When they showed up with Ken at the embassy, it was hard to imagine what they would say.

"Sooo . . ." Dodie would hold up Ken (now a diplomat) and gamely ask in a deep "male" voice. "You are enjoying your visit to our country?"

Barbie would flash the white of her teeth, cock her head, swivel on her torso, half raise her smooth arm, but she could say nothing. This was always the moment in playing Barbies when the play turned sour. For Barbie had no conceivable character or inner life. Her life force consisted of a filled suitcase, little hangers made of pink plastic, the flexible rubber shoes that matched every outfit, and her blank, mound-shaped breasts. It was easier to invent a character for Skipper: she still had no breasts.

Barbie's breasts and clothes seemed to blunt her personality. In Barbie's life, events were merely excuses for ensembles. Her story could really go nowhere. Which meant, perhaps, that once we got over the excitement of getting provocatively dressed and then undressed, our story too would go nowhere.

We were fixated on Barbie, but we also despised her. The secret game in countless American basements and playrooms involved (and still does, I am told) little girls doing bad things to Barbie. Sometimes we would make her take positions that were ludicrous or that looked painful. Other times, we would pop her head off the rounded stump of her neck. While this was a nice, French Revolution sort of vengeance, it also scared us. It was scary because even when you held her body in one hand and her head in the other, nothing seemed much changed. After all, she had been made up of parts to start with. Even when fully assembled, she wasn't whole. Her hands didn't grasp, her feet didn't walk, her face had no expression. We would never in our lives have as many clothes as she did.

Dodie and I wanted her to be in charge, but how could she be? What was Barbie's job? We knew perfectly well. We were not stupid little girls. Barbie did not have a real job, and she did not have a real husband. The insipid Ken was a front. The nurse's outfit you could buy for her was as unpersuasive as a French maid's uniform would have been. She wasn't going to wear it to empty bedpans in a hospital. These outfits, we knew or intuited, were about erotic fantasy.

Barbie's profession was open to speculation. How did we think Barbie paid for her wardrobe, the candy-apple-pink convertible, and the ranch-style bachelor-girl house with the plastic rock garden? We half guessed, without any sure sense of how such arrangements worked, that she lived in that fabulous house because someone out of the picture—some man, not Ken, not handsome and young—was picking up the tab. She wasn't an heiress. I think we imagined that Barbie was something like a call girl.

So, with these images were the ambitions of Dodie and me and our other friends on the block shaped. We sometimes wanted to be Marie Curie or Jo March or Harriet the Spy. But those girls and women were sexless, and we did not want to give up the promise of the sex and of the hot-pink clothes that went with the sex. Between a sexless Marie Curie and a hot-pink Barbie or Brandi or Kiki, even with the ambivalence we felt about their sexiness and thus about our own, there was no contest: Barbie, Brandi, and Kiki won.

Sandy remembers the earliest images she had of Barbie-style sexuality. "My very first memory of female sexuality," she recounted, "came from my baby-sitters. They were teenagers, pre-1968 version: miniskirts, hair that flipped up, pale lipstick. They looked like dolls. Women who looked like them were on *The Dating Game* in bright colors. On TV, female sexuality was about these dolls who were obsessed with getting dates with men. It was not a mature sexuality. They were like little pieces of candy. They wore baby-doll dresses and little flat ballerina slippers. There was no power in their sexuality. They were playthings for the Hugh Hefner types. There was a board game called Mystery Date, so I picked up that men were important and you were supposed to attract them—but for what? You were supposed to pick a husband, I guess. And then you got to go from *The Dating Game* show on to *The Newlywed Game*. Being doll-like was part of how you reeled in a man. But what you did with him after you reeled him in—I had no clue."

With the elevation of the Barbie ideal came the demotion of our mothers' status in terms of what they did when they cared for us. If Barbies didn't have much power, moms—who had no TV show we would want to go on—had none at all. According to the sitcoms of the early to mid-sixties—*Julia* and *Bewitched*—mothers dressed modestly. There were, we all knew, two kinds of women: sexy girls and moms. Sexy girls were essentially Barbies; Barbies were in James Bond movies and Millie the Model comics. The comic-book character Veronica, as someone has observed, was a Barbie; Betty, her lesser rival and sidekick, was a future mom. Barbies went on yachts, wore chiffon, and had high-coiled hair and interesting accents. Moms didn't.

Moms—the old moms, the stay-at-home moms—did everything else. No one wanted to be around them. They went nowhere and did nothing; they came on in commercials to worry about the dishes. They wore housedresses. (When asked what they wanted to be, many of the girls in our elementary school classes dutifully said, "A mom." The more adventurous said, "A stewardess." But that second answer was code. It meant "I want to grow up to be a Barbie.")

Unsurprisingly to us, the moms started changing. My mother had a ladylike fur hat that she put away one winter, along with two pairs of white gloves. After about 1967, these stayed forever in her right-hand bureau drawer, yellowing at the fingertips, along with the other disgraced accessories of her past life—the scratchy gold lamé cocktail dress, the circle-stitched brassiere that made two torpedo cones, and the baby-doll negligee with its floating layers of beige and biscuit silk. She bought an ankle-length Afghan coat with curly fur on the inside and embroidery on the skin side. It smelled of goat. By the spring of 1968, she owned minidresses made of triple blocks of synthetic Day-Glo color—fuchsia, tangerine, and lime—and a suede halter top with snaps.

For now, suddenly, our mothers were becoming sexy girls. Who, then, would be our mothers? Who would our mothers be?

Early on, you could ask a mother, anyone's mother, to do anything: get you a drink of apple juice or a place at dinner, provide a ride home. As time progressed, though, many of the mothers, certainly mine, would shut the door to an improvised study made out of a breakfast nook or dining room, and for a few hours every afternoon we would have to play quietly and not disturb. "Shh," we told our playmates, and they told us, humoring the change that for a long time we took, or hoped to take, as a game, "Shh. Mom's working."

Fathers, too, were changing. In some ways that was even more frightening. When we were smaller, the fathers had been uniform and reassuringly bland in their navy suits and white shirts, like politicians on television. Like Darren, like Dagwood, they always came home. But even that gave way. We became less afraid of them. Though we could still remember the days when they had come home from work like the walking embodiment of the law, everywhere, as the decade progressed, their discipline grew more lax. We could interrupt. There were whispered arguments between our parents while we watched TV—arguments about changing the rules, we gathered, that applied to all of us, the dads and moms as well as the kids—and these resulted in new, more permissive limits.

Someone gave my father a birthday present of a wide tie with stylized Peter Max naked ladies on it. He grew a longer beard. Then he grew sideburns, and his hair fell over his collar. At the end of 1969, for the occasion of my grandparents' golden anniversary, I saw my mother have her hair set for the last time. She never let hair spray come near her again. She let her hair grow out, wild and curly. Time was marked by my parents' growing brighter and brighter, furrier and furrier.

Up and down the block, the roar of social upheaval grew louder and closer. One by one, the families began to come apart.

In my girlfriends' houses, the most difficult thing they would face was the abdication of so many of the fathers. The boys shared equally in this pain. Every second kid in my elementary and middle school, it seemed, had a story about birthday gifts that their separated or divorcing dads had promised but which had never arrived in the mail, missing child support checks, custody visits abandoned for the sake of the dads' vacations, and the dads' new girlfriends, new wives, and new children taking all the money.

But girls' experience of the absence or abdication of their fathers marked them in all these ways—and in one more. The fathers' departure led directly to the girls' often shaky sense of sexual self-esteem. The boys lost their role models, but the loving parent of the opposite sex was still there to respond to them. Girls kept their role models, but just when the girls needed their fathers to be around to admire their emerging sexual identity from a safe distance—to be the dependable male figures upon whom they could innocently practice growing up—the fathers vanished.

This made sex all the more complicated an idea for many of the girls my age. We had understood as children from television and newspapers, and from those overheard whispered conversations, that the grown-ups were becoming preoccupied with something called "doing their own thing." This was a vague idea to us, but sex, or better sex, or sex with people other than moms and dads, seemed to us to be one of the most reverberating ingredients of this "thing." Sex, it seemed, in spite of their new Day-Glo colors, often made moms either sad or distracted, and it made dads go away.

To the female children on the block, then, there was a new kind of anxiety: How could one grow up to become, through sex, the kind of woman a dad would not want to go away from? The way they had to relate to their distracted, weekend or summertime fathers—the need to compete with the glamorous new wife, the other children, the father's self-absorption—was necessarily seductive. These girls could not sulk or rage too much, no matter how just their anger, and expect the man still to be there when the emotion subsided. They had to twinkle and caress and charm to get a father's attention. The romantic triangle with the rejected mother made that desperate seductiveness, and the conflict it engendered in the girl, all the more acute. Men could not be counted upon, girls this age often learned, but they could be lured into noticing you, if you were skilled and pretty and careful enough, for a little while. The fathers' departure created in many women my age a feeling of cynicism about the durability of the bonds of commitment and love and an almost blind religious faith in the strength of the bond of sex.

The undoing of Mrs. Brech's household was a microcosm of the general domestic disintegration. Michelle, her daughter and my friend, lived downtown. Her father was one of the first to go. He had grown out the lank blond hair under his bald spot and moved to an apartment complex in Walnut Creek with narrow balconies and a pool.

In revenge for what she saw as her husband's regression, Michelle's mom turned their house into a sort of commune—command central for the first wave of new and newly cool young divorcées. Mrs. Brech was now known simply, to her children as well as to her series of new lovers, as "Nora." Nora was the first mom to *have* boyfriends, a distinction her children's friends greeted with a mixture of fascination and dread. It was with the same confused feelings that Michelle and I stared at her mother's bras drying on the bar above the bathtub and tried to figure out, though we had a hazy sense of the possibilities, why Mrs. Brech had cut out the centers of the cups where the nipples would be.

In Michelle's house, suddenly, everything was permitted. She was ten when her dad left, and her sister, the noxious little Kyla, was eight. Kyla upended her mother's garden planters and taunted the dogs. Nora grew languorous and flip. Her hair, like my mother's, grew out. She lined her eyes with kohl and stopped cooking.

The chaos in the big, ranch-style house grew. The boss, the old-fashioned Father, was not coming home to dinner again anymore, ever. Dogs named Morrison and Janis urinated on the upholstery. Though the piano was still waiting in the formal dining room and the good china was still on display, they looked more and more like props from a theater piece that had folded. The parents had vanished, each in a different manner. With them had gone the idea of family law that they'd grown tired of wielding. And no one had stepped into the void. The ferns in the windows hung down in brownish strands. All was creativity and sensuality, flux and decay.

Nora smoked marijuana with her neighbors, her boyfriends, and, eventually, her children. By the time she was growing up, Michelle had more authority than her mother, and the hangers-on surrounding the family knew it. Instead of meeting at family dinners, the two kids and their mom would gather around the Formica-topped kitchen table to process marijuana. On a typical evening when I went over to play, Nora would be licking the tip of a joint while Michelle raked out the seeds from the leaves and Kyla got on everyone's nerves by fiddling with the volume control on the stereo.

Michelle and Nora created a bond that was replicated in my classmates' houses as the divorces spread: the two became "best friends." The divorcing mothers frequently wanted to be "best friends" with the children, it seemed, because their own emotional anchor was gone. The children, terrified that the family was half demolished and fearing it would fall apart entirely—and even sometimes relishing the status of honorary adult—in turn clung to that best-friend status. It was not just the mothers who courted the children's friendship. When the fathers showed up, they competed in this, though their courtship was through skis and stereos. From this moment a historical shift obtains, the effects of which we still feel today: adults, in an affluent country that had been premised on the notion of delaying gratification for the sake of one's children, began to put their own gratification first, and the children were left to accommodate the grown-ups' second infancy. Often, we became our parents' parents.

So that was how the center ceased to hold: one parent at a time decamped, folded his or her tent, and went off with tennis racket and pot pipes, a copy of *Siddhartha*, and boyfriend or girlfriend, leaving the children with everything they asked for.

Though tolerance, joy, and honesty were real legacies of the freedom of that time, there is no doubt in the minds of my friends and myself that children and parenting fell in value as the exploration of the self and the senses gained in value. The derision aimed at parenting was especially true of the popular culture's messages to men: we knew even as small children that a family man was considered "square." In the words of one young hippie guy interviewed in the film *The Summer of Love,* "These straights look at us and envy us. They're so tied down with baggage: the mortgage payments, the car payments, the wife, the kids." As the years went on, the popularization of "women's lib" made the life of a mother tied down to a home seem just as square. As children, we absorbed from that atmosphere a growing embarrassment at our childish dependence, a feeling that we were a weight, or an obstacle to our parents' self-realization. Many of us got the sense that, though our parents loved us, a part of them longed to be free of us. In that erosion of the emotional contract, the modern "kid" was born. Many of us responded to that elemental, if unspoken, rejection by acting out the wish to be free of our parents.

By the age of thirteen or fourteen, the children of these families would make their way to the unofficial meeting place in the forest behind our block. There they would huddle in the cool shade. Someone would take out a bong and scatter the old water. Someone else would gently pinch and smell the contents of a plastic bag. Farther in, on beds of dead leaves, children would separate into twos and learn to kiss and grope. Part of the appeal was the risky glamour of the drugs themselves. But a lot of it, for some, was just comfort. They were lonely. In some of those houses, there was no one, father or mother, really paying attention.

After a time, the "kids"—no longer children, since childhood now had few privileges—would rejoin the group, their hands in each other's back pockets. The person you made out with, the person you got high with, was a source of pleasure; but he or she was also, at least for a while, paying real attention to you. The boys, wearing down jackets, their hair parted in the middle, huddled over the flame of a lighter; the girls, wearing peacoats, their ankles cold in clogs, put their arms around the boys' shoulders. The pipe would pass from hand to cupped hand, each passing to each the glow of a little heat.

3

Activity into Passivity: Blanking Out

Becoming a woman, a *complete* woman, takes time. Your body must go through certain changes—gradual changes, wonderful changes. And so does your mind, your spirit.

At times, these changes are exciting for you. At times, they may be bewildering. . . . What's more, you hear so many *different* stories—many of them *conflicting*—that you may wonder what the facts really are.
—Tambrands, "Accent on You," 1973

Early adolescence—which for us meant the ages of about ten to thirteen—involved a twofold alteration of our identities in relation to sexuality. One aspect had to do with abandoning the activity of our erotic imaginations to become at least overtly more passive. The other had to do with relinquishing our excitement about physical space—which had been a sexual dimension for us—and accepting that, because of our sex, we would not be free to plunge headlong into the open world. This twofold change being worked upon us felt like preparation. Our unruly child's consciousness of eroticism was being smoothed over, as if with gesso on a canvas, so that the more socially acceptable, constrained, and yielding young-lady sexual consciousness could be applied to the surface.

When my friends and I were ten, whatever sensuality we had was definitely active. It was also in sharp focus. In the imaginations of the girls I played with, a general sensory excitement accompanied scenes of tension and adventure. Wrestling with one another, which we did continually, was vaguely erotic. We even made up elaborate games that would allow us to wrestle. At the park, for instance, we would play a game that went something like this: One of us would wait at the bottom of the slide. That girl would pretend that she was about to sink into a swamp full of crocodiles. The rest would cluster at the platform at the top, frantically reaching down and pulling the endangered one away from the snapping jaws of the beasts below. We could feel their crocodile breath and hear the sound of their jaws grinding. The San Francisco fog helped to mask the asphalt and monkey bars and rubber padding on the ground so it could become quicksand and creepers and jungle lotus.

The girls at the top would shriek louder and louder as the crocodiles climbed up onto the bottom of the slide with their huge, scaly claws. We would clutch one another to form a human chain. Two or three girls would grab the safety bars at the top, brace themselves against the platform, and hang on to the dress or arm of the delegated rescuer. She in turn would extend her body as far as she could down the slide, stretching every muscle, and the imperiled victim thrashing in the quicksand would struggle with all her might to reach the outstretched hand.

When contact was made, we would hoist with superhuman energy, and the beasts, enraged, would clamber halfway up the slide—almost to the top, where there was no escape for us!—before sliding back down the steel surface with a roar of disappointment. When we had lifted our comrade to safety, we would collapse together in a sweaty heap. And when one cycle was done, we would clamor to change places. We would quarrel over who would get to be the rescuer this time and who the rescued, and who had to remain in the less exquisite role of human ballast in the relative safety at the top of the slide.

When the new chain of girlish risk taking was configured and the crisis just averted, when our shrieks were released with their marvelous piercing quality into the moist, still air of the empty, late-afternoon neighborhood and our heartbeats slowed for a moment, we would scrabble upright, our heads spinning a little from being so high off the ground, adamant then, *right then*, to do it again.

It was the sense of struggling *toward* something together, and our skillful daring and power, that were erotic.

By eleven, though, I had learned my lesson. By observing the most desirable older girls, those creatures with the platforms and the lip gloss who did what the boys wanted when they were around them, we younger ones understood that you had to act a certain way to get boys to like you and that it did not include screaming with your girlfriends and running down the school hall together. Those desirable girls were completely different with boys than they were when they were being what we thought of as normal. They got quiet and hesitant and appreciative, and they broke off the string of clever, ironic social observations that characterized their usual speech—even as the boys grew louder and more extroverted than they usually were. Boys flocked around the girls who had mastered this trick. Being sexy meant waiting and not doing, being watched rather than watching. Behaviorists have a name for it: operant conditioning. You do this, you get that.

I began daydreaming regularly in Mrs. Claris's English class. I now understand that the images I dwelt upon were practice runs for a submissiveness that was unnatural and would take a lot of work to achieve. In my fantasy life, I was trying to figure out ways I could manage enough passivity to get Lucas Trujillo to like me.

Lucas Trujillo, seated across the room, was one of the class's acknowledged leaders. With his shock of black hair, he looked like Speed Racer. Even his name was cute.

I looked at him, and slow-motion soft-focus scenes would superimpose themselves before my eyes. I had a favorite image: an incarnation of "myself" had managed to swoon—the reason was unclear, I'd get back to that later—onto the linoleum floor in the center of the classroom. There "I" lay, half unconscious. Not the "me" that was familiar, the chubby, bookish, not-quite-social-reject wearing flared orange jeans with worn knees, my nails bitten to the quick, but a self that was transformed and even, to my conscious mind, silly. This self was pretty, older, darker, and more complicated, and for some reason she was wearing an Empire-waisted nightdress made of the sheer material that was also the stuff of *I Dream of Jeannie's* harem pants.

Somehow, my fantasy continued, Lucas would kneel to rescue me, perhaps using a little gentle CPR that would bring his attention (not crudely, but he could not help noticing) to the demure but definite bosom that, like the doll that grew breasts, I had arranged for my imaginary self. He would save me and become captivated. Not by anything I did; I knew that it was important, in this scenario, to say nothing and to remain very still. He would be captivated by what I, inertly, *did not do.*

What had so transformed the scenarios in which desire now fig-ured? We had learned that to become successfully sexual, we must not seek and initiate but wait and yield.

As we prepared for adolescence, our marching orders were con-tradictory, for some of the rules of the game we inherited came to us intact from the days of the dinner dance and had not been aban-doned with the sexual revolution. Passivity was one rule. Girls that boys liked were not supposed to ask for a dance. You were not sup-posed to kiss first. And while you were waiting for a boy to put his arm around you, you were not supposed to move more than a frac-tion of an inch. If you precipitated contact in any way, you would be going "too far."

Those confounding rules were hard for active, curious girls to put into practice. The culturally imposed process of "whiting out" our child's erotic consciousness—what Mary McCarthy has called "drawing a blank"—this intentional not knowing that girls are asked to yield to at moments of sexual experience, involved us, necessarily, in the task of becoming mysterious to ourselves. We began to notice that songs about "becoming a woman" centered on the woman's vagueness and lack of reality. In these songs, men were sexually infatuated with women they did not know, women who had no out-lines and no characteristics. One song—"Knock Three Times"—told the story of the sexual obsession of a man with his anonymous downstairs neighbor: "I can feel your body swayin' one floor below me, you don't even know me, I love you." The same scene was played out in the Temptations song "Just My Imagination": "But in reality she doesn't even know me!" "She takes just like a woman. She makes love just like a woman. And she aches just like a woman. But she breaks just like a little girl," crooned Bob Dylan. What did that *mean*? What was happening to her each of those times? How would we rec-ognize it? "I love you," a truck driver yelled out one day at a red light as my mother held my hand on Haight Street, and she smiled in spite of herself. Love you? He doesn't know you! I thought indignantly.

We would speculate with one another in maddening conversa-tions as we played in Dodie's basement. Our Mystery Date board game began to supplant our Barbies. What did it mean to "make love just like a woman"? How could we know? Clearly, it would not be enough just to grow up. There was something else involved. How would we learn? What if we didn't manage to "make love just like a woman"? What god-awful thing would we then be?

"Lay, lady, lay, lay across my big brass bed, . . ." Dylan sang too. "Stay with your man awhile, until the break of day, let me see you make him smile. His clothes are dirty but his hands are clean. . . ." Was a woman different from a lady? Better? Worse? Did it depend on the situation? What was she doing to him to make him smile? How could we learn that? Was there no deal in which he would make *her* smile? Why not? Sex, we understood by eleven, did not work symmetrically. "*Her* clothes are dirty but her hands are clean"—we already knew we would never hear that kind of line in a seduction song.

The woman's sexiness, when it wasn't a mystery, was often a thing or a single attribute: "She wore . . . an itsy-bitsy teenie weenie yellow polka-dot bikini" . . . "Every kind of girl there was, long ones, tall ones, short ones, brown ones . . . Spill the wine. Dig that girl." The message was that we had to be wanted in order to be allowed to want. We had to be mostly out of focus, except for a bikini or a hair color, to be sexy. It was not just a biological mystery that was enfolding us; it was cultural.

Carol Gilligan and Lyn Mikel Brown, in their classic *Meeting at the Crossroads*, eloquently described the way in which girls go from being distinct personalities at ten to amorphous, uncertain creatures at thirteen. An analogous process, I am convinced, takes place in relation to girls' loss of the "voice" of their own desire. The culture that surrounds girls signals to them that they must, sexually, forget themselves. They must become passive in relation to the energy of desire, or detached from owning it, even in the face of its increasingly active pressure.

This situation—the mystification that intervenes between girlhood and womanhood—reminds me of a scene in Lewis Carroll's *Through the Looking Glass*. Alice finds herself wandering in a beautiful, dark forest. She is joined by a young deer, which accompanies her in perfect amiability. The two share the journey with a sense of deep familiarity. But when they emerge from the wood, the fawn recognizes its companion for what she is: "I'm a Fawn . . . And, dear me! you're a human child!" The creature bounds away in alarm, leaving young Alice alone.

Something like this happens to us at the threshold of adolescence. "What are you?" the girl asks of her own desire—once her companion, now wary of the light. And: "What am I?"

The girl must now pass into the unforgiving glare of social reality in which human and beast—consciousness and appetite—confront each other in a state of estrangement before the relearning begins. The girl's consciousness and the animal aspect of her nature must assume names that insist they are separate beings ("And, dear me! you're a human child!")—rather than names that allow them to remain parts of each other. The girl, denatured, becomes a mystery to herself.

4

Free Flight to House Arrest: Slowing Down

Add some solo dancing to your agenda. Put on your favorite record and improvise freely. It's fun and excellent exercise too.
—Kimberly-Clark, "Your Years of Self-discovery," 1968, 1973

Cracklin' Rosie, get on board, we're gonna ride till there ain't no more to go . . . so hang on to me, girl.
—NEIL DIAMOND, "Cracklin' Rosie," 1970

T he second altering of consciousness that prepares us for becoming women relates to physical space. The young girl's lust for space comes at the same moment her culture tells her that her developing body puts her in danger whenever she roams "too far." She experiences at once an expansion of her desire for physical freedom and a contraction of her chances of gratifying it. The seductive world outside, forbidden to her when she was a child, becomes crosshatched with warnings and prohibitions. (In fact, child development specialists tell us that, at almost every age, boys have a larger allowable range of movement than girls do.) As little girls, we were luckier than most: we enjoyed a mobility that was erotic in itself. Almost every neighborhood was open territory. Public transportation in our city was cheap; with a student card it was almost free. And most of the time we were not bothered because, as little girls, we were mostly invisible.

Many of my earliest memories of moments that seemed clearly erotic involved moving fast. I recall three or four eleven-year-olds stretched out, mocking the events of the day, on the backseats of a streetcar, or bike riding along the Marin headlands, the vistas falling away too fast to see.

It is no accident that I remember so much of our preteen erotic awakening as being a form of movement. To little girls, the act of exploring the world outside is about the promise of growing up and an extension of exploring the body and the emotions. A distant landscape produces one of the little girl's first experiences of her individual self merging into the world, a feeling that is distinct from her childhood desire to merge with the maternal body. Losing herself in the physical world is an early thrill that a girl discovers her body can give her.

I noted earlier that few literary coming-of-age stories by women include the erotic journey. But when it does surface, it is often masked by an encounter between the heroine and the landscape. The young Maggie Tulliver immerses herself in what George Eliot called "the Red Deeps" in *The Mill on the Floss*; Catherine loses herself on the windswept moors in Emily Brontë's *Wuthering Heights*. As we prepared to become women, we had to learn that this sense of physical freedom would retreat into the space we must now reserve for fantasy.

I learned that lesson at ten. I was walking the five blocks from the bus stop to the day camp where I was spending the summer. Eager to get there—we were tie-dying T-shirts that day in big steel vats in the kitchen—I strode quickly in the straight, safe line my mother had pointed out to me: alongside the Sears display windows (then wait for the light); past the high, arched entrance to the firehouse—which I was to scurry past if I heard the fire bell. Eventually, I would reach the dusty playground with its throng of dreamy and distracted teenage counselors.

But that day, I met a danger that I experienced in the terms of the fairy tales and fables that were so real to me—stories of goblins under bridges accosting travelers. Just past the Fireman's Insurance Fund building and the firehouse itself, crouched in the triangular patch of ground where thick foliage grew, a devil waited for me in the underbrush.

"Little girl!" he whispered. "Little girl!"

I looked into the tangle of acanthus leaves. There, a young man was hunched over, his face just at the height of mine, barely visible under the overhanging bushes. He was handsome—I will never forget his young, vigorous face—handsome as the devil. He had a well-trimmed black beard and mustache and wore a woolen cap and blue jeans.

Losing my volition, I slowed down and then stopped.

"I've lost my contact lens," he said. "Would you please come here and help me find it?"

Why did I take those two steps toward him? The world is so without precedent to a child. I was flattered that he had addressed me as if I could be helpful to him. I had been raised to be polite to adults. And—fatal appeal, which of course he must have known—I wondered whether I could find it.

I moved slightly closer, halfway into the cave made by the brush. I left my lunch box as a sentry on the sidewalk. The bushes closed off the path behind me.

We were in shadow, piles of dead leaves all around our feet. The atmosphere was one of angry waiting.

Was he angry at me because I was hesitating? Was I doing something wrong? Was I being rude? I looked at the ground. There were a million dry, dirty leaves lying in heaps. I did not know what a contact lens looked like—except that it was very small.

At my hesitation, his tone of voice changed. It was no longer the seductive whisper that had so beguiled me. He inched closer, on his knees, and I could almost feel his breath. "Come on," he said roughly. "Come help me! Here—it's somewhere in here. You have to look harder."

He struck at the deep pile of leaves and scattered them. "Aren't you going to look?"

He had made a mistake. In a heartbeat, I understood that I too had made a mistake. The leaves were layers deep, and even I knew that if you are looking for something small you don't upset the surface where it has fallen. He had lied; and I was trapped.

Now I could see that his hand was moving oddly on something that could not exist: a white length, but alive.

I had not known anyone could be so afraid without dying. Except for the rattle of dead leaves, there was no sound. The noises of the day had fallen away. Nothing existed except my adversary, myself, and the thing that I sensed was the cause of the man's malevolence.

The grove, the leaves underfoot, the network of branches, all became electrified with a warning that I heard but did not understand. All I knew was that this adult man—the first such stranger who had paid courtly attention to me—and I were facing each other in a deadly serious match of wits, my first; and that I had for the first time ever to save my own life.

It had taken me several paces to enter this grove: there was no way I could leap the distance to the street without him falling upon my back. With one jump from his crouched position—he was young and strong and tall—he could bring me down.

I made a show of looking, my first purely conscious act of deceit. My brown shoes scuffed the leaves. The color in his face intensified. His hand was moving, moving.

"There!" I shouted. I pointed behind him. As long as he wanted to keep me there, he would have to pretend to look. I gambled. I prayed.

He twisted around, his coat hiding the fearsome thing; furious, he looked. He was on all fours, on hands and knees in the dirty leaves, and I, oh, I was standing. I ducked and ran.

I ran as if the devil himself were racing me down, into the playground at last, slamming the big gates shut behind me. I could not stop running. I ran around the softball diamond, around and around, my eyes filling up with tears, until my counselors caught up with me, gripped me by the shoulders, and made me catch my breath.

They took me indoors to an office, so I would not upset the other campers, and held my hands hard while they looked into my face and demanded to know why I was upset.

"What happened?" they asked. And I told them. But even as I told—using the only language I had—I understood that what had happened to me was not like what happens to children when someone has put a razor into an apple on Halloween. Here there was neither sympathy nor outrage. As I spoke, the female counselors became tense; a male camp administrator grew uncomfortable; and there was an imperceptible withdrawal from me and my fear.

Before they had finished with the questions, I was done talking. How could something that had hurt me make grown-ups mad at me? "We'll take care of it," the administrator said. "Don't go scaring all the other little girls."

So I set my teeth. Angry tears welled up but did not spill; I understood that crying would only make things worse. This event had made everyone angry for some reason; and I had to be big.

The tears I was not permitted to shed stung. They were a lesson to me: whatever the man had done, no matter how it had harmed me, no matter that no one had said this—it was all, somehow deeper than reason, my own fault.

That feeling I had in the grove—that I must think, hard and fast, to escape mortal danger, counting on no one else for rescue—is the loneliest feeling for a child. An extraordinary number of girls, it seems from the stories that women have told me, experience it young, whether or not they have actually been abused. It is an existential crisis. Many girls then associate that encounter with being sexual women. I think few boys who have not been abused associate the risk of sexual terror with becoming men. This could be the signal trauma that sets boys' and girls' confidence onto separate paths.

In a fairy tale, a heroine is asked to choose one of three boxes. One contains a magical stone; the second, a ring; and the third, a dragon. Being a young teenage girl negotiating the world sexually can feel as if one is standing before three magical doors, behind one of which lies a moment's ecstasy; behind the second, the love of one's life; and behind the third, a monster. Once you open the door, it is too late to alter your fate.

Because of the new dangers that awaited us in the form of "bad men" of all kinds, we were at once obsessed by physical freedom and fearful of it. Soon we understood that boys were, in effect, our bodyguards. A girl learns that the ecstasy of physical exploration is something she can now enjoy safely only in the presence of a boy. She intuits that the very same developing body that can carry her farther than her dependent childhood body ever could has suddenly made her a target as well. Why is it a cliché that a powerful car gets a teenage boy dates with the most desirable girls? Because the boy and his car have become the stand-in for the girl's relationship to the vistas now forbidden to her. She learns to project onto love relationships all the drama, discovery, and meaning that she would otherwise find on the open road.

Awareness that sexual pleasure meant sexual danger and that our own guilt would be held to be a causative factor in whatever harm might come to us was a constant drain on our energy. The shock was still fresh. Over the course of the following years, we would swing from outrage to denial to despair. By adulthood, we would have become numb to it and learned how to live with this everyday emergency. Perhaps acculturation to the unthinkable is one of the definitions of what it means to become a woman.

WE NEEDED SPACE so badly. When we discovered that, if we went with boys, space would open up for us, we found, to our surprise, that we needed boys. And yet boys were part of the danger. Thus, our balance of power with boys was thrown off. This inequity regarding moving fast into the world was the first real lesson I had about the inequities between men and women: We needed boys more than they needed us. We were more scared of them physically than they were of us. We did not know this, but we probably even desired them as much as or even more than they desired us. If we chose not to go with them, we couldn't go at all. But they were always free to choose to go without us.

5

Nakedness: Pride and Shame

So you see that to be a girl is very special. . . . Your body begins to mature beautifully . . . you'll begin to develop the pretty curves that make older girls so proud of themselves. Suddenly a waistline will show. Your legs and arms will become rounder and your hips curvier. Breasts will begin to form on what was previously a flat chest. . . . Each year from now on, that very special feminine quality that has been yours from the moment you were born will become . . . more noticeable.
　　　　　　—Kimberly-Clark, "The Miracle of You," 1968, 1973

The very consciousness of their nature must evoke [in women] feelings of shame.
　　　　　　—CLEMENT OF ALEXANDRIA, *Pædagogus*

G irls' normal anxieties about nakedness were intensified for us by the growth of the sex industry. Something new was happening, for what had been hidden from middle-class children since the Victorians had invented childhood's privileged space was now being exposed to them. During our childhoods, the sex industry moved from being confined to the world of adults—specifically adult men—to being an ever-growing part of the visible universe of children. During the 1970s, in many parts of California, "distribution locations" for the sex industry proliferated twentyfold. Our demographic counterparts in 1869 would have been exposed to almost no graphic images of female sexuality. In 1942, Anne Frank's ignorance of the adult world of sexual images may have left her better able to characterize with little ambivalence the sweet feeling she had for a boy whom she had a crush on. Her vague fantasies of being kissed are appropriate to her age. After 1969, my friends and I were exposed, just by walking to our schools and playgrounds, to fantasies that were in no way appropriate to our psychic ages, that belonged to the daily-more-expressive imaginations of adults.

The images we had of what it would mean to grow up and grow sexual were more complicated year by year. At eleven, my friend Cath and I would go on long bus journeys through the city. On our trips we saw scene after scene that we needed to think about. We understood that they bore intimately on the changes our bodies would soon undergo.

On Broadway, there was a line of huge neon signs demarcating what became the sex-club district. On that block was the famous club the Condor. As everyone knew, the stripper Carol Doda worked there. Even the breakfast-table columnists in the city newspaper wrote about her. I had the impression that she actually lived in the Condor. I understood that she was a joke and that what had happened to her breasts was a joke. They had always been huge, and they had become even huger because of silicone. It was funny that now she was a famous pair of breasts. There were lots of punch lines involving the local landmark, Twin Peaks.

A sign that stood about twelve feet high advertised her. It was made in the shape of her body. Perched on the sign's immense neon breasts were two red lights that blinked comically on and off. The whole atmosphere around her was absurd, and the absurdity was about what happened to women when they have breasts. I understood that someday my own breasts would grow and might make me a laughingstock as well. I wondered why some women's breasts were funny and other women got away with just having them, without being a joke; and I wanted to know how I could be sure to be in the second category.

Another sign on the block read: SEE AND TALK TO A NAKED GIRL FOR ONE DOLLAR. A naked girl? For a dollar? Cath and I discussed this but could come to no certain conclusions. "See and talk to": what was the importance to men, I wondered, of that—would women not talk to them otherwise, or let men see them? And what about this clearly valuable, desirable commodity: "a naked girl"? I did not yet understand where the special value lay in that. Underneath my raveling sweaters and the bellbottoms with the patched knees, even *I* was a naked girl; so were all my friends, and our older sisters.

"We used to drive to the Bay Bridge," Sandy recalled when I spoke to her as an adult. "And I was so shocked—there were these signs everywhere saying 'naked girls.' And my mind was blown away. What *is this?* There were signs saying things like 'topless,' 'bottomless,' 'totally nude.' And I pictured these torsos . . . half a woman."

"Did you ever talk to your parents about this?" I asked her.

"I knew I was not supposed to ask them. I understood that I was supposed not to see it, that it didn't matter and it wasn't there. But I thought it was exciting. I would cross my fingers and hope my parents would drive down that street so I could look at these signs.

"The one that really got me was a sign that showed a naked lady kneeling, wearing a mortarboard. It said: 'totally nude college coeds.' That was the first time I had ever heard the word 'coed.' And I thought, whatever a coed is, it must be really special because they've got a sign about them naked.

"That was the most prominent image of a college-educated woman that I had in my life. It affected my idea of schooling. It was not like you saw images of women in college attire anywhere else when you were a little girl."

We knew the women in those images were exciting but also silly. Was this imagery only a form of comedy? I wondered about that, too. I could tell that a sense of awe and almost of fear drove the comedy. Though Carol Doda was a joke, she was also a sort of deity. The sign of her body was bigger than anything else on that street. Behind her massive curving hips and the blinking of her nipples, the hill dropped off precipitously and you could see the sweep of the Bay Bridge and the white-steel shine of the surface of the bay, but none of it could dwarf the great figure of the woman mounted high over the street.

Farther down the block was the Garden of Eden; that sign showed Adam and Eve, and Eve was represented, again in neon, as a slim nude girl, seen from the back, standing, with a serpent coiled around her body. On the sign for the World of Eros, a sixteen-foot half-draped woman was painted on half a block of wall space, lying recumbent across from a parking lot. Another sign proclaimed: LIVE GIRLS. LIVE LIVE LIVE. I wondered at this too: What else would they be?

I wanted to understand how it worked, for this was Sexland. I wanted to explore Sexland the way I wanted to visit Disneyland. And though nothing was keeping me out, I had a sense that there would be a price to pay if I drew closer. There was always a man standing by a stack of magazines, yelling something as if guarding the gate. His hands were in his front pockets, making fists. I was afraid of him.

The "naked girl" seemed to have little value to the dispensers of sex newspapers that had begun to appear at child's-eye height on street corners. These were much more graphic and raw than the old-fashioned "burlesque" listings in the newspaper. Passing these dispensers on my way home from school, I would stop outside Cala Foods where we shopped; the cranky old crossing guard would gesture to me to stay where I was. I would look and not look at these newsprint representations of "sex"—of the fate of all big girls. These naked women were young—as young as our favorite, least authoritative substitute teachers—smiling their strained smiles. Their slender but quite ordinary bodies were contorted this way and that in hapless calisthenics. And I wondered: Are they there because they are having fun? How can they be having fun if there are no boys with them? What is fun about this for them—for big girls? I knew this imagery was "sexy," though it did not look to me like "sex." But I could not see what was in it for women. I still recall those bodies in all their postures, like a human alphabet, presented week by week on cheap newsprint on the street corners of my hometown. Like Sandy, I remember how odd it seemed that they were everywhere, but neither the crossing guard nor the ladies behind the counter at Cala nor my mother who took me by the hand seemed to see them at all. They seemed actively to avoid them.

There were more congenial images of female sexuality, too. My favorite was the scene in the bronze fountain at Ghirardelli Square, where two young mermaids played. They were surrounded by pond lilies, and on each lily pad was a welter of jolly toads. The scene was lewd: toads were kissing, small toads jumped on the backs of big toads, and water spouted over it all. One mermaid held out her arms, and toads leapt from her outstretched fingers. The mermaid bodies, though cast in metal, looked at once soft and strong. Each was a little pouchy in the belly and a little slack in the full breast. One mermaid cradled a merbaby in her arms. The baby was laughing. The grown mermaids were naked in the most public of spaces—yet merry, confident, young, and maternal. This also seemed to me to be part of Sexland but of a different kind. The fountain was reassuring to me. These mermaids were happy and playful as well as "sexy." The bronze mermaids were imaginary, of course, and Carol Doda was real; but to me they seemed more real than she did. As I grew older, the Carol Doda images proliferated and became active and three-dimensional, and the glimpses of what the mermaids represented grew rarer and quainter.

Wending our way among these divergent images, my friends and I had to follow complex and contradictory rules about girls' naked-ness. By the time my Bay Area friends and I were twelve, we had developed, as a way of creating order out of chaos, a byzantine sense of what was just naked enough and what was too naked. We were not sluts. The way we negotiated being "not-sluts" had to do with paying close attention to excruciatingly subtle rules. Midriff-baring shirts were fashionable that year. If you showed an inch of belly too much, the look was "slutty." But if too little belly showed, you risked being a "doggie," a loser in the sexual hierarchy.

That year I went away to overnight camp for the first time. In our barracklike dormitories, we practiced preparing and evaluating our nakedness. Bras and shaving were the mediums for this activity, which took place in communal dressing-up sessions for the Friday-night dance. Bras were important. Wearing no bra at all was consid-ered to be too naked; a bra made of what must have been some newly invented polymer blend, an early forerunner of spandex, that shimmered over the skin, hooked brazenly in front, and showed the shape of the breast was just naked enough; a training bra that showed nothing was not sufficiently naked. Bras—their outlines, their straps—were the badge. Panties were less important. No one, we reckoned, was going to see our panties for a good long time.

Shaving was important, too. Big girls shaved their legs. We would lather our shins up to the kneecap—beyond, up to the thigh, for the most daring—and then take turns shaving, using steady, unchildlike upward strokes and being careful not to nick. The shaving was full of implications: we were signaling that these particular expanses of tanned skin were to be transformed in anticipation of the touch of a boy. Beyond kissing, we knew that it was here—with these smooth calves—that it would all begin.

The first time I shaved my legs, that summer, it was in defiance of my mother's warning: "Once you start, you can never stop; it only grows back coarser." To me, this caution was exciting: "Once you start, you can never stop . . ." I recognized these words, on a subliminal level, as the eternal caution of mothers to virgin daughters. Her words echoed in my ears as I made the first swipe. There, Mom! My skin was denuded in my first irrevocable act.

Then each girl would put on her underclothing. The more developmentally advanced of the girls would wear real bras. These fastened with intriguing hook-and-eye devices and had underwiring. The wiring distinguished those who had arrived from those who were still aspiring. The most daring girls had obtained the new spandex brassieres that were so excitingly translucent. (They also discovered the bras pilled, and fell apart in the wash.) The less-advanced girls—including, predictably, me—did not subject themselves to the ridicule that pretensions to such garments would inspire. Facing the fact of our untransformed and unwished-for selves, we pulled on the simple white cotton brassieres that were sold folded up in utilitarian cardboard containers. Little corn-fed blond girls smiled on the boxes, just as they did on the white plastic Wonder Bread packaging. There was no mystery in that part of the girls' department of the store: AAA, AA, A ran the sizes, from smallest to "largest," and if you merited only the triple A, everyone understood that "bra" was a courtesy term for the seamless elastic garment with the babyish bow.

Through the bras, our nakedness was already graded. We understood that its quality corresponded to the quality of the prizes that went with it, and the bras were the prizes. Somehow, I would have to make the transition from the training bra to the Juniors' or Misses' section of the store, which smelled of perfume instead of starch, where the pearl- and rose-colored, even pure black, real brassieres hung on metal trees, shifting in the air-conditioning. It was entirely outside my control. There was no guarantee that I would ever make it over the threshold. In the meantime, I would try to follow the rules.

The problem was that the designation of "too naked" was not entirely within our control. The state of being too naked, we found, could inhere in the very structure of our physiognomy, no matter what clothes we wore.

Yet what were we to do? In San Francisco at that time, just about everyone, it seemed, was divesting him- or herself of clothing. Top- less women, fur visible under proudly upraised arms, were marching in women's liberation parades; we saw their pictures in our moms' *Ms.* magazines. Gay men hung out on the sunny sidewalks in the Castro wearing nothing but leather chaps and jockstraps. Our moms and dads went to Esalen on weekends, or Big Sur, and sat around naked in hot tubs with other kids' moms and dads and other kids. "Take it off," purred an ad for shaving cream; "Take it *all* off." That was what cool people did—but it seemed that everyone was taking his or her clothes off in public except the only people most of us girls really wanted to take a look at—the boys we liked. The straight boys kept their baggy army-surplus shorts on and smugly surveyed the scene.

In the autumn of my twelfth year, I was in Israel with my fam- ily. In some ways, that visit, which took me out of a culture increasingly influenced by the sex industry, gave me a perspective on my peers' new femininity that was both more innocent and more authentic. My girlfriends in the modern neighborhood in Jerusalem where we lived were less affected by sexual expecta- tions than my San Francisco friends had been—the Orthodox- dominated city had little sexual imagery on display—but they were much more curious on their own terms. When the Israeli girls and I played together we'd go to the house of whoever's mother was out, turn up the fans, take off our shirts, and inspect one another. Our interest was almost clinical. We would turn upon one girl or another and dare her to take off her shirt. She had to. The peer pressure against refusing was intense. We would ignore the girl if she declined. When she did our bidding, we would gather like medical students and scrutinize the buds of her breasts. We were both fascinated and repelled by the inflamed aureoli on the still-boyish chest, the first stage of breast development that characterized almost all of us. We knew these weren't real breasts yet. Another girl might share the information that if you pinch these buds, they would get harder from a rush of blood. A third might dispute this. Then we would pressure the first girl into demonstrating. She would blush and protest, but the pressure from the alternating taunts and cajoling would only grow more insistent.

"All right. I'll show you. But," she would bargain, "only if you will all come out with me on the balcony and flash the traffic."

A deal. This sort of bargain had an inner logic in the dreamtime of the room. We were fixated on dares and were always on the lookout for a good one. This was the kind of dare we longed to be goaded into, just as we goaded our day's designated specimen into taking off her shirt.

In a close, awkward group, we would edge out to the balcony. Then, huddling at the threshold, with little shrieks, our hearts pounding, we would push one another out into the sun. "You go!" "You!" "Now!" In one desperate moment, by unspoken agreement, all of us would rush out, flip up our T-shirts, and then duck, howling, back into the living room.

Afterward, our chests tingled. We were being girls together, flaunting what was happening to us and proud of it. We would tuck our shirts back in, thrilled with ourselves. And the traffic would flow on, ignorant of the little girls too high up anyway to be seen, who for an instant had felt electric with arrogance and power.

This "compare-and-contrast" ritual seems widespread. Sandy's took place at summer camp, a "hippie camp." "At camp," she recalls, "we spent a lot of time swimming around naked. At that age you've got girls at all stages of development. By eleven I had friends with fully developed breasts, friends who were menstruating, and everything in between."

The girls, she said, had different names for the different stages of breast development. " 'Nuzzies,' " she recounted as if doing an inventory. "They were the little mosquito bites. 'Squeeners' were where they get kind of pointy, starting to stick out. 'Dudleys' were when they got kind of round. 'Bonkers' were normal adult women's breasts. And 'bongaydie ladies'—I don't know how you'd spell that—were the women with breasts that hung down to the navels. My campmates and I just made these up. 'Cause we were all in these different stages. This was the vocabulary we had to talk about what was going on in our bodies. I remember singing this song about 'We are bosom buddies—some are big, some are small. But what the hell, we've got 'em all.' It had nothing to do with sexually interacting with boys," she explained. "This was just about being girls together.

"There was a part of it," she went on, "that made developing okay. That was the word: 'developing.' I got to see that it was normal. I think all girls had these questions about themselves and other girls, whether they were lying around together naked or not. But it was also a hazing ritual: you had to be comfortable being naked to be part of this group. We would tease other campers who didn't want to take off their bathing suits. We'd make them cry.

"I was a late bloomer," she said. "I felt very inadequate because boys were interested in the girls with larger breasts and they weren't interested in me. Girls with bigger breasts seem to have taken part in more sexual activities with boys—this is by thirteen. The friends I had who weren't virgins any more at thirteen were larger breasted. Because their bodies developed at a younger age, they got hit on younger. I had a few years' grace."

I knew what she was talking about. When I returned to California, that innocent sense of pride and pleasure I had had on the balcony became elusive again. Dangers loomed larger. It seemed that no matter how hard we tried to make and stick to rules about nakedness, we were confounded. You could wear a training bra and a work shirt and jeans, and a grown man would say "Mama!" to you, a little girl, on the street: you had been too naked. A judge in California ruled, at around that time, that a high school boy who had raped a girl in a school stairwell was not culpable because of the girl's revealing clothing: jeans. The other women remember the same ruling; a homeroom teacher told their class about it to scare them. The ruling did scare us. We all wore jeans.

A young woman named Daria, from a Baptist background, also told me a story about her own early experiment with nakedness. In this case, the moral of the story, in her eyes, is the shame her nakedness had first caused her.

"I must have been twelve or thirteen," she said. "I was just becoming an adolescent and had been changing, but there was no acknowledgment of my 'becoming a woman' whatsoever at home. I always wore baggy clothes, little girls' loose clothing. I didn't want to draw attention to the change: it was too frightening to do so; I was afraid that my grandfather would say that I looked like a harlot. And that my mother would disapprove: I would no longer be someone she liked, no longer deserve to be 'her girl.' "

One night in Albuquerque, where she, her three younger half brothers, and her grandparents, who were raising her, were living, the whole family went out to an old-fashioned restaurant.

The evening was a romantic prospect for Daria. The restaurant was grown-up: it had banquettes and a maître d'. The newness of the setting, the fact that she would probably never see any of the grown-ups eating there that night again, the southwestern springtime, the teenage coat-check boy who had been chivalrous as he took her jacket—all these made Daria take a risk.

She excused herself and went to the ladies' room. She washed her hands, using up all the pink soap. The restaurant had provided hand lotion: she spread it all over her face and throat. It was called "Cashmere Bouquet," a name that to her was suggestive of being adult and exotic. She then reached into her bag, took out the lipstick and mascara she had bought at Woolworth's and had kept hidden like a talisman in her sock drawer, and painted her face for the first time. She took off the detachable collar of her little-girl velvet dress and undid the top two buttons. The black velvet suddenly looked sophisticated. It was almost, she thought, as if she was dressed in "evening wear." Her skinny child's arms metamorphosed before her eyes into the arms of a young woman waiting to be caressed. Daria looked in the mirror and saw herself beautifully changed into her next and more powerful self.

Downstairs, in the restaurant, she joined her family. Everyone started to whisper urgently at her. "Go wash that off!" hissed her perfectly groomed grandmother.

"What is this nonsense?" muttered her grandfather.

"There's stuff running all down your face." Her little half brother giggled, picking up the cue. "You don't even know how to put it on."

What Daria heard was: You're no woman; just the thought is ludicrous. Your nakedness is a failure. She fled back to the bathroom. It felt to her as if the whole restaurant was laughing at her.

When she looked at her face and body, it was those that she blamed, and her desires that had led her to make such a humiliating mistake. There was no soap left in the dispenser, so Daria rubbed her face red with scratchy paper towels and hot water.

Later, her grandmother apologized. Nonetheless, Daria says that she got the message that her grandmother would not love her as much if she were sexual and that her "becoming a woman" in any visible way would embarrass her grandfather. She spent her teenage years hiding her body and denying her own growing up. "Well," Daria ended her story, "as you can imagine, I didn't try that again soon."

Daria's story is common. What feels like sexual pride one moment can turn into shame the next.

When I went home to talk to the girls, now women, with whom I grew up, we talked at a restaurant about how we learned to associate our emerging grown-up nakedness with shame. Pattie looked out the window, swirled the ice in her glass, and recalled: "No one has shamed my body like women have. The shaming experiences I have had, when I was just beginning to develop, were from other girls first. My best friend, Melinda, and me—we'd get dressed up together, at about eleven. And I'd like to look at my reflection. I really started developing early, and at that age you really love looking at your reflection. And she'd say: 'You really *love* looking at yourself.' And I'd think: So *what*? It wasn't okay to like yourself. And then, a little later, I remember my same friend telling me my breasts looked like 'blups.' "

"Blups?" I asked. It was a word that was distressing and funny at once.

"Big blups," Pattie said. "It was just cruel. Now, I can say, What was going on with you that you had to put me down? But then, it was awful. By then I was twelve or so. By 'blups' she meant big and no shape or something. I didn't respond angrily to that. I just absorbed it. There was no one to help me. No one I could go to and say, Why are people making fun of my breasts? Is something wrong with me, or is it them?"

Pattie leaned her head against a hand. "Yes," she reiterated, "it was the girls. Right when I was discovering my curves, I had this bikini. It was so great. And I'd put it on, and just *love* the way it looked. I liked my body at first. 'Well, what do you think of my bathing suit?' I'd ask my sister. And she'd say, 'Well, if you want to flaunt your body I guess it looks okay.' It made me feel . . . *bad*. Like, So: I'm not supposed to enjoy my body? What I absorbed was: there's something wrong with showing my body."

I asked her, "Any woman's body? Or yours in particular?"

Pattie answered: "Any woman's, because I remember, at about that time, becoming judgmental of other girls, the way they were being judgmental of me."

Sandy smiled dryly. "When my friends were getting breasts, but eons before I was, they would say I was on the Itty-bitty Titty Committee. They would also tease: 'You're a sailor's dream: a sunken chest.' Boys would never say that. Just girls. And—remember this?" Sandy began singing, making fists and flapping her elbows, somewhat startling the nearby diners:

> *"We must, we must, we must increase our bust.*
> *For fear, for fear, the boys will disappear.*
> *The bigger the better, the tighter the sweater,*
> *the boys depend on us."*

Trina said, "I used to tease girls myself. I remember as a group of girls—seventh grade—we would tease one another about our breasts or being fat."

I asked, "Would you tease the big-breasted girls or the small-breasted ones?"

"The big ones, of course," said Trina. "We did it to each other. It wasn't meant to be a competition, trying to cut each other down. At least, it didn't start out that way. It was more about our changing bodies and not being able to handle it or deal with it. And making fun of it as a result."

I asked the women, "Do you think the fact that there were not a lot of messages saying Don't laugh at the girls' sexuality intensified this inclination to mock one another or tease?"

Pattie said, "If only there had been some sorts of events for us, where girls were there to support one another about their changing bodies—*something*, saying that we were all of like gender, and this is what to expect, and that there's—" she paused, and thought "—a *goodness* for us in it."

"You didn't see messages that there was a goodness in it?" I asked.

Trina said gently, her confident voice now almost a whisper, "It was *so . . . scary*."

Like Pattie's bikini, a single article of clothing, which we remember forever, can symbolize a stage of the passage from childhood to nubility. At thirteen, I saw a dress in the window of a boutique on San Francisco's Judah Street. It looked like the hippest outfits that Millie the Model wore in the comic-book series. Made of blue-and-cream-striped Egyptian cotton that was a little nubby to the touch, it had the "midriff top," very fashionable at the time, that tied above the belly, and a wraparound skirt. It was definitely sexy. In my culture at home it said "Sexy hippie earth mama." I saved up baby-sitting money for a long time. It really mattered to me. It was the first outfit I ever wore in which I felt I could pass for a woman.

I went back to Israel that summer, and this time there would be no frolicking on balconies. We had all grown real, if tentative, breasts. I made friends with another American girl, Ofra, who was visiting her Orthodox relatives. When I went to get her one afternoon to hang out, I wore my dress. Her uncle intercepted me. He looked to me like Mr. Brocklehurst in *Jane Eyre*: a terrifying pillar of black. "You can't visit Ofra," he said in Hebrew. "Don't try to see her again. We don't approve of you. You are dressed like a whore." I was stricken mute, partly by the shock of being reflected in his disapprobation—no one had thought of me as a bad influence until then—but also by something in his cold eyes and voice that I had never heard before. He feared me; me, a little girl. He was shaming me because he was afraid of me. What I had considered something to be proud of—my emerging sexuality—was something to be ashamed of. In the Haight, I had absorbed the idea that God liked sexuality; through Ofra's uncle I saw the possibility, which I had never considered up to that point, that God hated it—and, in particular, that God localized it in women; in my belly, which I had passed up so many desserts to reveal; and in my nice blue-striped cotton dress with the ruffle along the skirt that had cost me all that money. What I offered was an affront.

In the West, it is rare for a woman to encounter this sexual shaming as late in life as I did. In Western culture's debate, images of female sexualized nakedness are assumed, by progressives and conservatives and apolitical concerned mothers alike, to be innately degrading to women. The trouble with this is that it locates the degradation of the women *within* the sex or the nakedness itself, rather than in the distorted value *assigned* to that sex and that nakedness.

In our culture, women's nudity is typically seen as exposing women—in the sense of making them vulnerable—for the sake of more powerful, less vulnerable men. But, as Havelock Ellis argued in his *Studies in the Psychology of Sex,* other cultures have organized female nakedness very differently. At the turn of the twentieth century, according to Ellis, among the Uapas of the Amazon rain forest, for instance, men always covered their genitals while women were free to roam about naked; the women of Tierra del Fuego, off the coast of South America, were comfortable in public wearing nothing but a tiny patch of animal skin between their legs, consenting to raise it only when they made love; and Moru women carefully covered their buttocks with aprons made of leaves at all times, but their genitals remained in full view.

Various attitudes to nudity have prevailed in the West as well. Fifth-century Alexandrian women aristocrats lent themselves to the pleasures of being washed and massaged by their slaves, including males, and were comfortable, according to a critic, stripping before spectators. In Germany until the sixteenth century, "the sight of complete nakedness was the daily rule" in crowded households, mixed-sex nude bathing in both water and steam was commonplace, women were often naked under their petticoats, and it was considered great sport by men and women of both the town and the country to play a game during dances in which the man hoisted his dance partner so high in the air that her dress flew upward.

In the early Middle Ages, some women in Ireland undressed as a sign of welcome; it is reported in G. Rattray Taylor's *Sex in History* that the Queen of Ulster and the ladies of her court greeted the hero Cuchulainn thus. One traveler in Ireland reported that, as late as 1617, naked young girls were to be seen grinding corn in public. At about the same time in Venice and Padua, in the summer, observers wrote that "wives, widows and maids all walked with naked breasts." Even at the end of the eighteenth century, in sophisticated circles in Paris that were responsive to the Greek revival, a fashion arose for dresses made of sheer gauze that outlined and even displayed women's nakedness. This style so charmed these aristocratic women that some were happy "even to walk abroad in the Champs-Elysées without any clothing; that, however, was too much for the public."

Could nakedness have many meanings? We knew of only two, and neither was of our choosing. For friends of mine like Sandy, female nakedness was not shameful, but it also signified total availability. For Daria, as for so many of the women who have told me their stories, the new revelation of female sexuality seemed to be partially constituted of shame. Was there yet a third way to think about what was going on with us, in us? If there was, we had no notion of it.

6

Girlfriends

In early adolescence, almost every girl . . . goes through a perfectly natural stage of life in which she prefers to share her pursuits and her ideas
with members of her own sex. . . . If sexual interest in the same sex continues into adulthood, it is a symptom of maladjustment. . . . Professional
counseling, in some instances, can reverse the emotional direction.
— Kimberly-Clark, "Your Years of Self-discovery," 1973

Rhiannon rings like a bell through the night . . . and who will be her
lover?

— FLEETWOOD MAC, "Rhiannon," 1975

Genevieve loved her girlfriends. A girl with straight dark hair
cut in a pageboy, she was my best friend at age twelve. The
sense of style she showed, the confidence she took in her
compact body, helped to redeem me a little from the triple stigma of
bookishness, awkwardness, and shapelessness. We all looked up to
Genevieve. A small, scheming diplomat, she seemed polite and
engaging to grown-ups; all the parents liked her. Little did they
know she was rolling around with their daughters during slumber
parties.

For most of us, these games really were, I suppose, "just a stage."
But it would be many years before we fell in love with boys the way
we were infatuated with one another.

For Genevieve, this passion was more absorbing than it was for
any of the rest of us. Her interest in other girls started at ten, when
she fell in love with her first older woman: a nineteen-year-old Japa-

nese college student named Grace. Grace lived in the apartment across the hall. She let Genevieve come over to feed her cat while she was away. Genevieve was allowed to loll on the bed with Grace when she was bored or had no date for the night. The younger girl got to wait on Grace as she watched *The Mary Tyler Moore Show*. The child painted Grace's nails and brushed her hair. Genevieve did not know that Grace only wanted her there because the girl made her feel glamorous and less lonely. She thought Grace knew that she was not just a kid from next door but a suitor. Grace thought Genevieve wanted to learn to be like her. She did not understand that Genevieve wanted to possess her, vague as that notion was to the child; to lie next to her and look into her eyes.

Late one night in the winter of sixth grade, after Grace had moved away, Genevieve was at a sleepover with me and a group of other girls. A girl we hardly knew, Shari, asked, "Do you know how to do a French kiss?" We didn't. "Watch." All the girls were watching. Everyone held her breath. The girl took a pillow and inexpertly mauled it with her mouth.

Everyone agreed that a pillow was not the best educational tool: you really couldn't learn properly that way, and boys would laugh at you if you didn't learn how to do it right. So, "for pretend," my new acquaintance, the golden Shari, looked around, considering whom to demonstrate upon. She chose Genevieve. And Genevieve let herself be taken into Shari's arms. Shari's hair fell all over Genevieve's face as she demonstrated "how to kiss a boy." Genevieve thought: Why ever leave this behind? It was girls she loved. There was nothing shocking to us in this kiss or her excitement about it. It was girls we loved, too.

Sandy recalls similar episodes: "By sixth grade, we used to play truth or dare with girls. A lot of the dares were kissing girls or bumping breasts together—such as they were. The massage thing was really big. We would give each other massages, and there was something going on there that was presexual. At slumber parties, we would practice French kissing with other girls. You could wrap your arm around someone and put your hand on their mouth and it would look like you were kissing them. We would be having some kissing event, and someone would always have to say, 'Imagine how much *better* it would feel if this was a boy doing it!' 'Cause then you weren't, like, lezzies."

Genevieve's father was one of the ones who had recently left home. But he still sent money. Of all of our rooms, Genevieve's provided the best stage for rehearsals. It had a soft, long-haired shag throw rug, a guest bed with satin covers, and a full-length mirror. There were more different kinds of softness in Genevieve's room than we had in our whole house. Irritable Cath, golden Shari, and I would gather there with Genevieve.

Shari and Cath, who were a year older than I and far more sophisticated, joined Genevieve in setting the script and the scene. Shari was imperious, critical, statuesque, usually coy, and sometimes somewhat cruel. An ex–rich girl with white skin, freckles, and floating yellow-white hair, she was situated at the pinnacle of the gang of kids we knew who lived close by. She was the first girl I knew whose mother shopped as a pastime and taught her how to do the same. Cath was her sidekick, more stolid and devoted, a dark presence, the daughter of people who ran a contracting business. I was so far below their status, with girls as well as boys, that it felt like a miracle or an accident to me that they noticed me at all. But they took me in for a few months, and I held my breath, waiting to be ejected.

The afternoons began with ritual food: when Genevieve's mom had gone for the day, we would make margarine-soaked grilled-cheese sandwiches in a device with two molded plates we called the toaster bra. We often held it up to our chests and pranced around the kitchen.

Then we would push the twin beds together. We would lie stretched out or all curled together like cats. We free-associated about boys. That conversation would last a good hour.

"Craig likes you," I might say to Genevieve while braiding her wet-looking black hair.

"Oh, he does not," Genevieve would reply. "I heard from my brother's friend at Galileo"—another high school, a tougher one—"that he likes this freshman on the drill team at Lincoln."

"But he leaned over you like that when he asked that question about English class in the hall yesterday."

"What question? What?"

"Well, he acted like he was asking a question, but I know he was just trying to get a better look down your shirt."

At which Genevieve would leap onto my back and pummel me with a pillow. That was the signal for everyone to pillow-wrestle. We all tumbled together until we could not stand any more, then we separated and resumed talking.

As we gossiped, the throat of one girl would press against the back of another girl's hand or a hipbone would nudge the underside of a neck. We would all smell the Love's Baby Soft ("Because Innocence Is Sexy") mingling with Jovan Musk and Revlon's Charlie, and with the scent of freshly washed hair (Clairol's Herbal Essence) and cotton fabric. We were great believers in the powers of scent. We had to be: perfume was, we believed, just as the magazines promised us, a way for us, all still virgins, to connect seductively without touching.

All this talk about boys was still a pretext. The truth was that we were not ready to splinter off into love relationships with the opposite sex. We talked about crushes on boys because we knew it was forbidden to breathe a word about the way we felt about one another. Everyone was in love with clever, observant Genevieve, and Genevieve flirted with me and with Shari, Genevieve's rival for the role of the alpha female. Shari and Genevieve were wary of each other, as two stars must be. But when we were all together, it was a group crush. We were giddy with the charm of ourselves.

But scared, too. The mid-sixties sex education manuals or the "growing-up books" still on the shelves in the junior high school and high school libraries always had a passage, early on, that read like this one from the widely used *Love and the Facts of Life*, by Evelyn Millis Duvall:

> Sometime when you were about halfway through elementary school, you quite possibly had a very close buddy or pal of your own sex to whom you were devoted. . . . You did everything together. You may have worn the same kind of clothes and sent for the same gadgets advertised on cereal boxes and over the radio. No treat was finer than having a meal together or being able to spend the night in the other's home. . . . You shared your most precious confidences, told the darkest secrets.
>
> These early friendships between persons of the same sex give a special sense of security at a time when one is hungry for companionship, yet not quite ready to take on friends of the opposite sex. . . .
>
> Hidden fears of the other sex may halt one's love development at this point. An attachment to members of one's own sex in preference to persons of the opposite sex is called *homosexual* (same

sex). This is normal during certain periods of childhood, and even for a while in early adolescence. Later it may become a cause for concern, for it may indicate that one has stopped in his love development. . . . A boy or girl who does not seem to arouse the interest of the opposite sex, or to be interested in the opposite sex, has no reason to fear that he or she is a homosexual by nature. Time and growth are on his side.

Time and growth were *on our side?* As I lay with my head pressed against Genevieve's warm shoulder, I felt nothing but pain at the thought of that imminent separation. I knew that I was about to lose this world forever. I would have to transfer my allegiances or close down all feelings for girls: it was a law. What we did not have in the school library were books with passages like these from Sappho:

> *To me it seems*
> *that man has the fortune of the gods*
> *whoever sits beside you, and close, . . . my heart flutters in my breast,*
> *whenever I look quickly, for a moment—*
> *I say nothing, my tongue broken,*
> *A delicate fire runs under my skin, . . .*
> *I am greener than grass. . . .*

But lying beside one another, with no safe way to think about it, a delicate fire still ran under our skin.

Tonya remembers a similar love: "My friend Shane and I spent time together constantly at thirteen and fourteen. I remember those moments in her living room or in her basement. We'd be sewing or something and be very close physically. Shane smelled like . . ." Here Tonya paused, looked away, and smiled. "Her dad was really into natural foods, so she smelled like some funky oatmeal wheat soap, and she had that cocoa butter smell. I'd be showing her something or she'd be showing me something, or I'd have to reach over her shoulder to show her how to do something, and our hands would be close together. Or we would be in deep conversation about my relationship with my mother and then we'd get into the whole philosophical picture—why were we here on the planet, what is our role on the planet, what's wrong with the world and how can we personally fix it—when we would be so close. And there would be that sense of emotional connection and then that hesitation in the air—

that feeling that I recognize now but didn't then: this is the moment when you're supposed to kiss."

"Whenever I look quickly, for a moment—"

"And then one of us would laugh and go get Doritos or something from the kitchen. The laugh was regret and relief. Relief that there was this intense conversation and then that funky moment, but we had done nothing irrevocable—that it had been so intense but that we could still get out of it."

As adult women, those of us who are heterosexual sometimes have a sense of a lost Eden. We are determined to seek out a love as perfect again: a love at once so intimate and so charged; to be once more as teenage girls are when they are in love with each other. This is why teen idols—the David Cassidys and the Bobby Shermans or, later, the Bay City Rollers—always look like girls. They are our disguises; they are cover for these feelings. An editor of one of the preteen girl fan magazines said that they are careful never to show the teen idols' chest hair because their young female readers find such signs of masculinity too scary.

In a way, there will be nothing as exciting as this love between girls ever again. This love has codes and repression, innocence and distant obsession, all intensified by the secrecy of the feelings involved and the knowledge of the world's disapproval "if they only knew." These are all parameters of love that, by the time we were coming of age, had died out everywhere but in our all-girl subculture. If thirteen-year-old Juliet were to fall in love with Romeo today, she could get a condom in the ladies' room of the train station and instructions from *Cosmo* ("Your Sexual Style"), and Shakespeare would have to look elsewhere for his plot.

But our loving other girls was still the stuff of great dramas or nineteenth-century novels, rather than of women's magazines, for a simple reason: it was doomed. We understood already that the price of being intimate with women beyond that first stage of early adolescence was just too high and that if there were another path we could take, we should do so, with all the strength we could muster, and not look back. Even as we flirted and left little love notes filled with sparkle in one another's lockers ("My lady of celadon eyes," read a favorite note, addressed to me by an older girl with long blond hair and a *car*; as she must have known, I had to look up the word "celadon"), we knew that time was running out on us. But our regret at the separation was wrenching as we began to move away from our infatuations with girls, whom we saw as captivating, civilized beings, into the world of sex with boys, those ill-spoken, skateboard-wielding Visigoths. It was like moving a love life from a Henry James novel into a Spiderman comic.

7

Sluts

I want you, I want you
I want you . . . so bad . . .

—Bob Dylan, "I Want You," 1966

The instant gratification of your senses, at the expense of your feelings of self-worth, can only lead to deep unhappiness.
—Kimberly-Clark, "Your Years of Self-discovery," 1968, 1973

When I was thirteen, I went off to a Zionist summer camp located near a dusty resort town.

There was a girl with us that summer who was appealing to every one of us, male and female. She was named Tia. Like everything else about her, her name took on cachet. Tia's voice was gravelly; soon we were all pitching our voices lower. Part Russian, part Albanian, her olive skin was perfect. In a subculture that worshiped golden-brown skin, her complexion set the benchmark; we all labored to become more tan. While the other girls wore expensive braces with tiny rubber bands or slept with watermelon-colored retainers at night, Tia's teeth were naturally straight and white. The rest of us had to really swing it to give any suggestiveness to our little-girl hipbones; Tia's hips curved with no effort on her part. Her thick hair hung almost to her waist, and it curled back naturally from her face at a time when elaborate blow-drying around big round brushes was necessary to achieve the requisite roll away from either temple that we called "feathering." Whatever was in fashion, Tia took to a level that verged on mockery: her hip-huggers were

slung lower, and her midriff tops knotted higher, than anyone else's.
Under her midriff top she revealed the ultimate status symbol of the
time for California girls: a completely flat brown belly. The labor-
intensiveness of being a woman was beginning to become clear
to us, and we were having flashes of boredom already. We stole
envious glances at Tia because she did not seem to have to work at
it at all.

Later, as an adult, I read about research on attraction to personalities that asked the subject whether he or she would want to lick a
given person's hypothetical already-licked ice cream cone. By virtue of an enduring associative magic, everyone wanted Albert
Schweitzer's ice cream cone. Same with Einstein's; no one wanted
Hitler's. A similar associative magic seemed to apply to Tia. If Tia was
using root beer–flavored lip gloss that day, it was an honor if you
could let it be known that she had lent some to you. As for her high-
arched feet with their pearly toenails, access to them became an even
more intimate mark of status. It was she who initiated the ritual of
the girls' "doing" one another's pedicures. You would place your foot
in the lap of your chosen groomer; your girlfriend would scowl and
turn your foot this way and that; and she would wield the tiny acrylic
brush like a workman in a Florentine studio. And if you were chosen
by Tia to paint French Seashell lacquer on each toe—the toes held
apart by tissue—you had, for that day at least, ascended to a higher
level of adolescent achievement.

Tia's story soon got around. Its drama would have sunk a less popular girl, but in Tia's case it only deepened the general consciousness
of her rareness. Back home, in the Lower Haight, she confided, there
was a love triangle. Herself, her thirty-two-year-old mother, and her
mother's twenty-five-year-old male friend.

During the hour of quiet time at camp, after lunch and "bug juice"
in the flyspecked mess hall, the girls of Redwood Cabin would wander down to the creek in a small clearing in the Valley Oak forest. At
our feet was a savory, crackling layer of dry green bay leaves. We
would lie on our stomachs on fallen logs, look at the sun bouncing
off the water, and listen to Tia tell her stories.

She had been raised in an always-changing household. Her
mother had listened to the contemporary wisdom that a formal education squelched children's creativity, so an old boyfriend of hers

who had a room in the apartment and shared the rent—a middle-aged hippie—had been charged with providing Tia's home education. He had taught her to read by using his collection of 1950s science fiction comics, and that was about the extent of her schooling. "We learn by doing" had been his and her mother's premise. At thirteen, she knew about intergalactic travel and the death of Superman's parents; she spoke with scorn about long division.

Her mother was a cocktail waitress, dance instructor, and artist. In our circles, it was common for kids from single-parent homes to tell wild tales of their "real" fathers' status and accomplishments. Tia alleged that her real father was the owner of the San Francisco Forty-niners, and this sort of assertion was routine enough for the rest of us to accept it for what it was: a statement of an emotional, not a literal, truth.

There was a children's book, still current at the time, about a girl who cried for the moon. Tia, it seemed to us, was allowed the moon. She could stay up until one with her mother's new boyfriend on the nights her mother got home late. She was allowed to put on her mother's work clothes and high heels and pretend she was waiting tables. She could watch *The Twilight Zone*, her mother's friend's favorite program, with him until it was over.

Her mom did not know, but we, thrillingly, did, that during the commercials the friend allowed her to make out with him. The game was so easy—so much an extension of their bored, brother-sister rivalry and affection—that it was simple enough, when her mom came home, for them both to revert to role.

The glamour of this arrangement was staggering to us. Each of us nursed an emerging sexual competition with our mothers—women who thought of us as being children still. Tia's vengeance was the most audacious, and the most poetically just, that we could imagine. Besides which, the photograph of the boyfriend confirmed the rightness of this romance in our eyes: he looked just like Peter Frampton.

By the first week of the camp session, Tia had consolidated her reigning position not only by these daily extended tales down by the creek but also by her bored-face conquest of the coolest moves at the Friday-night dance in the cleaned-up mess hall. She had also learned to shoot an arrow straight and had stolen away from her nearest contenders the starring role in the camp play.

By week three of the session, though, Tia had grown shaky. On Friday night she refused to dance—ignoring even "One Toke over the Line," our risqué favorite (slipped in by the kid playing DJ; the adults did not seem to have listened to the words). Even though none of us had yet smoked pot, we would chant its words in a sassy all-girl circle right in hearing range of the camp director.

"Forget it," said Tia, turning away from us and in one gesture making our ritual of belonging seem babyish.

By Monday of the fourth week, she was beginning to withdraw. That Friday night, she refused even to make an appearance at the dance. She would not go to macramé; she would not even go to swim class. She lay on her bunk and wrote in tiny script in her diary.

The girls of Redwood Cabin delegated Jenna to go to her. Jenna was the warmest and most tolerable of the girls' counselors. By the time Jenna reached the bunkroom, Tia had gotten wind of the betrayal and had bolted the door. We hovered behind Jenna, listening.

"Come on, open up!" cried Jenna. "You're not the only person who lives in there. Look, Tia, whatever is bothering you, I bet we can find a solution. Come on, open it.

"You're wasting a perfectly good summer." Jenna had said the wrong thing: adults were always obtusely instructing us that this or that intolerable quantity—sweater, teacher, summer—was "perfectly good."

"Why don't you go work on your tan, Jenna?" said Tia from within. The shaft hit home; Jenna, who had attained an all-over golden-brown shade, was famously obsessive about maintaining it. Even on white-hot days she refused to wear sunglasses because they would give her face an uneven tan. Perhaps contrite, Tia slid back the bolt. Jenna angrily pushed open the door. Tia lay back down on the bunk.

"You're absolutely right. I am just a Sulky Teen. Nothing *could* be That Bad." She was using the deadpan capitals that were our code. "I'll just go out now," she said, leaping up again and breezing past the counselor. "Macramé calls." She flung herself out the door.

That time, the secret remained intact. But by week five she looked, oddly, like a child again. Her moon face was neither sly nor radiant, only frightened. Her skin was greasy, and her hair hung lank. The wild tendrils were a memory. The flat brown belly was now covered, always, by an oversized Grateful Dead T-shirt. This

abdication allowed other popular girls' almost-flat bellies to preoc-
cupy both the boys and the girls. Tia was slipping. Her supporters
were worried, both altruistically and selfishly; their fortunes rose and
fell with hers.

During quiet hour that week, Tia, two of the Redwood girls, and I
were resting in the Valley Oak grove again. We had a transistor radio
with us. A little brook ran through the bottom of the glade, and the
slanting light played over it. We sang along with the deep male voice.

As we sang along with the radio, we carefully frayed the hems of
our cutoffs. The frayed part had to be about three quarters of an inch
wide. More was posing; less was geeky. It was particularly good if
there were white cross-fibers hanging by threads through which mil-
limeters of tan thigh could be glimpsed. The cutoffs had to look neat
but worn: not by intention but by summers and rivers and sun.
Another song loped along:

> In the summertime, when the weather is hot
> You can stretch right up and touch the sky
> In the summertime, when the weather's fine
> You got women, you got women on your mind. . . .
> If her daddy's rich, take her out for a meal.
> If her daddy's poor, just do what you feel. . . .
> We love everybody, but we do what we please. . . .
> Yeah, that's our philosophy.
> Sing along with us . . . yeah we're hap-happy.

That song sounded good to us, really cool. But even as we were
singing along, patting the bark of the tree to the beat, I was worrying in that now-familiar anxious inner monologue. "You can do what
you feel"—to the girl in the song, presumably. But what *did* she feel?
"That's our philosophy"—the phrase evoked in my mind's eye a
bunch of sexy guys, brown and black and white, with their shirts off,
wearing bandannas, maybe, and hot patched-up jeans, sitting in an
old open-topped car, singing, bopping to the music, having a blast.
What girl would not want to go along? And that would mean going
along with that happy-go-lucky "philosophy." Once again I found
myself immersed in that anxious internal monologue of questions,
now growing familiar. But what about our gang? Who would come
along with us and on what terms? What was *our* philosophy? "We

love everybody, but we do what we please." It sounded great. But that would make us sluts. It was okay to be "free." But you could still be a slut.

Tia asked us to pay attention. I do remember her lowering her voice. As cool as she was, she was still ashamed. She asked us if we knew of a place she could get a cheap abortion: "My period is late."

"Well, maybe it's just *late*," her nearest rival said, resenting this sudden accruing of even more drama into Tia's corner.

"I know what I know," she said. And the way she said it—flatly— we believed her.

The air was full of insect noises. As so often in those days, I realized I did not know what to say.

Our peaceful moment was changed; no one knew what to do with the change, how to contain it. We were furious and silent. Tia was supposed to be the leader, to show us how to brazen our way past all the discomforts and awkwardnesses that besieged us. What the hell was she doing?

Tia jumped down off her log, feet first into the stream, splashing us hard. "Just forget I said anything. *Jesus*," she said. "Fucking infants." She grabbed the low-lying branches along the edge of the stream and pulled herself up onto the path, walking away from us and not turning back. We scrambled and caught up with her. She let us. She had no real choice. We walked four abreast when we hit the main road, just as we had done before. We all made the right sounds: "God, Tee, when did you find out? How long have you known?" We put our hypocritical arms around her; we hugged her. "Don't worry, 'kay, Tia?" We produced the tearful smiles that were the currency of moments of great girl importance, and forgave and were forgiven. ("Sorry, guys, I'm just really fucked up about this." "No, no, I was a jerk, I should have guessed there was something." "No, it's cool, I know you're all there for me. I just didn't want to talk about it.") But a wall had come down between us and her.

Her secrets were no longer thrilling. They were too much for us. Even as we stroked her hair and reassured her that "We'll find something—there's got to be something out there that you can afford," we knew that we were so scared that what had happened to her might contaminate us that we could scarcely refrain from wiping our hands on our shorts.

Tia kissed us, laughed her hoarse laugh, and wiped her eyes. "It's not a big deal," she said. "It's not the end of the world. Anyway, I've still got my sources to check out," she joked. "You're my buds." She ducked into the cabin to change some money for long-distance calls.

But we weren't; not the way she thought we were. That was what happened, then, when you gave in—when you followed your inclinations and touched that ravishing twenty-five-year-old that every one of us, given the opportunity, would have jumped at the chance to please. We looked at one another, our eyes immense. Without speaking, we knew that each of us was glad, glad that we were carefully guarded middle-class girls with some limits still in place. *Not sluts. Like Tia.*

By the end of week five, Tia was gone. Just gone: bunk stripped down to the striped-ticking mattress and an old toothbrush and a plastic ponytail holder with sparkles in it left on the top of what had been her shelf. None of the adults explained clearly why she had gone. She wrote to no one.

A year later, we heard a rumor that she had "had it"—the baby. Then we heard a rumor that she had had an abortion. She was somewhere, still in the city but gone, dimmed, done for, lost to our preadolescent world. We heard that her mom was still mad at her.

Tia, we heard, had cut off her wild hair; she had feathered shoulder-length hair now, just like everyone else. And she was fat now, we were told. Someone who'd seen her had said so. She wasn't . . . part of things anymore. In our world, that was almost like saying: Tia was dead now.

We were not sluts . . . like Tia. Tia was dead now. Though still children, we were girl children, and already we understood the situation without anyone—certainly not our liberal parents, who would have been appalled at the clarity of our vision—telling us in so many words. If we took one false step—if we did something that could expose us as "sluts"—there would be no way to overstate the danger of the fate that awaited us. We could die, socially; in terms of our identities as good children, we could die to our families; we could even die literally. We already understood that our own death could be the shadow side of our desire.

If we were out of line sexually, we could become sluts; if we became sluts, we could die several deaths. This equation was so much a part of the air we breathed that we could scarcely examine it. The impulse to equate women's being sexual with their suffering a swift, sure punishment is reflexive.

IN ANY GROUP of girls, it seems, someone has to be the slut. In her book, *Schoolgirls*, Peggy Orenstein describes the same dynamic. In our extended group, now that Tia was done for, Dinah was called the slut. She found that role—or rather, it found her—and she did not deign to fight it. She put it on with dignity.

We were fourteen and a half now; it was our eighth-grade year in junior high. After school, before she was fully placed past the margins, I used to go over to Dinah's house almost every day. It was in a shabby stucco apartment building the color of a dirty eraser. The wood of the front door was battered, and there was a neo-Tudor-style entrance with straggling grass by the steps. When Dinah opened the door with the key she kept on a loop of red yarn around her neck, we were met with a warm, sad smell: cat litter, bubble bath, and packaged cinnamon rolls going stale on the counter.

Indoors was what, to my adult eyes, would be a scene of squalor. At the time, though, it looked like a scene of freedom. There were never any adults around during the day, and I was never invited to stay to dinner. There was a sense in the afternoon that the adults had given up; and in the evening, when they came home, the mood was one of private struggles that an outsider was not invited to witness.

Both her parents were tall, thin, raw-skinned people, transplanted from a rural province in Canada, ill at ease on the West Coast, and both equally defeated in their bearing. When they came home, the first question usually had to do with chores far beyond expectations I was familiar with: Had Dinah deposited the check? Had she called the social worker and explained why they couldn't make the meeting? Had she given the cat her medicine? One of her errands was to throw out the plastic bags full of rinsed empty mixer bottles and throw out the steady supply of empty liquor bottles. Her little sister, a seven-year-old, could never sit still. Already unable to look another child in the eyes, she veered around making airplane noises when we had to take her with us on errands and would crash into us so hard it would hurt.

Dinah had her own compulsion: every morning she would creep into the chipped-tile, peach-colored bathroom while any adults who might be around were still sleeping and take a hot shower. She would then wrap her body and her head in the one set of towels that was free of stray cat hairs; she kept these in her room, for no one's use but her own. Then she would take her hot cocoa into her room. (The cocoa was a luxury on a food-stamp budget. The cashier who rang it up would flick her eyes at it for the benefit of the cashier at the next checkout counter. At those moments Dinah would stand perfectly still and present her lifted-eyebrow, crossed-arms, hip-out-thrust, Myrna-Loy-being-patient-but-amused-with-the-loutish-delivery-boy face.)

In her room, alone, she would begin her ritual of the nails. She would sit at the rickety child's vanity table, a white ruffle pinned around it, that had been a gift from her father at an earlier, more prosperous Christmas. She would spread out each hand in turn and lacquer each nail with colors that sounded like experiences she still wanted to have: Tangerine Sunrise, Parisian Gala, Mist on the Moors, Bronze Fandango. The bottles were ranged in rows around the table, like her own army. Outside there might be adults sleeping off a bad night, a cat in need of distemper pills, a younger sister menacing the cat, a phone that might or might not emit a dial tone. Or, worst of all, her mom whispering apologies through the door. With her bulky headphones on, Dinah listened to the Bee Gees and painted. She was a miniaturist, and everything within her range of vision was perfectly under control.

She had the gift not only of inventing a more alluring world but of extending it to others. Alone, a glamour would descend on the two of us. Dinah had a chewed-up collection of records of musicals, and for her these created an alternate world. Singing along with them, her pointed chin would lift upward, her red-rimmed eyes would light up, and she would lose her tough scrapper quality. The headache-tight Lee jeans, the hair darkened with auburn streaks by henna, the pookah-shell necklaces, the run-down hiking boots would all disappear. She became Gypsy Rose Lee bathed in a spotlight, Auntie Mame loose in Manhattan.

Dinah put the record on the turntable that was propped up by old *Life* magazines. Then she would stand at the picture window behind the closed drapes; with a single gesture she would pull them open, a leg, a rounded arm would emerge, and she would be performing "Luck Be a Lady Tonight." She would roar in her throaty contralto, her eyes beckoning the mighty audience, her lips and slightly crooked teeth giving a rogue's smile. The floor would vibrate and the cat would leap onto a chair back to stare. Dinah would open her arms and throw back her neck and arch her back and her breasts for the finale, the crowds lifting her up with their applause and the mud colors of her household all gone, sung away into less than a memory.

But Dinah was called the slut. She was defined as the slut because of conditions so tangential that they could almost never have been, or it could as easily have been someone else. She was poor; that is, poorer than the other white kids. And her body changed faster than many of the other girls'. By seventh grade, her breasts were large and high—but that visitation had come to other girls, too. So that was not all; it was how she decided to carry them that did her in.

It was her posture. She refused the good-girl slump, the binder held crosswise across her chest (cool boys held the binder loose by their side in one cupped hand, like a club). She would not back down and rest her weight on her pelvis and ruin her line. Instead, she flagrantly walked with her spine extended to her full height, her back slightly swayed. Knowing the dusty afternoons in front of the proscenium in her living room, I understood what she was doing with her tailbone tucked under, her torso supple and erect like a figure on the prow of a ship, her feet turned carefully out: she was being a star. She was thinking of the technique of stage movement she read about in her books on the Drama and trying always to imagine a fine filament connecting the top of her talented head to the heavens. She was walking out to her public, graciously, for an encore.

But there was no visual language in our world for a poor girl with big breasts walking tall, except "slut." And rather than bow her shoulders, she took that name onto them.

By watching what happened to Dinah, we discovered that sex— for girls at least—was a game of musical chairs. It was very important to stay in the game, if always nervously moving; but finding yourself suddenly singled out was nothing short of fatal. And—just as in that game—the rules that isolated one or another of us were arbitrary and capricious. One thing was certain: if you were targeted, no matter how randomly, whether you had moved not fast enough or had moved too fast for the music, in some sure way your exclusion was your own fault. For what were you doing between chairs?

Who did she think she was? What was she doing, walking like that? "Moving," as Dinah might say, exhaling cigarette smoke sharply. Or, in another mood: "dancing, *asswipes*."

She was a spectacular dancer. On late afternoons, she could usually be found practicing steps alone in the shabby music room, head up, facing solemnly into the wall-length mirror. She was more than disciplined with herself, she was almost brutal in the service of what she thought of very levelly as her art. There was a genre of teenage-girl novel, left over from the early sixties, in which a hardworking and usually orphaned ballet student pits her all to attain the great performance and accolades, and then a life of grace and ease. There was always a scene in which the ballerina takes off her slippers backstage and they are full of blood. In spite of my teasing, Dinah devoured these books. Her kicks were higher and her splits deeper than those of any of the other girls in our eighth-grade class.

Given those hours spent alone, begged from the demands of her parents' errands, and the flamboyant 1940s musical style she developed, it was no surprise that when the call for cheerleader auditions went out, it provoked her competitive spirit.

We were not the kind of girls to approach the cheerleading squad with straight faces. But the idea of a test—even more compellingly, a test of skill and charm—seduced us. We let ourselves dwell for a moment on the prestige implicit in the susurrus of the pom-poms and the red-and-white skirt that flipped up to reveal red velvet undershorts. Cheerleading was sexy, but for once it was a sexuality that was also absolutely safe.

As the tryout date neared, with great concentration Dinah substituted visions of herself as a squeaky-clean teen aristocrat, projecting radiant school spirit, for her usual fantasies of being Lotte Lenya in a smoky, debauched cabaret.

One problem, though, was that our crowded, underfunded junior high had no school spirit. Though there were some dedicated and creative teachers, in some ways the school was a warehouse for the students of the city's poorer neighborhoods. Many of the kids, distracted by home struggles, saw the school as a mutely oppressive presence forcing them to mark time. But Dinah had such faith in the untried power of her stage presence that she was sure that, as cheerleader, she could budge that mood of student cynicism. And maybe she could have. Dinah was popular with the disaffected kids.

The second trouble was one the power of her talent could not touch. The junior high school's cheerleading squad would be chosen not by PE or drama teachers on the basis of physical merit but by a panel of regular-subject teachers.

These teachers were not outsiders like the eccentric elective teachers—like the drama teacher who thought of Dinah as a future Gypsy Rose Lee or the gym teacher who saw her as a hardworking athlete. The regular-subject teachers thought of themselves as the conscience of the school. "And," as one was overheard to say, "the cheerleaders represent the school." In the manner of conventional middle school teachers everywhere, they saw a heavily made-up girl, in her short red leather jacket and cropped T-shirt, leaning against a graffiti-stained wall every afternoon with the guys in the drill team, smoking; and they thought they knew all about Dinah.

For weeks, nonetheless, Dinah prepared. She believed in merit. When she was done, she could do the "Fight" song—"We're going to F! I! G-H-T!"—and the "Pep" song—"We've got the sun in the morning and the moon at night!"—with flair and even an approximation of sincerity. Her pivots—a tricky step that I never mastered in spite of nights spent trying—were exemplary. In the tryout red plush outfit that Dinah had sewn herself, she played the role of "wholesome cheerleader," the only jarring note being the crease of metallic blue eye shadow that, against the dictates of *Seventeen* magazine, she insisted on applying daily to her light brown, tired-looking eyes.

On the afternoon of the audition, Dinah was tense. But her performance of the two cheers was, insofar as such a crude and bouncy set piece could be, a star turn. She held out her arms to the dark and silent auditorium seats, pom-poms lifted in an exuberant V, then swooped them low. The panel of teachers sat in the center of the pit, their faces impassive.

Then the other girls and I tried out, sheepishly, in jeans. None of us was any better than pedestrian in contrast to Dinah. We went outside to wait for the panel's decision.

Sex negated Dinah's grace and her skill. The panel passed her over. Forty-five minutes after we had started our wait and Dinah had gone off to get a Tab, a secretary—as I recall, a woman who had glanced in at the auditions—posted a typewritten list outside the gym door. She avoided our eyes.

All the new members of the team consisted of commonly acknowledged "popular" older girls. And me. In a mostly poor or working-class school, almost all of the chosen were daughters of the middle class. And—in a student population that was mostly Chinese, Japanese, Filipino, or African-American—almost all were white. Dinah was not even an alternate.

I felt sick. Without Dinah, I did not want to be a cheerleader. Without her, it would not be campy; it would be dire. It would be our idea of middle school purgatory. What had happened?

Dinah rejoined me and looked at the list on the door. She made her Judy Garland chin-out "struggling" face, then laughed at herself.

"You," she said, "don't know *what* to say."

She shrugged her shoulders under her leather jacket. "It's that I hang out with the wrong group, that's all," she said. "I should have anticipated it." Looking past me to the hills above the playground, she changed her face and tone back to the ironic detachment she was so good at. "Well," she said crisply, lighting a Marlboro and then making one perfect French curl of smoke, "it can't be because they think I don't know how to dance."

And I could not contradict her. We filed to the bus stop together in silence. We had been classified differently, and we knew it. Our companionship was never exactly the same again. Together we had learned something new. Sex was not just sex, then, for girls. It was class too. And we had already learned that it was color. The stigma of it was not derived only from what you did but from who you were thought to be. The girl named head cheerleader, called "the cutest girl in ninth grade" and a paragon of her church group, was no angel. But her parents were "nice" and her clothes were good. The popular girls whom the teachers approved of conducted their budding sex lives after sneaking away from their parents' cabanas on the white-sand beaches of family vacations. Dinah went out with nineteen-year-old store-clerk motorcycle rockers and lay around listening to music on foam mattresses in garages in a low-rent district. That was the difference.

I will never forget Dinah sitting up in the back of the bleachers with the tough kids, illegally smoking, watching us quietly, almost technically, at the first appalling "rally," as her friends jeered. I was a failure, of course, and dropped out—to the team's relief. But it didn't do any good. By joining, I had betrayed her.

By high school, Dinah had found a new gang. They were mostly guys, the tough guys who hung out in the Mission District. They wore the uniform of the streets: plaid shirts cut off at the arms with waffle-weave long underwear worn underneath, and Ben Davis navy blue work pants.

Class considerations, which were like an invisible, undeniable hand moving us over a school-sized chessboard, directed Dinah to a whole new group of girls. The whole school spread rumors that the girls in that gang had mastered every technique in *The Sensuous Woman*.

Another girl familiar with what was becoming Dinah's world said, when we were adults, that fellatio was the first genuine adult skill she ever mastered other than driving, and that it made her feel just as powerful, just as valuable and free of her childhood helplessness. She spoke about the feeling among the girls in that subculture that sex was a performance for the benefit of boys.

Making out took place in the hilly shadows at the top of Twin Peaks, where all the kids drove to make out on weekend nights. The performances would begin with a sensuous, chilly striptease, furtive and exciting, in the dark grass, with the guy drinking or smoking a joint and guardedly watching. It ended with the girl twining herself around him, he protected from the wet earth by his Ben Davis jacket, she unprotected but high and warm with her power, the finale a demonstration of her skills and the boy unable to catch his breath, beside himself with his good luck. As an adult, I thought anew about Dinah in that setting, surrounded by those expectations. I wondered what she thought of that idea of a drama and a stage.

As we got older, her reputation worsened. She was said to be good at the performance. But the irony was that she *wasn't* a slut, in that her behavior was tame compared to ours. I also guess that during the same time in her life as her name became a fixture on the boys' bathroom walls, she was probably studying and trying to keep her family life together. I gathered from the junior high and high school grapevine that when she heard about the graffiti in the bathrooms that talked about her blow jobs, she thought it was funny. At least, I heard she laughed. I believed it. She liked to shock the world that had repudiated her.

By high school, her clothes tighter and her makeup heavier than ever, Dinah still seemed proud and she still carried herself with that head-held-high fuck-you regalness. I can't be sure what she was thinking because I stopped "knowing" her—both of us victims of that adolescent social dynamic, when class or race or gender pulls friends apart. Though my complicity was the more weak-willed, somehow we both understood we had to stop being friends.

But I could see that something was getting worn down in her. By the time we started high school, there were always dark circles under her eyes. She seemed to me to look fatigued from the effort it all took.

I have to imagine her thoughts after that; that she must have grown sick of the expectation that she and her friends were supposed to go over the dunes to "get down," as the language went, with the guys of the moment who asked them to. She must have tired of slam-dancing on a fake ID at the punk clubs. She must have become aware, during those mornings when the members of her gang and she were waking up still high in somebody's unfurnished Victorian apartment that stank of cats, that she was smarter than all the boys who talked about her.

Class had declared her a slut by fourteen, while she was still technically a virgin. It kept her there and kept me and my other little middle-class friends, who were wilder than she was, just on the right side of safe. With every year Dinah's face grew more and more impassive as she passed us in the halls. That still haunts me.

What happened to Dinah was brought back to me the first time I was touched in a place that only my clothing had touched before. From her story and from dozens of others I knew that "keeping control" of my desire was the key to keeping myself and my emerging identity safe. But—paradoxically—that same knowledge of where I had to go in order to possess my woman's identity made me want to move on fast into adult sexuality. So much depended on my taking the careful, balanced paces of a tightrope walker. Go—but *don't jump!!!* Go, but go slow and keep watching. Yet part of me wanted above all else the experience of shutting my eyes and falling through the air.

I knew I was dangerous to myself the day, a year later, that I let a boy named Ben, who would become my first boyfriend, walk me home. He drew me into the overgrown alley that ran alongside the stone staircase up the hill. A tangle of growth hid us almost from view, except that I could see the dark windows of my own house.

He pushed back my hair and kissed my forehead first, as if to make everything all right. He kissed down the side of my face to the corner of my mouth, too shy to look me in the eyes but moving always closer to my lips. All I had to do was turn my face up toward him and hold perfectly still. It was the easiest important thing I had ever done.

I knew that arching my neck just a little meant, that's all right; go on. His hand lay against my clavicle and then against my chest above my collar. Finally, he slid just the tips of his fingers not even to my breast but to the skin between that lay just inside the line of my clothing. It was skin that no one else had touched since I was a child. Through my closed eyes the light went red.

He withdrew his hand and watched my face. As the cold air rippled my shirt, his fingerprints were still burning.

He was watching to see if it was all right. It wasn't all right. I was capable of anything. I was capable of being Dinah.

A Short History of the Slut

Young women tend, in their peer groups, to act out in microcosm the splitting off of female sex from "legitimate" identity that the larger culture is intent upon imposing on them. We learn to identify the girl who most embodies that sexuality and to do to her, in a form of scapegoating that is a ritual to ward off the fate she represents, what the culture is doing to us. Why should these social paradigms exist? How did it happen that Dinah would be a "bad girl" and my friends and I, at least for the time being, "good girls"?

The fear of being out of control—in relation to food and money as well as sex—is characteristic of contemporary women. We understand loss of control to be inappropriate—and that it could turn a woman into a monster. We understand from books and movies that something terrible must happen to the slut. Where do we get our sense that our past must be immaculate, that our "promiscuity," our being in any way out of control, can lead us, if discovered, into symbolic or actual annihilation?

It is neither natural nor inevitable that women's lust should be punished. The idea of the slut in our own culture is deeply embedded.

There have been many ways of looking at "loose" female sexuality. Obviously, there are no sure data about the relationship between men and women before recorded history begins. Some theorists, such as Riane Eisler in *The Chalice and the Blade* and Marija Gimbutas in *The Language of the Goddess,* believe (though, given the uncertainty of the evidence, the debate is ongoing) that in the earliest civilizations, such as the Minoan, women's sexuality may have been considered holy magic. They date the reign of the Great Mother, with her divine sexuality, from the beginning of the Paleolithic period (20,000 B.C.E.) until the Bronze Age (ca. 3000 B.C.E.). They also hold that agrarian Mesopotamia, Egypt, and northwest India, with their pantheon of powerful goddesses whose sexuality was sacred—the magical child creators and the sole cultivators of the soil—were overrun by the more masculine-defined, male-god-worshiping pastoral nomads. This conquest, these theorists suggest—and it remains a controversial contention—consolidated by 2500 B.C.E. the rule of what we have come to call the patriarchy. After this period, they maintain, the sexually sacred goddesses were demoted to the rank of "subsidiary to husbands or brothers."

Though we can't possibly interpret this as part of a pro-woman belief system, it's interesting to know that some early recorded civilizations saw women's sexuality very differently from the way it looks today. In Sumer and Babylon, looseness in women was part of the religion. Temples were once staffed by sacred prostitutes—young women from the most aristocratic households—whose earnings helped support the temples. This practice of sacred prostitution may have derived from more ancient fertility rituals. The Babylonian *Epic of Gilgamesh,* dating from around 2000 B.C.E., tells the tale of a wild man, Enkidu, whom the hero Gilgamesh must tame. Gilgamesh dispatches "a temple prostitute to conquer him / with her greater power." Shamhat the prostitute "showed him her breasts, / showed him her body, . . . she showed him the things a woman knows how to do." For seven days the wild man "in his wonder / lay with her in pleasure" until he was too weak to hunt. The prostitute herself narrates this sexual tale.

The memory of female sexuality's sacred and religious aspects, though degraded, did not die out at once. A millennium after Hammurabi, Herodotus noted of Babylonian society that "Every woman who is a native of the country . . . must once in her life go and sit in the temple and there give herself to a strange man." Thus she did her duty to heaven and to the goddess, who welcomed the offering of female sexuality. (This practice was so widespread among the young women of Babylon that typical advice from a Babylonian father to his son was that the young man should avoid taking a sacred prostitute to be his wife, since "her husbands are beyond counting.")

Slowly, the many well-documented ways that male-dominated societies used to punish women for their sexuality became institutionalized. Strabo, the first-century B.C.E. Greek geographer, asserted that the Egyptians "excised" the women of their culture—a practice, of course, that certain Egyptian women, along with millions of others, still undergo today. From this time forward, history records a range of practices that fall into the category of female circumcision. These varied and still do from ritual hymen breaking to the excision of the entire clitoris and labia. Only by literally cutting women apart from their pleasure, it was and is still believed, could they be deterred from licentiousness.

Our own direct Western lineage of sexual valuation derives from the Hebrews. Though the Jewish tradition consistently held that, within marriage, the woman's erotic pleasure, as well as the man's, was part of God's legacy of joy and that pleasing one's wife could be a *mitzvah* (a camel driver was expected by divine law to make love to his wife at least once a month, and a rich man, who has more leisure, daily), the Hebrews took a lead in formalizing the attitude that sex without procreation was illicit. The Hebrews refined the sexual double standard that we have inherited: sexual constraints tended to favor the man. "The usual remedy" for a woman's adultery seems to have been divorce, in which the woman lost her dower, right of maintenance, etc. Deuteronomy 22:20–21 warns that if a bride is not found to be a virgin, "Then they shall bring out the damsel to the door of her father's house, and the men of her city shall stone her with stones that she die," because she has played the whore in the house of Israel. And in Numbers 5:15 women are warned that the wife who has gone astray "and commit[ted] a trespass against [her husband]" must drink an "offering" of jealousy: "The Lord make thee a curse and an oath among thy people, when the Lord doth make thy thigh to rot, and thy belly to swell; and this water that causeth the curse shall go into thy bowels, to make thy belly to swell, and thy thigh to rot" (Numbers 5:21–22).

Other nonprocreative forms of sexuality became taboo. While Babylon still had its legions of homosexual prostitutes, among the Israelites homosexuality was denounced in the same terms as bestiality. By the time the Old Testament was compiled, hatred of prostitutes was entrenched, and that hatred echoes the fear and disgust felt for the Babylonian societies, which had codified holy prostitution.

The Book of Ezekiel (23:8) compares the sinning city of Jerusalem to a loathsome harlot: "In her youth [men] lay with her, and they bruised the breasts of her virginity, and poured their whoredom upon her," it reads. The harlot "doted upon her paramours," men "whose flesh is as the flesh of asses, and whose issue is like the issue of horses," reads the text. The venom that from here on characterizes descriptions of loose female sexuality is clear: "I will deliver thee," said the Lord to this promiscuous, feminine city, "into the hand of them whom thou hatest . . . and they shall deal with thee hatefully, and shall take away all [the fruit of] thy labour, and shall leave thee naked and bare: and the nakedness of thy whoredoms shall be discovered, both thy lewdness and thy whoredoms." The Hebrews equated female promiscuity—meaning any female sexuality outside marriage—with shame, destruction, and just punishment, as we consciously or unconsciously still do.

The Roman Empire, though guided more by civil than by religious law, also established and defended the sexual double standard. Roman law, like Greek, seems to have defined adultery as "the violation of another man's bed." Male unfaithfulness in itself was not seen as adulterous.

In contrast to the sacred prostitutes of the earlier civilization, Rome maintained a cadre of sacred virgins. Their celibacy was seen as crucial to the well-being of the entire country. Being a sacred virgin for the good of the city was a serious business: in the first century before Christ, three of these young women were accused of having had sexual intercourse. Each was buried alive to starve in an underground cell.

In Rome two millennia ago, a woman's drinking more than a little wine could have been punishable by law since that behavior suggested sexual looseness. We still take for granted that "loose" behavior by women must provoke punishment. In 1993, a debate arose around the issue of "date rape" in which a strong consensus formed among many commentators that if a woman got drunk, she deserved what was coming to her. This view shaped the defense even of brutal gang rapes in which the women had been drinking, such as the notorious Governeur, New York, pool-table rape of an unconscious young working woman and the rape of a half-conscious student at Saint John's University in Queens, New York, on March 1, 1990. O. J. Simpson's attorney Robert Baker pursued his defense of a man accused of murdering his wife in a jealous rage with the charge that Nicole Brown Simpson "drank excessively" and "apparently used drugs herself." In the case of the Saint John's University date-rape trial, half the public blamed the twenty-two-year-old victim, Angela, for her assault, because she had gone to her assailant's house and accepted a drink. According to the defendant, " 'she asked him for a drink and this meant she wanted sex.' " "Taking advantage of drunk women seemed to be an accepted part of the house code," notes Peggy Reeves Sanday, a commentator on the trial. "As long as Angela was drunk, whatever happened was within the code." In Rome, while women's drinking, even in moderation, was grounds for divorce, men's drinking was institutionalized as part of elite social life.

Another ground for divorce in ancient Rome was behavior that could come under the heading of "perverse and disgusting conduct." In our own culture, as Phyllis Chesler documents in *Mothers on Trial: The Battle for Children and Custody*, sexual behavior on the part of a divorcing mother—dating, having a man spend the night in the same house with one's children, certainly maintaining a lesbian relationship—can mean that the woman is seen as "unfit," jeopardizing her chances of gaining custody of her children. In her study of sixty custody suits in which the fathers won—suits that, Chesler holds, reveal a trend toward giving inadequate or uninvolved fathers an advantage over "good-enough" mothers—57 percent of the cases turned on the point that the mother was "seen as unfit by father, other family members, or by a judge because she was sexual during marriage or after divorce." (Poignantly, "Two lesbian mothers were privately allowed to keep their children by agreeing not to live with their mates; not to allow them or any woman lover ever to spend the night.") In Rome, the charge of female licentiousness in a divorce meant more than merely the ending of a woman's marriage; it was in some ways the end of her life. By early imperial times, an adulterous wife had to undergo banishment and be stripped of half her dowry, and for any other man to marry her was considered to be a criminal offense. The historian Tacitus felt that Rome in the first century was too easy on loose women. He praised, in contrast to his own society, the Germans. Among them, when a woman was accused of adultery, "Punishment is swift, and is the prerogative of the husband: in the presence of relatives, the husband expels the wife from the house nude, with her hair cut, and drives her through the whole village with a whip."

Women's groups around the world still battle with the judicial tolerance of women's murder by their husbands on the grounds of adultery—the *crime passionnel*. On October 25, 1996, for instance, O. J. Simpson's defense lawyer "attacked the character of the former football player's murdered ex-wife . . . accusing her of consorting with prostitutes. . . . Attorney Robert Baker opened his defense in Simpson's wrongful death civil trial by describing Nicole Brown Simpson as a promiscuous woman 'who . . . partied with "lots" of boyfriends. . . . Nicole was exercising her wings. She had many boyfriends. . . . She was the pursuer.' "

"And they shall deal with thee hatefully."

Simpson's attorney in Los Angeles at the end of the twentieth century is playing on assumptions descended from Mediterranean laws two millennia old. Until the end of the first century B.C.E, Roman law ruled that a man could kill his wife with impunity if he caught her in adultery. Sometimes the Roman husband could have his wife sentenced to death even if she was not caught *in flagrante delicto* with her lover.

In a repressive male world, the force of female desire can in fact be subversive. There have been moments in history when the safeguards have broken down and a civilization's worst fears of the slut have been confirmed. In Rome in 186 B.C.E., according to the historian Livy, women's misbehavior sent a shudder through the highest echelons of society. The women of Rome—particularly the highborn matrons, who were leisured, bored, and, like their earlier Greek counterparts, excluded from much of public life—became leaders in the many cults that flourished in urban society. These cults in turn created for the women a central place in pantheons and rituals. The worship of Bacchus—the god of wine, ecstasy, and promiscuity—was especially popular. Women were allowed—even encouraged—to indulge in religious cult exploration because it diverted them from political intrigue. Roman society was generally content to let this religious subculture thrive, if it harmlessly absorbed the energies of these well-educated women.

The scandal started out innocently enough—as a women-only festival administered by the older wives. But eventually, "divine revelations" to participants served as cover for a change in religious practice: selected men were allowed into the activities.

Once this happened, the women-dominated festivals were held much more frequently; worshipers felt the need to commune with the deity not three times a year, as they had before the revelations, but a good *five times a month*. Then the festivals were held in the dead of night. In the darkness, it was charged, all sexual restraint was cast to the winds. Cult members, respectable wives and mothers by day, ran screaming and bearing torches to the river. As the riotous women and the selected men intermingled, the scene became orgiastic.

Inevitably, the nature of these rituals was exposed to the community at large and public worship of Bacchus was legally curtailed. The male participants were killed; the women were returned to their families; and the families, held responsible for the women's behavior, were charged with their punishment.

The early Church built upon the reinforced control of women. In Justinian's time the straying wife was held to be a criminal, her lover only an accomplice. Early Christians were instructed that a faithless wife must be divorced, but not an unfaithful husband. By the early Middle Ages, it was well established in Western Europe that women were more lustful than men. The Christian twist on this ancient view was that women were therefore more culpable. The Latin term for passion—used later to denote an unreasonable and possessive erotic drive—was "libido," and this drive always was understood to derive from the woman and to be associated with her.

Eighth-century penitentials developed by ecclesiastics in Rome gave adult males only a year's penance for masturbation but assigned three years' penitence to a woman who masturbated. The more severe prohibition for women was necessary, in the eyes of the Church, "to punish an excess of desire [libido] greater in women than in men." "Women," the historian Michel Rouche writes, "blamed as the source of the destructive folly of love [libido], had to be wrested from the cosmos, or at any rate from the world of wickedness, and made safe for the dignity of marriage and tender motherhood, the basis of society. The sacredness of the body and the need to exorcise passion account for the status of women." Since women were considered lustier, they had to be more carefully controlled.

An edict of 517 C.E. speaks of a Burgundian widow who, "burning with hot desire [libido]," breaks her vow to the man to whom her parents have promised her. She runs away to her lover, risking a death sentence that is averted only by a royal pardon. By the time of the Merovingians—the Frankish dynasty that dominated the region now called France from around 496 to 750 C.E.—it was taken for granted that an unmarried girl's desire for one mate rather than another counted for little and could put the girl into grave jeopardy. Though the Merovingian councils and the decree of Clotaire II in 614 prohibited forcing a woman to marry against her will, in practice a young girl's rejection of her parents' choice for her was thought as serious as adultery. Such disobedience turned her into a moral exile from her entire community.

Many European law codes, such as those of the Franks and the Burgundians, early in the Middle Ages, set rigid consequences for adult single women who acted upon their desires. The Visigoth Code of Euric decreed that a *widow* who had sex could lose her property. The only fate left to single women, once convicted of having acted upon their desire, was a miserable life of prostitution. Even if a Burgundian widow was committed to marrying a new husband, she forfeited the right to do so if ever, when "overcome by desire [libido]," she "freely and spontaneously has sexual relations" with her intended groom. Such sexual desire was seen as degraded, and not worthy of the sanction of marriage.

Our modern stigma against rape victims was legally codified at this time. Among the Franks and Burgundians, there was a penalty for raping a slave. But once she was raped, whether slave or free, a woman was beyond redemption. She was "corrupted," and "a corrupted woman had no further value."

During the early Middle Ages, from the sixth to the eighth centuries, extramarital sex on the part of women carried even more severe penalties than did single women's sexual expression—deadly ones. Adultery included lovemaking outside the institution of marriage. According to the law of the Burgundians, the "stench of adultery" was so loathsome that women found to have had sex outside marriage— whether the women were wives, unmarried girls, or widows—were banished from their homes and condemned to die from strangulation, their bodies to be discarded in a marsh. Among Gallo-Romans, in what is now France, a husband was entitled by law to kill "with a single blow" his wife and her lover caught in the act. The Franks, living in the region north of the Loire, strangled adulteresses, burned them alive, or tied a heavy stone to an accused woman's neck. If she sank, she was guilty. If she managed somehow to rise to the surface, she was innocent. The Burgundians, who had extended the definition of female adultery to unmarried girls and to widows who had sex, treated such women forever as being marked and untouchable.

As much as to say, Tia was dead now.

Almost every society punishes its sluts in its own ways. Right now, however, our own sometimes pretends that it does not. The summer I went back to ask my friends about our girlhoods, there was a rash of sex industry films coming out of Hollywood. *Indecent Proposal, Striptease,* and *Showgirls* were following *Pretty Woman.* Teenage girls were reading about how Demi Moore had worked out for hours each day to play the stripper in *Striptease,* how she would go to the strip joints and hang out with the dancers to "get it right."

As we drove through the hills above Marin, I asked one young woman who had grown up with us what she thought about those films. Her opinion was better informed than most of ours, for she had spent time as a sex worker: as a stripper and later as a professional mistress. She embodied the contradiction we lived under: a college-educated, happily married, community-minded woman with curly black hair, tailored clothes, and a timid grin—indistinguishable from any of the rest of our tribe. But by the standards of the culture she had been a real whore, a true, dyed-in-the-wool, no-argument, verifiable slut. She had gone all the way. Bad girl, good girl—the dimorphism was a fantasy. They were both here in the car; in her, in myself, in us all.

As she drove, the carefree mood of two women in their early thirties reminiscing about girlhood in an open car, feet on the dashboard and reggae on the radio, evaporated. "Here is all I have to say about how they are glamorizing those images for girls, who are just sucking it in," she said. Her words became slow and deliberate. "When men think a woman is a whore, it's open . . . season . . . on her. They can *say* anything to her they want, they can *do* anything they want, they can be absolutely as crass and vile and violent and cruel and uncaring as the darkest part of their personality wants to be. And it's okay. They don't have to afford the woman *one ounce* of respect for being a human being. She's not a human being. She's a thing."

"From your experience," I ventured, "is there such a thing as a line that exists that we're right to sense and to fear? That once you cross it, anything can happen to you?"

"Absolutely," she said. "And I think it happens to prostitutes more than to women who just sleep around a lot. But the danger is something you can feel in the continuum. It's a coherent system, in effect. Since the sexual revolution, there's license, and there's terror, and we're living under both."

Then the words came out in a torrent. "I was shocked. I was shocked. I thought that because of the progress women have made in our society, men would have a *clue* that prostitutes are human beings and that they don't deserve to be treated so poorly, but they don't. It's almost as if now they see sex workers as the *only* women that they can be so aggressive and cruel to. They can't get away with it in their jobs anymore, they can't get away with it in their marriages, but with sex workers it's okay. That's what they're paid for! They're paid to be sexually harassed, they're paid to be assaulted. Women outside the sex industry won't put up with it now."

I was quiet. I was thinking: if all women, even nice women, can do what only whores used to do, but you can no longer treat all women who do such things like whores—that is, if feminism is succeeding in breaking down some of the penalties that used to be applied to nonprofessional sexually licentious women—then society will all the more rigidly professionalize and demarcate the "bad girl" for sale, the girl to whom anything can be done. My friend was explaining that "real" prostitutes used to bear the burden of the fact that nice girls had a limited repertoire; now they bear the burden of the fact that nice girls have gotten wild.

The feeling of foreboding that had hung over the word "slut" in my sexually libertine girlhood became clearer. The culture had said: Take it off—take it *all* off. The culture had also said, of the raped girl, of the hitchhiker, of the dead girl: She was in the wrong place at the wrong time, doing the wrong thing, wearing the wrong clothes.

Suddenly, as the soft round hills sped by, I saw flash before my eyes a photograph from one of the social histories I had been reading. It was of the nearly intact mummified remains of a fourteen-year-old German girl from Windeby in Schleswig-Holstein, dating from the first century C.E. Her long, shapely legs and slender feet were intact, and her right arm still clutched the garrote that had been used to twist the rope around her neck. Her lips were open in an "O" of surprise or pain, and a twisted rag was still securely bound over her eyes. At fourteen, according to scientists and historians, the girl had been blindfolded, strangled, and drowned, most likely as retribution for "adultery"—for what we would now call a teenage love affair.

Thank God. Not sluts like Tia.

Given these origins, it is no wonder that even today fourteen-year-old girls who notice, let alone act upon, their desire, have the heart-racing sense that they are doing something obscurely, but surely, dangerous. It is also in part because of this inheritance that a modern woman wakes up after a night of being erotically "out of control" feeling sure, on some primal level, that something punitive is bound to happen to her—and that if it doesn't, it should.

8

First Base: Hierarchy

The unfolding of the sequence of "bases" began, moving us on from the first kiss, well behind us now, through the sequence of what was called "getting to third." For most of us girls, it was an extraordinarily important process that ended too soon. For with each level, each gradation, we learned a little more about where we stood and who we might become. The progression through the "bases" was not only a physical exploration, it was also a social one: it told us about who we might be in the social hierarchy. And it was about trying on personas. Who we could be was determined by whom we were allowed to touch. As we got better at investigating this erotic territory, it became a way we could try to resist, subvert, or manipulate the identities imposed on us by peers and parents.

"My first crush," recalls Tonya, "was in seventh grade. I remember that I wrote love notes in my little locked diary that I wanted to give the guy at some time. But he was in the in crowd, and I was not in a crowd at all. When I tried to go up and talk to him, I was laughed away—according to the rules, I wasn't allowed to be in conversation with this guy. This was a guy I was supposed to want but couldn't have.

"So instead I tried to get a crush on this big geek and waited every day under a bridge that he had to walk across to school. I would see him coming, and then I would come out and be casually picking berries. He was the first guy I kissed. He was skinny, scrawny, and not very cute, but I could fantasize enough by altering my picture of him. It was more okay than wanting this unattainable guy.

"All my real crushes were unrequited until I was a sophomore. By then I had joined the official radical-youth out crowd. I was wearing the radical-outcast style that came in with punk—brocade 1950s dresses from thrift stores that we would shorten into miniskirts and, my favorite, little white boots like Blondie wore. I had my hair shorter in the back—you had to have some part of your head buzzed, that was required—and longer in the front. You couldn't have your hair your natural color. That was unacceptable. So the front was black and the rest was bleached blond. I looked like one of those dogs that can't see anything. You weren't supposed to be able to see. You had to be able to throw your hair around when you slam-danced.

"This guy I liked had a reputation. By then I had picked up on how to flirt from watching TV. I was just one of those little girls who liked being coy. I guess I caught his attention. By then, too, I had 'developed.' I had all the feminine accoutrements. When I got to kiss him, I realized I did not have to be a mainstream reject. I could be a successful rebel."

My own introduction into the peer-group sexual hierarchy was no more successful than Tonya's. The summer I was fourteen, we started to have slow dances in kids' homes in our neighborhood.

Shari, Cath, and I—Genevieve had moved away to the suburbs—used to get together in the bathroom, locking the door, to prepare ourselves for the Friday-night dance parties with the boys. The kids in Shari's gang had decorated her basement with totem paintings: motorcycles, musical notes, and imitations of the artwork on King Crimson album covers. An old stereo had been set up on the floor. This was where the dancing took place, that solemn inquiry in which the women would be separated from the girls.

Each one of us looked at herself and the girl standing next to her. She looked with the imagined eyes of a lover, gauging which of the two the imagined lover would choose and why. If there were things the projected boy might prefer, they would be attacked openly and slyly: the threatening charms would have to be slashed away in the mental calculation, no matter how dear the friend who possessed them. This was not the gleeful curiosity of preadolescence. Instead, we were engaged in something that felt truly Darwinian: organizing ourselves into a pecking order.

"Your breasts are twice the size mine are," Shari might say to Cath.

"You'll grow," Cath might respond coolly, thus engaging in an act of aggression, since the conciliatory answer would have been "No way, stop joking."

One day Shari actually retorted, "You know, they say bigger woman have twice the chance of getting breast cancer." None of us was too shocked, for this preparation for the dance had such serious implications that of course the long knives would come out.

After we had stared at the mirror until it could tell us nothing more about ourselves, we put on the jeans we had pressed and our cotton tops. Sometimes we wore "sweetheart blouses," floral-print shirts that had puffed sleeves and tied in the back. Our jeans were so tight we could not move very freely. We took the stairs to the basement like a theater ensemble before a performance, mentally checking our makeup and lines. The boys, and the rival girls, were waiting.

Down in the musty room, the most sexually advanced boy would lead the most sexually advanced girl out onto the floor. The initial fast dances were merely social, and couples regrouped in such a way as to keep the fabric of the "gang" together. But with the slow dances, sexual status mattered. The well-liked but sexually immature kids goofed around in a corner, pretending to show one another dance steps. The more grown-up boys clasped the girls with the B cups or higher, while the rest of us sat up straight, waiting to be claimed.

During all the slow dances except "Stairway to Heaven" (which, at eight minutes, was reserved for serious making out; dancing it together was a statement to everyone), girls like me, not yet "developed," could ask to dance with one of the desirable boys. For three minutes once or twice an evening, we could let ourselves feel wanted in spite of knowing that a boy like that could not really want us. Not "did not"; could not. It wasn't even worth trying to make conversation. It was, as Tonya also recalls, one of those unwritten laws.

Low-status girls knew that the high-status boys would keep their hands firmly on our shoulders rather than let them wander, the way they did when they danced with the more desirable girls. But sometimes someone would turn the lights down and someone would be passing a bong around, and the high-status boys would get bored and make out even with the girls they would never want to claim in full view. This could get you a sort of temporary exemption.

Theo was the most desired boy in the gang. He was disruptive in class, which was considered a killingly attractive quality. He lived with his father, who owned a movie theater. Suddenly, on one of these Friday nights when not too much was happening socially, Theo took my hand very casually, the way the dominant males of the tribe did. But he had not realized that the song was the infinite "Stairway to Heaven." It had only started groaning out its opening chords, but I wasn't about to let this opportunity pass. I stood up in a hurry. His face fell: he was cornered.

We danced. As I knew he would, he kept his hands immobilized on my shoulders. He did not even begin to move them down my back. He held me with perfect propriety. I was mortified.

Finally, my luck turned. Maybe he just didn't want to waste a whole "Stairway to Heaven." He kissed me. At first he was kissing me with the exact same self-absorbed, distracted air with which he constantly combed his hair. Pretty soon he was kissing me more or less for real.

But when the lights came back on, he removed his mouth with dispatch. He brushed back his hair and, turning away, patted me on the hip like an obedient handmaiden. "Yo! Shari!" he called, taking no more chances.

My feelings were mixed. I had failed the test of sexual allure so obviously that my girlfriends tactfully avoided even mentioning my experience. But privately, when I was alone, I replayed the memory and put it into its best possible light. I might not be unthinkable forever. I had gotten the alpha Theo to kiss me.

9

Second Base: Love and Control

Come on now, try and understand
The way I feel under your command.
— PATTI SMITH, "Because the Night," 1978

E ven as we were trying to explore, the physical horizons continued to close in.

Shari and I, intimate friends by now, used to creep up onto the warm shingle roof of my house and perch there, eating, drinking, reading, and planning our assault on the future. We lay in the sun and read Kerouac and Tolkien alongside our *Cosmopolitan* and *Mademoiselle*. We were in love with Dean in Kerouac's *On the Road*, wanting both to have him and to *be* him, too. "For to him," we read, "sex was the one and only holy thing in life. . . . Dean just raced in society, eager for bread and love, he didn't care one way or another. . . . 'Oh man . . . dig the street of life . . . wow, and that woman in that window up there, just looking down with her big breasts . . . whee. Sol, we gotta go and never stop till we get there!' " The books lied to us: they equated youth with liberty. The magazines told the truth: they offered rules. With the books, our vision of the future would expand; with the magazines it would contract.

We undid the straps of our bikinis (thus avoiding unsightly tan lines) and held still beside each other, aware of the very outlines of the other's body, not touching, for we were older now. At that point, we were always on the Grapefruit Diet. We peeled grapefruits with our teeth until the fragrant oils sprayed our necks and our fingers were sticky. Our chins rested on our folded arms; our ribs, our hip-bones (day four of the diet), and our toes dug into the slant of the roof; our eyes peered over the crest of the house into the immense blue distances, where the bridges hung suspended, steel gray to the east and golden red to the north, the sun shaking flashes of white light across the bay. We looked out over the immense cityscape, and we wanted to devour everything—everything we saw.

We would argue about our plans. It was always the same argument, like that of a long-married couple.

"Let's just go, Shar. Let's stop thinking about it. Let's just go."

("*Where we going, man?*" "*I don't know but we gotta go.*")

"We can't 'just go.' You know that. We're not 'of age.' We'll get busted."

"Let's just get in the car right after school lets out for the summer and just take off. Just drive to Tijuana. To Baja. Let's go camp on the beach." Dean and Sol had driven straight to Mexico.

"Yeah. Let's drink tequila and throw up. Let's get nailed by the Mexican police force. I'm sure our parents will understand. I'm sure they'll rush to help us make the arrangements."

"Your stepbrother got to go. My brother went last year."

And then anger would rise up in both of us, a hot uneasy wave that was always within us, turbulent or slow. We couldn't go. "It's—" said Shari in a singsong "—not the same." All at once the vista, which had been a fantastic gateway, became as tight and circumscribed as a postcard. Girlvision.

Her mockery of our parents' nonanswers stood for an injustice that was too big even to think about. "Fuck 'em all," she said.

We did not go to Tijuana. We had changed: we were big girls now. The climate had changed; it was the ungentle 1970s. Our parents let us spend a night in Point Reyes, a safe bus ride away.

What was it the world so feared in two young women setting off alone with each other? Why was it that when Shari and I sat in a café, deep in conversation, young men and old would make their way toward us belligerently, as if they were fulfilling an assignment? "You girls want company?" They didn't just want sex. They also wanted, it seemed, to make sure we didn't get too far without them. Many people, in many different ways, were helping us learn about our being under sexual control.

That closing-in teaches quiescence. It prepares girls to react sub-
missively in the face of more overt controlling, even to the point of
abuse.

The couple of guys I had kissed did not wait around for me. I was
way behind most of the girls I knew. So it was with real relief that at
fourteen I found Ben, that first actual boyfriend. I fell "in like," as we
said, with a guy who was sweet and popular, a good student, and, it
turned out, physically violent.

Ben, the son of a WASP mother from an old family and an Italian
American father who was a local attorney, was charming to my
mother and father when, wearing a clean flannel shirt, he came over
to pick me up before a movie. But in the streets around the tough
school he went to, he was known as a daredevil. When I first met
him, in the alley beside the bike shop where the older kids hung out,
he had been describing his skateboarding injuries to a friend: "The
side of my leg," he had been saying, "looked like hamburger."

To my amazement, he did not see me as an insignificant little girl.
He wanted to "date." The importance this bestowed upon me
seemed immense. It equalized me. A sophomore was interested in
me, and so I graduated into the same league as Shari and Cath. I also
won territory separate from, and not subordinate to, the grown-up
territory of my brother and his gang.

Soon I was traveling around the city with Ben and his skateboard.
When we went to the movies, the skateboard occupied a third seat.
When we went to kiss in the forest, Ben first laid his skateboard
down tenderly, wheels up on a bed of vines so it wouldn't get rusty,
and only then turned to me to help me lie down on his old lumber-
jack coat.

We did "make out." Again, his willingness to do so was a surprise
to me. I still had no breasts to speak of, and I was under the impression that a boy would find the whole thing a waste of time if I could
not provide them. But he seemed happy to fool around; and when he
did, when we "French-kissed"—which I had not attempted on anything but a pillow before—it was one of the shocks of sex that I will
always remember. "French kissing" had sounded so much more delicate and palatable than something that involved so much of someone else's saliva. I sat on his lap on a fallen log and experienced the
pure oddness of someone else's tongue *in my mouth*. It was more weird

than fun. But in spite of it all, I was relieved that everything was finally going to happen. I would not be left behind altogether. He was a Boy, and so whatever I did with him made me real at last. And becoming real was reason enough for me to suspend judgment and forge ahead.

We dated for a month or two before I saw his temper. One day I was walking alone by the Palace of Fine Arts, along the man-made reflecting pool of the neo-Roman landscape left after a World's Fair. I was lost in that adolescent girl's experience of having almost an out-of-body level of self-consciousness. I became aware of myself against the columns and pediments as a picture, a moving, fascinating picture. I saw the picture as a Romantic one: Young Woman amid the Ruins. Part of the frame was the dull sky, the rearing geese, and the white-fleeced, yellow-bellied swans that, from where I stood, did not look as bedraggled as usual. The arches and columns were reflected in the pool, the waterfowl leapt back, skipping over the water and plunging. I watched myself.

I thought of the Young Woman, noting myself from the outside: here she is with her whole life waiting inside her. Since I did not have in my mental bank of pictures the one I wanted—an image of a female adolescent Lord Byron—I chose for the fantasy of "myself" a scene from a liqueur ad: a woman (I left out the chignon but kept the pearl choker) waiting, leaning against a ruin, arms slightly outspread, fingers splayed against the stone, her pelvis tilted at a provocative angle, wearing a flame-colored chiffon dress. In the original ad there had been a man strutting in a black suit and turtleneck in the foreground, but in my mind's eye he vaporized and the woman moved to the foreground. She became not a model but a tormented heroine—my self-projection—thinking not about the man but about Mont Blanc, or language, or death.

I kept walking. The fog began to wet the cuffs of my jeans and lay a scrim of moisture on my hair. I liked that touch; *I am cold and solitary, a street-wanderer, a poet, versifying in the wind.* It was like the turned-up collar on the cover of the Bob Dylan album. My solitude and this pose of self-importance were both novel.

A man passed and gave me a sidelong glance.

In my inner monologue the story began once again: He was a filmmaker, or maybe a playwright. Could he tell, from my haunted expression, perhaps, that I too—*wrote?* The man's face darkened; his eyes were dark and red-rimmed. *He knows,* I thought.

I wore a Danskin leotard, and my skin prickled with the cold; a gauzy white overshirt covered it, and one sleeve slipped off my shoulder. I had seen a shirt in a magazine layout that hung loose on the shoulders, the way my overshirt now fell. It had been described as a "poet's shirt." Maybe there was a uniform. The dark eyes tracked me.

Someday, I thought, I would find my soul mate and we would write facing each other at an old kitchen table in the south of France, as I had read that Katherine Mansfield and John Middleton Murry had done.

You are too early, I wanted to telegraph to the man. Wait just a few years—till I'm seventeen—then come get me.

But he smoked his cigarette and came no closer, ground it out under his heel and passed over to the prosaic bus stop. Eventually I was chilled through, and the real moment came back. Through the wrought-iron bars I could see the Chinese grocery store on the corner, with its posters for Winston cigarettes, and I could hear the rush-hour traffic crossing the Golden Gate Bridge, a far-off honking. It was getting late. The fun was over. I was a high school girl with no name, no car, not tall, not thin, not blond, bad posture, no breasts, not noble, not facing into the future like the prow of a ship.

Looking for comfort, I hopped a bus across town to Ben's apartment building. I went down the familiar dark hallway. His room smelled dark, like something I was coming to know; like boys: shoes, sweat, cinnamon. Ben was sifting through the metal bowl on his desk. That was where he kept loose change, skateboard bearings, quaaludes, and safety pins.

"Where have you been?" he demanded, not looking at me. His fingers chinked through the coins and his foot jiggled under his desk.

"Just walking around the Palace of Fine Arts."

"Making people look at you," he said.

"What are you talking about? The place was empty. I was walking."

"Look at yourself," he said. He turned his face to me. All the features were thicker. His face looked like it was under a watercolor wash of black. "Your clothes are falling off you."

It was true. My overshirt was still loosely slipping off my shoulder. "Look at you, showing your body." I looked down. It was true. You could see my shape under the leotard.

"I can't believe you!" I snapped. "What a weird thing to get upset about. I could say you're showing your body too." Ben's legs were stretched out beneath the desk, and the edges of his boxers showed under his army-surplus shorts.

"It's different," he said. "I'm waiting for you here, and you go out like *that*—anyone can see you—what do you think I'll put up with, treating me like—"

One instant he was seated and speaking; the next, I was flying up against the wall. My shoulders and spine slammed into the plaster. I lurched into the corner. "You won't," he said hoarsely. I felt myself spun around by my wrist. His fingers gripped my bicep. He forced me down on my knees and hands. My face was to the floor. Standing, then staggering, then kneeling, at each level I tried to right my balance. I simply could not go down. If I did, that would be to acknowledge that this impossible thing was happening.

"You won't," he said again, "do that to me." His hands under my arms, he picked me up and once more shoved my shoulder blade against the wall before letting me drop.

"Ben—" I sat back on my knees away from him. I was too stunned to cry. "You hurt me."

His rage faltered at once. He was grief-stricken. He fell to his knees, put his arms around me, and stroked my hair and face.

"I'm sorry, I am so sorry I hurt you. Let me see. Oh, God." He put his head against my chest and held me around the waist. All those gestures were new—too intimate for the relationship we had had until he hit me.

I was stunned but also moved. Ben had never before shown such need. Now need was leaking out of him. How strong, how extreme this scene was! This felt real: like the white-hot center of the mystery between the sexes. I was not hurt. I could not help thinking: what an intoxicating arrangement. I forgave him, just as he asked me to.

That was how I tacitly gave Ben consent to play this game.

I got caught up in a spiral of excitement. The extremes of sensation and emotion—"love" and sexuality and violence—took me miles away from the constricted world of our high school. I would show up for homeroom, and both extremes would make me feel special, differentiated from the banality of the teacher rapping the map with a pointer, the kids slouched in the yard.

My friends did not know how to integrate this relationship into our moral world. Neither did I. What Ben was doing was clearly appalling. But he was so popular. He was funny and self-deprecating, with enough of the little boy lost in him to elicit tenderness in girls like ourselves.

And he loved me. We still talked, as my friends and I put it when we meant something was perfect, "about everything." He still cooked me oil-soaked omelettes on Sunday mornings at his house and squeezed me when he lifted me in a hug. Though we were still virgins, he was an exciting lover to me. We would shower together in his parents' bathroom, both of us in our soaking-wet underwear, observing what passed for the limits. At other times we rolled around on his parents' king-size bed. The feelings between us were genuine. He still made me laugh. Food, sleep, secrets, opinions, affection. It was a relationship, my first.

But he shoved me again, during an argument in a movie theater lobby. A week after that, when I said I needed to go home early to study for a test, he body-slammed me onto the concrete pavement outside the public swimming pool. There must have been five or six adults on the sidewalk, and no one stopped to see what was going on. Once, after I told him I thought he had been mean to a friend of mine, he smashed his hand into a white garage door on Clement Street. The blood came out of his knuckles in an arc. It was a startling color: magenta.

But he was always so tender afterward, and so sorry.

"Walk out on him next time he does anything like hurt you that way again," Cath and Shari warned me. "I will, I will," I swore. And then we would all turn to our notes. My friends would cast sidelong glances at the hickeys under my collar, "hidden"—in fact, highlighted—by a scarf. They did not approve. But they understood.

The first time Ben did something brutal to me in front of my friends was when he leapt onto my sleeping bag at a sleepover at a friend's father's empty apartment. I had said something wrong, and he reacted so fast I did not even know what it was. He rolled me, in the bag, out into the hallway and straddled my chest with his knees, knocking the wind out of me. I could not take a breath or speak. There was so much intrigue—wrestling and flirting and betrayal—between the sleeping bags in the semidarkness that no one even really noticed it, except one or two boys who later said to me in private, "Ben is crazy. And you shouldn't put up with him." But the girls' society stood firm: he was just troubled.

One evening, four or five months into our relationship, the two of us were staying over with some other teenagers in the still-unoccupied apartment. Again there was that familiar sense of there being no adults around—a celebratory, nihilistic feeling in the air that the kids got privileges because the adults wanted to be left alone, too.

The group of us could see a telephone booth from the corner window. We knew the number and made the phone ring for passersby. Some of them would answer it.

I flirted over the phone with a cute guy whom I could see from the window. When I got off the line, Ben pulled me over to the wall by my neck. I suppose he decided at the last minute to smash his hand into the wall rather than my head. The drywall of the old Victorian building shook under Ben's blow. When his fist fell away, there was a mashed-in hole in the particleboard. Crumbs of brown furry insulation showed through the shards.

The other girls did not know exactly how to react. Neither did I. I backed away from him, into the kitchen, but all at once he was normal again. "My dad is going to kill me," said Zoe, whose father owned the house. But nothing happened beyond that. I helped Zoe sweep up some of the plaster. Ben let the blood dry on his hand. He liked the way it looked. Then everyone decided to order Chinese food.

When I told my parents that Ben had struck me—I lied, and said it was just the once—they immediately made me stop seeing him. I was allowed to say good-bye in their presence, and that was it. I have no doubt that the fact that the women's community was "raising consciousness" about domestic violence at the time helped them to be so quick to intervene and so uncharacteristically firm. It was the only thing in my adolescence I can recall them actually compelling me to do. Even at the time, I was glad they made me. At that point, I could not have made myself. (I would like to describe that intervention to everyone who has ever dared to assert that "feminism failed." For all I know, it saved me from real harm.)

When I told him I could not see him, he expressed sorrow, then moved on to the next girl. I erased or dissociated from the memory of his fingers digging into my neck. The memory of the affair itself, cut short by "outside" forces, like all great teenage love affairs, was something I remained nostalgic about. I still think of him, hurtling through rush-hour traffic down Lombard Street on his skateboard, the sun in his eyes.

I do not remember the pain of Ben's violence. I still want to type the words "It didn't hurt." But it must have. He was big, and not a few times he really slammed me around. I still want to trivialize what happened there, and I feel myself wanting to apologize for Ben—to tell you that he was loved by everyone who knew him, and that he somehow could not stop himself. Maybe that is part of the way I, like so many, rationalize such experiences. Maybe learning that impulse is part of what it means, and shouldn't mean, to "become a woman."

This relationship has been a secret I have kept. I don't like my old friends, or my brother, mentioning it at all.

Is it shame? Yes. I do not want the words "abused" or "victim" applied to me. But it is also a reluctance to reduce Ben to an "enemy." He messed up, badly, and that was his fault. But that fact was not the totality of him, nor of his relationship to me.

My inability to understand this paradoxical experience is the same reason it is important to me still: he really liked and believed he respected me, and he really hit me. I really liked and mostly respected him, even after he had hit me. No pure ideology about male violence against women that takes the violence out of a subjective human context has helped me make final sense of that.

Dr. Amy Holtzworth-Munroe, a psychologist at Indiana University, has found that there are three categories of men who hit women. Men in one group fear abandonment; those in the second are hypersensitive to criticism; men in the third more deliberately use violence to control their partners. Only the theory of male violence as a way of controlling love and sex sheds some light on what Ben did, and what I accepted. And the cultural process that prepares girls and women to accept such control is subtle and starts even earlier than the violence itself. When I was with Ben, in spite of my upbringing—

which one would think would have inoculated me against such tolerance—I thought of it as being not unnatural that he would try to control me. To the extent that I did tolerate it, I must somehow have
absorbed an expectation that I should be controlled, and a fear of
what might happen if I were "out of control."

10

Crash Course: Their Bodies

It makes just as good sense to understand the male reproductive system
as it does to understand your own.
—Kimberly-Clark, "Your Years of Self-discovery," 1968, 1973

While other girls and I were fourteen and fifteen, through
trading information—through Cath's mom's copy of *Fear of
Flying,* Shari's after-the-Friday-dance making-out sessions
with whoever was the main "dude" of the moment, my nostalgic if
half-informed description of Ben, and through books, and older
girls' gossip—we had created a reliable composite of the male
physique and its changes during arousal, and had a fair idea what to
do about it.

If anyone had bothered to describe to us in detail the male sexual
apparatus in all its cycles before we had experienced this new terrain
for ourselves, we would have laughed at the improbability of it all.

A lot of explicit popular sex guides were lying around the houses
where we hung out and baby-sat. ("It was an all-points bulletin
search for the sex stuff as soon as the parents were out the door,"
recalls one woman of baby-sitting as a young teenager.) Week after
week, we would obsessively read out loud, in Shari's room—which

she had hung with almost-life-sized posters of a bare-chested, glistening Mick Jagger—from the pop sex manuals of the time. We mused over the little information we had, refining it and examining it in light of our new experiences, which each of us contributed, like poker players, to the pot of shared knowledge.

"All right: 'Penis-mouth technique,'" Shari would read from *The Sensuous Woman* in a mock-professorial tone, crossing her legs with exaggerated fastidiousness, her face a parody of hauteur. " 'Bend over and take the penis and place it gently in the palm of your hand. Run your tongue . . .' Okay, this is where you do the 'flick' thing—'To drive him straight to ecstasy, take your tongue and flick it *lightly* back and forth. . . .'"

Cath and I screamed in unison. "Now, that sounds really romantic," said Cath. "Oh, my God."

"You're extremely mature about human sexuality," said Shari. "I'm sure your partner is going to feel totally understood. 'Now run your tongue down to the base of the penis and back up again a few times and then return to the Butterfly Flick, only this time flicking all the way up and down. . . .' That's true. Guys actually do really like that. 'And always keep your nails short. You should try to practice relaxing your mouth muscles by letting your jaw hang slack.' I read that you can do this while watching TV or driving." None of us drove yet.

We're all going to be out on the freeways eventually looking like we've had lobotomies, I thought.

"And listen: 'Now stretch your mouth until it comes over the top of both rows of your teeth.'"

"How do you always cover your teeth with your lips?" Cath could not help asking.

"Look," said Shari. She stretched her lips in an odd-looking grimace.

"That doesn't look very sexy," I said. "You look like a tortoise."

"No, I know, but look," she said again. She rummaged in the bathroom and came out holding a stick of Love's Baby Soft cologne. It had the shape of a phallus, with a domed plastic top. "Here: see?" She pretended to stick the tube in her mouth. "No teeth: they'll love it."

We shrieked. "No way!" I said. "Never."

"Oh, you two, get over it."

And of course, we did get over it. Within a year, we were obsessed. Not so much with what penises did (that was how we thought of them—separate beings, willful third parties, often more interesting than were the boys who had the custodial role), for that was still quite new and we were tentative and clumsy. But rather with what they were—the improbability of them, the beautiful weirdness, the way they oddly rose of their own volition and oddly defied gravity, their unfathomable responsiveness. We could have taken it more calmly if men's penises had done all the elaborate things once or twice a year, perhaps with the change of the seasons. But *each time*—it seemed awfully operatic.

Penises were exciting. They were cool. Cath and Shari and I almost felt as if the ones we were beginning to encounter, even if only through blue jeans, while tumbling around with our boyfriends, were our responsibility, like babies or pets. They were certainly represented to us as being our responsibility. Nonetheless, they made *us* feel exciting, skillful, soft, elegant, magical, even protective. Like new mothers, we were consumed with a fascination for every detail of something we could share only with one another. They were a favorite conversational topic. They had lives of their own, so it was as if we too, in connection with them, had new and amazing and secret lives separate from our own familiar ones.

Sandy's memories of her adolescent gossip sessions confirm my own. She brought back the scenes when we were sitting on the floor in Pattie's house. "While we were told there was nothing too wild for us to do, and some of these sexually active girls were heroes to us, to boys they were still sluts. This had to do with the two cultures the two genders were living in. Women were in fast-forward and men were still in reverse. A lot of our friends had older sisters—they were seventeen, we were thirteen or fourteen. The big girls were showing off, and we looked up to them because they were older and they were cool and having sex and we wanted to be like them. It was cool to give a really good blow job. And they'd tell us detailed stuff, like what it tastes like to go down on a guy, and they would take the Coke bottle and show us. Those girls at seventeen were so tough. And those boyfriends were totally unaffected by feminism or the gay awakening. The archetypal seventies guy has a beer bottle in one hand, a joint in the other, and this teenage woman is giving him a blow job, and he's saying, 'This is totally excellent.' And the bubble over the woman's head says, 'Wow, I'm so liberated.'"

The sexually active girls were, to us, as often intriguingly glamorous as they were threatening. Kirsten, a woman four or five years younger than I, mentioned to me that the first image she had had of female sexuality was a sixteen-year-old woman who took swim class with her when she was fourteen. "I had no breasts at all," Kirsten said. "And this woman was big—she was built big all over—and when I watched her put her really big breasts into the cups of her bathing suit, it just seemed to me that it took her forever. She amazed me. And she went with a lot of the guys. She would stand by her locker when I was around and talk to the other girls about how great sex was. 'I like it,' she said. 'It feels good.' Some people called her a slut. She minded that. But she was into what she was doing. And I was blown away. All this guilt I felt about sexual feelings just fell away. I thought, I can grow up, I can be like that."

The young woman Kirsten remembers was called a slut because she did not pretend not to like what she was doing, yet her persona was alluring to Kirsten. When we were growing up, the message we got was exactly contradictory: it's the Age of Aquarius—you can do anything and probably should; *and* you can get called a slut for it.

"When I finally saw a man naked," recalled Sandy, "I decided I liked how smooth men were. They were so streamlined—no extra flesh. And strong. Adolescent boys are very strong in a way that girls just aren't.

"They were very easy to please. It made me feel needed and important that I could please someone. But it also gave me a sense of power that I could just reduce a guy to this helpless . . . blob. They seemed to be so much at the mercy of their sexual sensations. They ceased being who they were in real life and became slaves of pleasure—which meant, I guess, I was the mistress.

"Did I like penises? I liked them. I liked the way they felt, inside and outside. They were something I didn't have. Like a new toy. It was a fascinating thing to figure out how they worked; they were obviously very sensitive, and there was something appealing about men being tough on the outside but—there's a vulnerability to penises. A lot of my friends were scared of penises, especially if they hadn't grown up around boys. I think I was an anomaly."

Pattie was one such girl. "I remember," she added, "when I went to third base with my boyfriend for the first time, and there I was holding this guy's penis and I thought, *This feels weird.* And *dry.* It felt drier than I'd expected. Maybe because I wasn't aroused. I remember feeling a little shocked. It was hard and hairy, and it wasn't pretty and gentle and soft. I was a very prissy person. Maybe there's a better word for that . . . 'feminine'? 'fastidious'? The penis is kind of crude. Growing up the way I did, with only women around, I would hear a lot of bad things about what men do. And a lot of bad things they do with their penises. I was never primed to feel it was going to be a great thing."

And Tonya, who is younger but had some parallel experiences, remembers "the aimless groping around—trying to reach down into pants that were a little too tight, trying to find something I wasn't sure I wanted to touch in the first place!

"About penises, I felt that they forced me to do things I wasn't sure I wanted to do. When I dated boys, I felt I had to do something with this thing because all of society said that the center of their pleasure was their penises and that nothing else you could do with boys could possibly make them happy. They were groping me, and I felt like 'Gosh, well, I should do something.' That was presented as the right and proper, the polite thing to do if you wanted to keep your boyfriend."

As Jeanne reminisced, she rolled tiny cigarettes and put them to her mouth with her small hand, the nails painted in brown-black polish. "Aesthetically," she told me, "I thought men were kind of boring. Probably because of all the nudity I saw growing up. You know—hippie nude beaches and nude retreats. The Sonoma School of Herbal Studies—I was always seeing men nude by the time I was eight. In the Sonoma County mountains, you stood out if you had clothes on.

"I did not like male sexuality, particularly, until once, when I was making out, I had an orgasm for the first time. I thought, 'Oh, my goodness!' I liked that, of course, who wouldn't?" She laughed. "And then I had them all the time. For me it was a time of learning about my body. I was in love—or lust; it's kind of confusing when you have your first orgasm. I would have married him.

"Then the first time I saw this guy I was in love with masturbate, that was totally incredible. I was falling in love with him at the time.

He was completely gorgeous, and I was very interested in what was going on. It was just the most amazing thing I'd ever seen—beautiful and elegant to me; maybe because it was something I was just learning about for myself too. It was like nothing I could have imagined. I can't make an analogy because I never experienced anything like it ever."

"No analogy of any kind?"

"No . . . I'll have to think about it."

Then, some moments later: "I thought of an analogy—if this isn't strange to say. It was like a gorgeous trick of some kind."

" 'A gorgeous trick.' "

"Yeah . . . I still haven't gotten over it—that feeling—just that someone would be that comfortable with me. It totally was not strange. It was the most natural thing in the world. That's when I *realized*—something."

"What was that?"

"It was the first time sexuality was not scary or weird to me. It was actually kind of beautiful."

Weird, neat, scary, crude, threatening, empowering—the male body was all of these to us, and somehow, too, it was actually kind of beautiful.

To truly acknowledge the sweetness and intensity of the initial, revelatory experience of desire, that we were learning at about this time, is a rare enough event that, when a woman my age confided the following, the feelings she recalled seemed shocking to me in their unspoken familiarity.

"I was thirteen," she said, "and I had gone to a dance with some older kids, part of a science fair held in a hotel. What was I wearing? I know exactly. I was wearing a peach-colored leotard, a crimson wraparound skirt. I was wearing my new breasts! I had on a lot of makeup, and I must have looked seventeen. I was like a dancer, flexing, pushing my strength; but what I was flexing was my femininity.

"This man came in. He was a grown man—twenty-four or so. He had been driving by and heard music and had just come on in to see what was up, and probably to see if he could score with some high school chick. He asked me to slow-dance. While we danced—and I was counting the seconds because it was just a matter of time before someone got on to this man being here and made him leave—I suddenly realized that he had this erection. And instead of recoiling away or resisting, I did the opposite.

"Something clicked in my head; it was an epiphany, a paradigm shift. Pressed against this guy, I got it. I got the picture. I suddenly understood what it all meant and how it worked—the whole potential. And what fun it could be.

"I had decided I would have sex when I turned seventeen. And I remember at that moment thinking: it's four more years till I'm seventeen. Four years. *I'll never be able to wait that long.* I'll die if I have to wait that long."

11

Third Base: Identity

Tell me, who are you?

—THE WHO, "Who Are You," 1978

We could learn who we were by whom we touched. Tonya and I, as well as the other girls I knew, were finding out who we were and who we were not by entering into intimate scenes that were not the ones expected of us. The physical experience of self-discovery was enhanced by the psychological insight we gained.

By the time she was in high school, Tonya had gone from being an unhappy "mainstream geek" to being a "successful rebel." She found she became happier still when she made yet another unexpected discovery. "My friend," she says, "took me to a lesbian party. There were girls in high school and also older women in their twenties. And this older woman Amy was relentlessly flirting with me. She told me how cute I was. She was well dressed and articulate, and she began putting her hands on my thigh and caressing me in a way guys never did. They were just gropers, whereas she was light, and able to give me that tingly feeling that sent shivers up my spine. . . . I told my friend, 'Help!' And she laughed. 'It doesn't look to me like you need any help.'

"We set up a date, to hang out over at some friend's parents' house. The parents were out, of course. And even though I said nothing was going to happen, I spent two hours getting ready. I wore this slit skirt and see-through shirt. I was definitely testing the waters.

"When I went to comb my hair in the bathroom, she put her hands on me and said, 'So when am I going to get a kiss from you?' It was so nice to have someone assert themselves in that way, and yet it was safe 'cause she was my size. It was intriguing because it was something I hadn't done before and yet felt familiar because I was familiar with myself—I wondered what it would be like to kiss myself in the mirror. And when it happened I thought, 'God, this is sort of like kissing a boy—except that she knows how to kiss!'

"When things progressed over time, the relationship was so great. It was so nice—her body was so soft—her shoulders were small, and I could really wrap myself around her completely and, instead of feeling enveloped, feel interlocked. She was pretty. Boys just don't have any fashion sense! It was cool to be with this woman who had fashion sense. We could get dressed up together, and when we went out I'd be on top of the world. With boys, I'd want to re-dress them before we went out, but you knew they'd have nothing better in their closets. They couldn't dance—and she could dance. And I felt so safe in her arms. I could reach around her and pull her into me and feel so complete. She had her arms around me because I was me. I always felt with boys, because of their size, you never know if they think you're just somewhere comfortable to put their arm, like an armrest, or if they really want to put their arm around you. I felt she really meant it.

"Plus she knew what she was doing. No ambiguity—she knew right where to go, and that was great! And since I knew what gave me pleasure and she knew what gave her pleasure, we were able to complement each other and bring each other satisfaction that I'd never found with any of the boys. And it kept going on for hours and hours, so I never felt like it was this culmination and then boom, it was over. We'd doze off, and it was almost like transcending consciousness in a way, a dreamlike state. There was no sense that I had to do some mechanical maneuver whose effects I didn't really understand. She gave me a profound feeling of safety that gave me the courage to get up and do other things."

The lessons about defining ourselves through our sexuality were not just about gender, social hierarchy, and physical space; they were also ideological. In the summer after I left Ben, I had an experience that informed me in sharp terms that our emerging sexuality was not presumed to be ours but rather was something we were supposed, like Roman vestal virgins, to devote to the service of a larger, impersonal worldview. My adventure revealed not only that whole belief systems felt entitled to appropriate my sexuality; it also taught me about the erotic allure of the forbidden.

It all started when I went with a branch of a national Jewish youth group on one of the trips to Israel with which middle-class American Jewish kids often mark a rite of passage in their acculturation. These junkets, subsidized by various Zionist organizations, are designed to introduce youngsters to a heritage more compelling than that which they are likely to find at their suburban Hebrew schools and to solidify, in a three- or six-week excursion, an identity that will withstand the lures of American assimilationism.

The group consisted of about a dozen kids, mostly from affluent suburbs on both coasts, and a houseparent husband-and-wife team, a young, progressive, bearded rabbi and his loquacious bride. We spent our time as we were expected to do. We went to Yad Vashem, the Holocaust memorial; to the sheer cliffs of the Sinai; to the Holy City; and finally to a northern kibbutz, where each of us was assigned four hours of manual labor a day. We were to learn the value of working for the collective Jewish good and have the softness of our everyday, materialistic lives muscled out of us.

I was assigned to pick bananas and grapefruit in the orchards. Every morning at four A.M., we American girls were hustled by Israeli overseers, irritated almost beyond speech by us, as we fussed about our hair and our nails, onto open-platform trucks. The convoy of kids would make its way out of the modern compound in the slowly intensifying daylight. At the edge of the still dark otherworld of the banana groves, we left the truck to continue on foot between the thickly planted trees. Moist stalks of tropical green hung in midair, casting cool, damp shadows; green bunches of fruit grew upward; and between the shadows and the moving light, young men, Irish temporary workers with their shirts off, their upper bodies reddened from the sun, stepped all morning a little ahead of us, slicing with their machetes at the heavy, plate-shaped leaves, which we gathered up behind them.

What a contrast we saw before us: the boys from Marin and Great Neck did not look like that. They talked about getting into Cornell.

They did not take their Lacoste shirts off under the sweet-smelling, sticky leaves. They did not look particularly persuasive handling machetes.

It soon became the opinion of a few of the other girls on the trip, and mine, that the nature of most of the boys with whom we were traveling was not sexy.

But the young men in the banana grove were sexy; they were also off limits. They were Irish, hence, Christian (whether Catholic or Protestant was immaterial in this scheme of things). Therefore, it was made implicitly clear, they were not for us. It was understood to be inappropriate for us to visit the Irish boys' cabin. That would mean crossing a divide, for the Irish boys were sited in a separate part of the kibbutz, nearer the orchards than the dorm where the precious Jewish-American girls were billeted.

When Friday night came, the whole extended kibbutz family and its visitors changed into pressed white shirts and modest dresses. While the kibbutz went prayerfully silent on the hill, the Irish boys, making fun of their ostracized status, played the Sex Pistols at full volume in the dark of the banana groves. They sent Palestinian teenagers they befriended on runs to Haifa to buy them black-market Johnnie Walker Black Label and Marlboros. Under a single red lightbulb, they stayed up all night long before their one day off, playing poker, smoking, and drinking. They were poor boys doing underpaid work in a gorgeous, alien country, laboring for a people who half feared and half distrusted them and whom they themselves half feared and half distrusted. Their jokes were scathing.

On the ride into the fields, where they knew they occupied, in the eyes of their "hosts," almost the same status as the untouchable Palestinian workers, they kept their blond heads high and trailed smoke from their cigarettes in the dawn wind. They sang "Onward, Christian Soldiers" in their lilting accents, mouths twisted with irony, in full hearing of the Israeli foreman.

There was nothing the kibbutz could do about it. The kibbutz fathers needed the labor. All they could do was to keep their daughters safely out of reach.

The other girls and I schemed to get at them.

I managed to work alongside the Irish boys. We arranged our flirtations in between the lifting of a bushel of fruit and the scything of

a sticky branch. The heat, the hard physical work, and the forbid-
denness of the exchanges made two of the bright-eyed young men,
Devin and Christopher, into everything masculine and unacceptable
to our chaperones. Perhaps they could confirm us as being finally,
beyond doubt, real women.

I got Devin. When we made out on the front stoop under the lurid
red light, I tasted for the first time the harshly sexual melding of low-
level poisons: cigarettes and whiskey. In his complete otherness from
me and the world I knew, he was an endless source of surprise: in his
excitement, he'd grab my waist and bend me backward. When we
ran out of conversation—which never took long—he'd fall upon my
neck.

One could say, looking back, that at such moments he was aware
of me only as a "sex object"—but his helpless lust seemed so honest
and direct compared with the blandishments of the Pacific Heights
boys. Those "94123 boys," as we called them for the Zip code of
their expensive neighborhood, tried so hard to be cool that their status symbol was the ability to unhook the back of a bra with one
hand. They would say to girls, "How does that feel?" or "What are
you thinking?"—but their agenda was the same as Devin's when his
unmasked, full attention was focused on the clasp of my brassiere.

Even more interesting to me, his excitement seemed to be kindled
by a sense of furtiveness. This, too, stood in contrast to the sensibil-
ities of the liberal, "sex-is-only-natural" boys I knew. For boys in a
town that prided itself on dismantling sexual mores, with easy access
to contraception and abortion, sex held no terrors. Sex itself, for the
94123 boys, seemed to be something kind of fun but by no means
the doorway to ecstasy and perdition that, I intuited, was the reason
why tough, street-smart Devin sometimes actually trembled. San
Francisco boys, permitted everything, trembled at nothing. I loved
the feeling that I so consumed Devin that he would climb over a lifetime of taboos to get at me.

Our accord was very simple and very much without friction,
compared with the struggles over sexual boundaries I knew my
hometown girlfriends were engaged in week after week. His ardor
stopped at the threshold of "third base." I was reserving my virginity, however "technically," and he, with his own belief system, was
adamant about not interfering with my decision. He approved of it;

he liked the fact of what we could and could not do. Through him, I learned about the degrees of complexity implicit in the phrase "everything but."

No boy at home that I knew of thought particularly highly of virginity; they saw a girl's attachment to it not as an honorable philosophical position, however interim, but as the unacceptable opening gambit in an adversarial negotiation.

That alien flesh, the exotic pinkness of his skin, and the golden quality of the hair on his head and his body were all pleasing to me. Years later I would read Philip Roth and consider that men did not have a monopoly on expressing the appeal of the "other." I loved to take long, careful looks at Devin, and I believe he was shocked by that, but he eventually came not to mind it. "I'm pretty, then, am I not?" he would tease.

When we could absorb no more of each other, we would lie on his narrow cot, on his sleeping bag, and be peaceful. As conversation, he sang for me the lyrics of songs by his town's punk rock bands.

There was such a strong unspoken caste system on the kibbutz that it took real nerve for Devin to use the community pool with me. But he began to swim with me in the afternoons when his work was done and keep pace alongside me in the mornings. We made fun of each other, just waiting until we could stop pretending to communicate and simply, more intelligibly, kiss.

The young, progressive rabbi and his wife, our chaperones, noticed the flirtation. One evening as I sat writing letters, they both came into the dorm room. "We need to talk to you," said the earnest, blue-jeaned wife, Karen. She sat on my bed, on her face the expression every adolescent hates most: "This is serious—and you can *talk to me.*" Her husband stood in the doorway, his arms crossed. There was clearly going to be no easy way out of this.

"You are spending a lot of time with Devin and the other immigrant workers down at their bungalow," she said. I waited.

"You know, Larry and I take our responsibilities as your chaperones here very seriously. We need to watch out for every single kid we have with us, and when we see a danger or a difficulty that someone might be about to struggle with, it's our job to let you know about situations you may not be able to handle on your own."

"Well—thanks. I appreciate that. I don't know what you mean."

"You are spending too much time with the Irish boys, and we think you should back off."

"I'm never out past curfew."

Karen looked meaningfully at Rabbi Black. This is a job for you now, she seemed to be telegraphing to him. Rabbi Black came across the room and sat down next to his wife on the bunk bed, thus making me move my legs up so that there could still be a civil distance between us.

"You are misunderstanding us," he said. "Think about what you are doing here in Israel. You are supposed to be getting in touch with your heritage. Learning about your culture and your identity. As a Jew."

"How does my seeing Devin keep me from knowing about my identity as a Jew?"

"First of all, those boys are terribly disrespectful of this community. But more importantly: there can only be a Jewish people if individuals like you make the choice to date and marry people of your own faith." Rabbi Black began to sound quite angry as he warmed to his theme, a refrain he had clearly played a number of times before. "Right now, Jews are falling in love with *goyim* and marrying them at such a rate that by the year 2030 there won't be a Jewish community left in America to speak of. You're here to find out more about Jewish culture, but also to spend time with boys from your own culture and get a sense of just what's lost if you stray beyond it. Remember: it's up to you to determine if there are even going to be Jews left in the middle of the next century. So please: I have to ask you to consider not seeing your friends down by the fields. It's for your own sake. Think about it."

Karen bestowed a pat on my knee, and the two left. Their argument shocked me: if they believed that God guided history, and if Jews were marrying outside the faith, maybe God had decided that he didn't need the Jews to stay just as they were—at least not the way people like Rabbi Black thought God needed the Jews to be. Rabbi Black's God seemed awfully insecure. I was disturbed to consider that Rabbi Black felt—and seemed certain that he was articulating God's feelings as well—that the future of my tribe rested upon whether or not I abstained from making out with a cute laborer from north of Dublin.

Shortly after I was warned against seeing Devin, I cashed in all my traveler's checks, knocked on his door, and told him to dress and pack and come with me: we were going to Jerusalem. All of us on the trip were allowed three days' free travel—usually spent looking up distant relatives—and by God, these days would be mine. Devin had no money; I bought his ticket.

For those entire three days we stayed in a Palestinian hotel in the Old City. All through the evenings and into the nights, we exhausted all the outer terrain of virginity. Culturally indistinct to each other and surrounded on all sides by language, mores, and even currency and food that we could not begin to understand, we became isolated on an island of the senses. In a square ringing with the call of the muezzin, we ate pigeons served with their heads tucked under their wings. Like children, our minds shut down as our senses were overwhelmed. Our bodies were chafing. We did not know where we were.

For the first time, I felt that apotheosis that is the aim of adolescence: total freedom from familiar social pressures; from the identity imposed on me by family, school, friends; the humiliations of peer judgments; the frustrations and limitations of youth itself. If to my trip counselors I was a miscegenating rebel, and if to Ofra's uncle, whose censure I still remembered, I was a godforsaken secular Jew, and if to Devin's mates I was that locker-room joke, the lubricious JAP, and if in the eyes of the Muslim men observing us while they played *sheshbesh* in the market cafés I was a representative of dissolute America, the country of women who are beyond whoredom, then the weight of these clashing systems of control and expectation around female sexuality was just too much. In my mind, under the burden of all those dictates competing to stereotype rather than support me, the legitimacy of the notion of such control simply collapsed. If, no matter what step I took, I outraged some one of those dictates, then I might as well please myself. And, in doing so, please my soft-spoken friend.

And no one could punish me too much, because I was leaving.

At the end of our flight—when Devin had to return to the fields and I had to resume my education about my roots (the next stop on the trip being an advanced-irrigation date palm collective)—he borrowed some of the money I had left over after I had paid for our meals and our Maccabee beers and the hotel room and a T-shirt he had admired that was printed with the Coca-Cola logo in Arabic. The sum represented a term's after-school work at minimum wage. I had a little more than enough left over for my bus ticket.

When I kissed him good-bye, I guessed I would never see that cash again. It was all going to go straight into Johnnie Walker and Marlboros and imported stout. When I waved good-bye out the back of the Egged bus, I wished him well of it, pleasure in every drag of each cigarette and every sip of whiskey. Considering all the pleasure he had given me, it seemed money well spent.

WE WANTED THE Irish boys precisely because they were considered unsuitable for us. (That may well be the same reason they wanted the Jewish girls.) Because we were told they inhabited an erotic region outside the safe parameters of our community, we wanted them all the more.

And here you have the conundrum of the routine badness, the apparent inappropriateness, of the objects of heterosexual feminine desire (there is an alluring bad-girl image in lesbian iconography, but she is less predictable). In art as in literature, in film and on the mass-culture page, those desirable bad boys are always in the act of riding away, leaving behind the feminine indulgence of their rottenness. The "victims" recover slowly, tending their wounds, but the irresistible nature of the bad boys' glamour means that those women receive a sympathy not unmixed with envy.

Robin Morgan, in *The Demon Lover*, pointed out, after tracing the bad boy's lineage, the appeal of *l'homme fatale* to men; but, characteristically of much second-wave feminist theories of sexuality, she derides his appeal to women as being a reflection of female false consciousness, of abject desire for male approval. And they are indeed of a long lineage, both fictional and historical, the desirable bad boys: Lord Byron, club-footed and addictive, leaving scandal and broken reputations and rumors of incest across the continent; Heathcliff, introduced into the overcultivated gentry to torment his Catherine to death and beyond; Stanley Kowalski, dangerous and cruel in *A Streetcar Named Desire*, falling on his knees in front of Stella of Belle Reve and not one woman in the audience wondering why she had chosen to leave her social class behind.

Think of the Mickey Rourke character in 9½ *Weeks*. With the trade-mark "help me" eyes, weak chin, and feral mouth of many such demon lovers, he scatters dollar bills in front of his humiliated lover. She comes back for more. In *Thelma and Louise*, the soulful drifter's confiscation of the innocent heroine's money is a small loss, we are given to understand, compared with the value of the night of sexual awakening that brings her downstairs in the morning, lips still swollen with kisses, to confide in her friend. Clint Eastwood drives away from domesticity through the rain in *The Bridges of Madison County*, and Meryl Streep never forgets him. The jackbooted, pierced antihero in *Decline of the American Empire* summons his lover away from the sophisticated pleasantries of a gourmet dinner, and she follows willingly. The Who smash their guitars. Women scream.

Why do so many young women get excited when a young man breaks an expensive and delicately crafted instrument on a stage? Understandably, this persistent strand in female eroticism has disturbed many feminist commentators. The temptation to pathologize it is strong. In such readings, the "demon lover" appeal to female desire is counterfeit from the beginning. Robin Morgan's reading is a summation of this classic second-wave position.

But let us ask the familiar question: What if women's more troubling passions actually aren't defective or reactive? What if their less acceptable desires aren't merely a desperate response to a crippling "phallocracy"? If the female lust for the "demon lover" is valid in itself, what should it teach us?

Certainly there is truth, for too many women, in the traditional feminist explanation of female "self-subjugation." Too many women, beyond question, experience violent rages or simple abandonment from fathers or stepfathers or brothers in childhood and then as a consequence experience brutality or distance as love—and as erotic love. Certainly, too, many of us have become conditioned sexually by the violent and loveless sexual images in modern culture, a phenomenon that has been analyzed thoroughly by writers ranging from Morgan to Susan Griffin and Andrea Dworkin.

But what if women's innate sexual wildness is always, by definition, in a state of low-level rebellion against the very domesticity and commitment it is incumbent on women to seek out? The demon lover's tendency toward chaos and escape and risk and selfishness may be seen as a projection of inadmissible female longings onto the male—a way of safely handling and vicariously experiencing the release of women's own wish sometimes to be "out of control."

Unsurprisingly, the more forbidden women are to own their sexuality lest they become "sluts," the more inclined they are to project an out-of-control sexuality onto men. The more a woman's "appropriate" social and sexual persona is defined as being for others, the more the demon lover—Bacchus—stands in her mind as promising a sexuality that can be, subversively, for herself alone.

It was precisely because I knew Devin would wipe away my reputation among the authority figures in my life that I wanted him. Devin was, in himself, a friendly, pale, foul-mouthed kid from a depressed country town. When I knew him, he wore a rotation of white T-shirts—he kept his cigarettes rolled up in the sleeve—and his shock of colorless hair stood up in all directions in a suggestion of punk. But that fall he sent me a photograph of himself outside the carpet store where he had at last found work as a salesman, a good job for the region. In his jacket and necktie and with the proud expression of a wage earner, he made my heart sink. I never showed the picture to Shari, who had heard the whole story of my adventure, and in my callowness I never even wrote back. I hope he forgave me.

For my own entirely selfish and private purposes, I wanted to remember him as he was when he was my alien, dangerous, costly suitor, stung red in the neck and along the arms by the light, speaking with his melodic inflection, and completely unlike any of the safe, familiar youths from the suburbs of my home territory. I wanted that imago, rather than his everyday self. At midadolescence, love and the love object seem interchangeable. But it's pretty clear now that by fifteen, various forces had powerfully conspired not just to turn me, sexually, into "a woman" without my active participation, but to turn me into a very specific kind of sexual woman: I was being taught in no uncertain terms how to be a straight sexual woman; how to be a middle-class sexual woman; how to be a white sexual woman; and how to be a Jewish sexual woman. And I was being taught that deviating from those paths meant walking among land mines.

My friends and I were forced to try to learn on our own how to be the kind of woman who at least attempts to resist such rigid scripts. Teenagers are intent on freeing themselves of burdensome personas so that they can find out who's emerging inside their heads. Both Tonya's experiences and mine with Devin were about fantasies that illuminated a hidden potential in the evolving teenage-girl self. Tonya's older girlfriend did this for Tonya. Devin did it for me.

My early attraction to men completely unlike the boys I knew at home in terms of class, temperament, religion, and even hair color, however questionably it can now be read in terms of cultural politics, was functional to my growing "as a woman" in a way that had meaning for *me*.

Tonya's attraction was to the illumination of sameness; mine was to that implicit in otherness. Feminist thinking about eros has shed more light on the first than the second. Tonya's experience opened up a world that has been hers ever since. Devin's otherness burned some of the bridges of the expectations of childhood, and helped me be freer, in sexual terms, to guess at myself, and see what would happen next.

12

Fourth Base: How to Make a Woman

So [in the South Pacific] the life of the female starts and ends with sureness: the period of doubt . . . is brief, and comes early, followed by the long years of sureness.

—MARGARET MEAD, *Male and Female*

"Today, I am a woman," wrote Francie in her diary . . . she looked down at her long thin and as yet formless legs. She crossed out the sentence and started over. "Soon, I shall become a woman." She looked down at her chest which was as flat as a washboard and ripped the page out of the book. She started fresh on a new page.

—BETTY SMITH, *A Tree Grows in Brooklyn*

You want to be a full woman, don't you? Then down to business.

—"J," *The Sensuous Woman*

What, then, in our world, makes a woman? Who gets to decide? We were sophomores and juniors now, and we were going mad in the effort to find out.

Adolescence is, for girls, a time of fanaticism. Those few girls in my school who could afford it became obsessed with horses, devoting themselves to currying and caring for them and collecting ribbons and trophies. Others underwent the rigors of anorexia or bulimia and attended to the evaluations of the scale and the dressing room. Others danced until their joints hurt; still others pierced their ears again and again, then their navels, then their noses. There was strict vegetarianism, and there was growth-stunting gymnastics; for girls a few neighborhoods over, there were the girl-on-girl fights and gang initiations. Shoplifting was the ultimate daredevil behavior for girls of all backgrounds: there was danger, the hunt, and the kill. Women I knew later described to me the ways in which they developed complex mystical and religious conversions; Roman Catholicism, with its devotions, was a popular choice. What were we doing with these ritualistic behaviors and obsessions? At any given time, our fanaticisms had a perfect internal logic. All of us were, in our different ways, trying to create tests for ourselves so we could know we were graduating the stages into womanhood.

My own testing ritual was one of classic rebelliousness. I began to fight with my older brother, who, I was certain, both oppressed and ignored me; and, more important to me, against my father and mother. Though they were more conservative than the families of most of my peers, it was a relative conservatism. I couldn't have my new boyfriend, Martin, spend the night if I didn't clean my room, for instance. And even the few limits they did set were powerless against the push of the culture, which set almost none. More important than the lack of limits was the absence of hurdles set up for us as rites of passage. This made us push against the tolerance of our families until something, anything, would let us take the measure of our maturity and our actions.

Loving, distracted, indulgent, my parents would never follow through on threats to ground me. Would a mounting pile of filthy clothes, leftover food, and unretrievable textbooks that had to be expensively replaced do it? No? Well, what about hitchhiking to Mount Shasta with Martin and not phoning in when I got there safely? No? How about spending the night on the couch in the *Hustler*-strewn living room of the hippie bikers there who took us in and, miraculously, gave us nothing worse to remember them by than their hospitality? No? Well, what, then? My parents trusted me. It drove me berserk.

Could I take drugs—that is, more drugs? My dad had hung out with the Beat poets; no doubt my parents had taken drugs I didn't even know the names of. Could I wear slutty clothes, throw my sexuality in my mother's face? By my midteens, moms had truly completed their transformation: my mother now picked me up from summer camp looking like more of an adolescent male dream than I had ever managed to in my life; her clinging turquoise top was provocatively tied together with psychedelic embroidered ribbons. I had no chance there.

Could I declare myself a lesbian, a declaration that a few other friends were making to their families to satisfyingly thunderous effect? In my house, such an announcement would have been met with benign curiosity and, no doubt, a Lavender Menace T-shirt in just my size. My mother's doctoral thesis on the S.F. lesbian community was leading her to spend the time when she was not driving us to Hebrew school in interviews at the local women's bar about what it meant to be, say, a pierced-leather femme. Our house filled up with her interview subjects and evidence of her academic interests: copies of *Off Our Backs* and stacks of the *Edward the Dyke* poetry collection. Increasingly, the people who helped around the house, doing odd painting jobs or taking care of our pets when we were away, were Marxist women with very short hair, members of a loose-knit lesbian alternative economic subculture. The all-woman house-painting team, for instance, charged one and a half times the going rate, used the wrong color, dripped nonremovable primer all over the floors, parked their motorcycles illegally in our neighbors' parking places, and left their stubbed-out Djarum cigarettes in the sink. Still, my mother paid willingly, eager to support such pockets of pro-woman resistance. Many of these new additions to our lives had changed their names: Earthwomon, Goddess Child. Upon departing for camp, I was compelled to leave my pet rat, Ratty, with a very sweet biker—an occasional baby-sitter for us—who had renamed herself after a collectively farmed province in China. When I returned I was surprised to discover that, in solidarity with the rodent's femaleness, and seeking to empower the unsuspecting creature, she had changed Ratty's name to Madame Mao.

Could I hang out with socially marginalized people, with rebels and outcasts? At the time, my father was interviewing people in San Francisco who thought they were vampires. For an article, he had placed an ad in the local paper asking "Are you a vampire?" and had received dozens of enthusiastic letters and phone calls in response. Several times a week, as I sat at the battered dark oak dining table trying to focus on my homework, he courteously questioned the decadent and the deranged: deathly pale young men with shocks of black hair, furtive twitchers in heavy tweeds, bald men with tattooed flesh wearing black T-shirts, the occasional languorous teenybopper. As my father's interest in horror literature intensified and his article turned into a book, our house began to display decorative items that were more and more difficult to explain to casual visitors: a framed engraving of Vlad the Impaler, whose serene gaze rested on the telephone books on a hall table; a four-foot replica of the stake used to kill Bela Lugosi in his classic thirties' version of *Dracula*. What shocking imagery could I gather around me to outdo this heterodox display? A Sex Pistols album cover? What bad company could I associate with—some kid who grew pot under the cover of backyard geraniums? My dad was hanging out with the *undead*.

What could I possibly do to my parents if my parents had done it all? How could I separate from them, using the poor tools of adolescence—recklessness and disrespect—if I, in fact, respected them and they did not even know that I was trying with all my heart to find some way to disobey them? My adventurousness got wilder and wilder, and I scared myself more and more thoroughly.

In comparison with the limits to which I might have gone as I pushed against nothing in my search for rites of passage, devoting my energies to losing my virginity seemed like a sane and measured goal. That fall, when I was a junior, still fifteen, I managed the crossing. But the event alone did not solve the larger problem I, and the other girls, faced. The whole experience, while being good in many ways, was a series of episodes that kept falling short of being momentous.

Martin was an earnest, even-tempered kid with a strong scientific bent. His idea of a great date was to take me wading in the muddy flats by the freeway, peering at guppies—and in its own childishly contented way, it *was* fun.

He and I could have been a poster couple for the liberal ideal of responsible teen sexuality—and, paradoxically, this was reflected in the lack of drama and meaning that I felt crossing this threshold. Conscientious students who were mapping out our college applications and scheduling our after-school jobs to save up for tuition, we were the sort of kids who Planned Ahead. But even the preparations for losing one's virginity felt barren of larger social significance.

When Martin and I went together to a clinic to arrange for contraception some weeks before the actual deed, no experience could have been flatter. He waited, reading old copies of *Scientific American*, while I was fitted for a diaphragm ("The method with one of the highest effectiveness levels, if we are very careful, and the fewest risks to you," Martin had explained after looking it up). The offices were full of high school couples. If the management intended the mood to be welcoming to adolescents, they had done an excellent job. Cartoon strips about contraception were displayed in several rooms. The staff members were straight-talking, and they did not patronize. The young, bearded doctor who fitted me treated it all as if he were explaining to me a terrific new piece of equipment for some hearty activity such as camping or rock climbing.

In terms of the mechanics of servicing teenage desire safely in a secular, materialistic society, the experience was impeccable. The technology worked and was either cheap or free. But when we walked out, I still felt there was something important missing. It was weird to have these adults just hand you the keys to the kingdom, ask, "Any questions?," wave, and return to their paperwork. They did not even have us wait until we could show we had learned something concrete—until we could answer some of *their* questions. It was easier than getting your learner's permit to drive a car.

Now, giving us a moral context was not their job. They had enough to handle, and they were doing so valiantly. Indeed, their work seems in retrospect like one of the few backstops we encountered to society's abdication of us within our sexuality. But from visiting the clinic in the absence of any other adults giving us a moral framework in which to learn about sexuality, the message we got was: "You can be adults without trying. The only meaning this has is the meaning you give it." There was a sense, I recall in retrospect, that the adults who were the gatekeepers to society had once again failed to initiate us in any way.

For not at the clinic, at school, in our synagogue, or anywhere in popular culture did this message come through clearly to us: sexual activity comes with responsibilities that are deeper than personal. If our parents did say this, it was scarcely reinforced outside the home. No one said, at the clinic, "You must use this diaphragm or this condom, not only because that is how you will avoid the personal disaster of unwanted pregnancy, but because if you have sex without using protection you are doing something antisocial and morally objectionable. If you, boy or girl, initiate a pregnancy out of carelessness, that is *dumb, regrettable* behavior." Nothing morally significant about the transfer of power from adults to teenagers was represented in that technology. It was like going to the vet: as if we were being processed not on a social but on an animal level.

Well, the Act Itself will take care of that, I thought. How did I decide on the day? A civics class drove me over the edge. The thought of plowing through the electoral college—which, in its stubborn irrationality, seemed to represent all the rigidity and hopelessness of the adult world closing in on me—was finally too much. The sun drenched the linoleum floors of the classroom and lit up the soft gray undersides of the eucalyptus leaves. Was I going to spend all this day's beauty, all my young self, in denial, learning to do the things adults told me I would someday—when it was too late anyway—be glad I knew how to do?

At the classroom threshold, before the teacher noticed me, I suddenly turned on my heel. Down the hall, I intercepted Martin before he walked into his biology lab. I easily persuaded him, ordinarily a conscientious student, to cut class. "Today's the day: this is it." It felt special to be the one whose decision was so attentively awaited. We seized our backpacks from our lockers, he took my hand, and we ran up the lawn to the street car tracks just as the class bell was shrilling.

The ride on the N. Judah streetcar—nearly empty at midday—felt very slow and very important, like a processional. Martin was just there, waiting beside me: friendly, nervous, and patient, knowing what he (who was not a virgin) knew and what I did not yet know. He seemed to be the way he always was: the responsible one, readying himself to get me through this experience safely, just as he would check the gas level in his car before we drove to the beach. Martin had waited until I told him I was ready; he would not press me. The son of a fragile single mother, he was well aware of women's feelings about the harm that male carelessness can do.

While the tram jolted along its track and the hills of the neighborhoods gave way to the caverns of downtown, I thought about his forethought and his patience. And I admitted to myself, this is not the way my fantasies want it to be. It is not a Rod Stewart song.

That spring, 1977, they were playing a hit song by that singer, listened to closely by every young girl I knew. Stewart's cracked, roué's

voice had been heard and reheard on inexpensive radio sets on virginal dressers all over the city. The louche ballad painted a picture of
the loss of virginity that we were all wishing for but that none of us
would in fact experience: parents too far away to worry about at the
moment but not vanished altogether; a knowledgeable, yet safe, yet
dangerous, yet boyish older man who appreciates, teaches, reassures,
and helps us into another state. "Don't say a word, my virgin child;
just let your inhibitions run wild. The secret is about to unfold
upstairs before the night's too old. 'Cause tonight's the night, it's
gonna be alright, 'cause I love you, girl, ain't nobody gonna stop us
now." And it had a line that was shockingly frank at the time: "You'd
be a fool to stop this time. Spread your wings and let me come
inside."

Now, that! That was the seduction that, in my wilder dreams, I
wanted; that many of us wanted. A hint of menace, of transgression;
a sense of wildness controlled and then not controlled. I wanted
something to commemorate the specialness of what I was about to
give up, give away, give over.

Martin sat beside me, deep in his own thoughts, a protective arm
around me. Martin, with no father at home, was valiantly engaged in
trying to figure out how to be a good man in the world; he had seen
his mother suffer; and the gender tensions of the times confounded
him too, for he was a truly nice guy. The car lurched. The mood was
tender but matter-of-fact. It was not mysterious, what was about to
happen. Not dramatic.

I did not even have language in which to phrase what was mean-
ingful about what I was preparing to do. And that really bothered
me. According to the views of the West Coast of the United States
in the 1970s, there was nothing particularly special about what I
was parting with. The ancient sense that virginity was precious was
now, I knew, held up for ridicule. The guys who were rats took sexual access to women for granted. The nice guys, perhaps in reaction, seemed almost preoccupied with protecting us from their own
wish to look at us sexually. The virgin/whore split had not been
integrated; rather, it had collapsed—leaving us, in some ways, with
the worst of both personas to contend with and the glamour of neither. Virgin? What's your problem? Whore? Whatever—what's your
number?

"Here it is," said Martin, and we got down onto the curb. We had arrived at the Olympia Hotel, a seedy flatiron-shaped building on a corner of San Francisco's transient district. Some entrepreneur had bought the decaying pre-earthquake structure and outfitted its lobby with mirrors, an irritable clerk, and a stack of tourist guides to the city. Young Dutch and German tourists with little money crammed themselves four and five to a room, and local high school kids saved their allowances and the pay from their after-school jobs so they could be alone together on the cold white sheets.

The stairs sagged. As we made our way to a room, a kid our age suddenly opened a door. His eyes were red; a billow of marijuana smoke emerged behind him. He almost fell across our path. "Hey, want to party?" he asked.

Our room was hardly larger than the bed. The television was locked onto the top of the bureau, and the lamp was bolted to the desk. Through the narrow window we could see a patch of that high gray-white cloud cover, unique to the city, that makes you feel cut off from the rest of the continent, intimate and melancholy. It is, I think, one of the reasons so many people can go to San Francisco and shed old lives for new. It made me feel that all there was was Martin's body and mine.

He was shy and undressed in the bathroom. I, somewhat less so but still nervous, undressed under the sheets. When he returned, I was stunned: he was so beautiful. He shivered but let me look.

This was not sweet old Martin, whose grandmother bought him his shirts. I had been taking art history and had spent many hours memorizing fifth-century statues of male nudes. The walls behind Martin were grimy, but he looked like one of those statues, only alive.

My train of associations connecting Martin to Praxiteles and the sublime came to an abrupt end with the production and deployment of the condom. We had the diaphragm, but there was no way I was about to deal with that yet. I was grateful not to have to think about the little rubber disk, but grateful, too, not to be directly involved with the alternative. Putting the condom on looked terribly complex. It seemed to me, watching, that if you were dextrous enough to gift-wrap an independent-minded amphibian, you could just about manage a condom.

When we made love, it hurt, but only a little. It was nice but strange. I realize my relative good luck with every disastrous loss-of-virginity story I hear. For a seventeen-year-old boy, Martin was a rarity—a sensitive, respectful teacher. After we dressed and left, we were very hesitant, even solicitous, with each other. It would take a long time and a great deal of trust to create real erotic love between us.

I remember kissing him good-bye, going home to think about what had happened, and . . . getting angry. Not angry at him—just angry. I vaguely recall going through some brief phase afterward of being quarrelsome and withdrawn with Martin—irrationally "hard to get." It had nothing to do with Martin or even with my feelings about what we'd begun, which were mostly very happy. It had to do with the larger context. That's it? I recall thinking, not about the physical connection but about the absence of the event's significance as a marker for the journey. That's all? A phrase repeated in my head that made no sense at all in the liberated context of my surroundings: "That's all my virginity is worth?"

Few of the "first times" I heard about were any more truly initiatory.

"I felt it was high time, my God," Tonya told me. "I wasn't with my girlfriend anymore, and I wasn't sure if I finally was going to like guys or girls. So I chose this guy at work who was really popular when he was in high school and was really nice to me. He was an alcoholic and I knew he was too messed up to be a boyfriend, but he would fit the bill to be, I guess, the 'defiler' of my 'purity.' I wanted to get it out of the way. I thought I would clear up the loose ends.

"He had just worked an all-night shift. He came by my house at eight-thirty A.M. I had bought condoms and spermicide lubricant 'cause I was so scared of getting pregnant. I got no pleasure out of it whatsoever. It was in my room, in my house. His semen stained my quilt, damn it—eventually I couldn't bear to look at it any longer and gave it to Goodwill. He was very nice, there was nothing harsh about it—but I remember seeing his eyes close when he really got into it, and I felt like I could be on another planet and he really wouldn't know.

"I wasn't sore afterwards or anything—I just felt empty. Even though I was being, quote, 'filled,' I felt so empty. So we had a fight afterwards about his drinking—and I knew we would never have any relationship afterwards. Because I knew I would need to be able to trust him completely or have nothing to do with him."

On another occasion, Sandy, Trina, Pattie, and I sat up in Pattie's living room very late talking about virginity. Her apartment was in the untouristed Eastern suburbs, long and narrow, dimly lit in the center, with pink and green tiles on the fireplace. Sandy and I sat on the carpet, drinking mint tea and wishing for something stronger. Trina, tired from her day's work, stretched out on the floor. Pattie curled in her armchair. The talk was fitful. These three had been so absolutely in possession of themselves in their high school that, years later, I was still struggling to put aside the stereotypes I held of them. They had seemed "perfect"—that teenage-girl word of words—and so at ease with their sexuality. To hear them reminisce in halting, musing tones of voice about struggles as hard as anyone's startled me.

"First intercourse," said Trina, "was not a good experience. I was sixteen, and I really had this crush on a guy. He was a babe. He was two grades ahead—a freshman in college. I was up at this country home of one of our schoolmates—right in line with the whole parents-aren't-there-during-what's-going-on kind of thing—and we were having a party. We were having a ball. I'd gone out a few times with him, and we'd done a lot of heavy petting. I remember during the dates feeling this hard penis under his pants and thinking, I'm being aroused . . . and kind of liking it. Because first of all, it was not out of the pants. It wasn't like I had to do something with it. I wasn't ready anyway. I wasn't giving him the cues that this was something I wanted to do.

"So he shows up and I'd been on acid all day. I wasn't prepared, psychologically or any other way. I was having so much fun with my friends that I didn't want to have to turn into a 'girlfriend.' To me there was a whole difference . . . but we all went off to go to sleep and it was just *given* that I was going to sleep with this guy. I was under the influence of a very strong drug. And it's hard to say exactly what I felt when I walked off with him, but I just figured we'd go to sleep—I didn't really know what to say to him because we hadn't been developing this great friendship. The guy's in the sleeping bag and the next thing I know, it's practically like what today would be called date rape. He's on top of me and this is *going to happen.* It just *happened.* Nothing was even talked about. We were kissing and all like that, and the next thing I know, my underwear is coming off and I'm being penetrated. And it . . . hurts . . . really . . . a lot. And then I realized: this is it. It's going to happen right now."

I noticed Trina had shifted from the past tense to the present, as if reliving the painful event. Then Trina's voice grew slow and she shifted back to the past. "I think he realized at that point that I'd never had sex before. It certainly didn't go in easily. I remember eventually it penetrated the hymen and broke it. The whole she-bang. I didn't feel that he was raping me exactly, but at the same time . . . we hadn't talked . . . about it or anything like that. So it was not a pleasant experience. I remember feeling—after it was over—I didn't want to talk to him. I just kind of . . . turned away. I felt very alone. I felt . . . this is not fun. This physically hurts. Probably emotionally, too. I feel like I shut my emotions off. I felt everybody else knew he was coming except me. And . . . everything couldn't be so changed. All of a sudden.

"Did I become his girlfriend after that? I don't even remember what happened after that. It was a separation of me from my girl-friends. Then, afterwards, I was just so worried about getting pregnant."

I said, "You didn't use contraception."

"No, I didn't even have any," said Trina.

Pattie shook her head and said something that, given the exaggerated attention directed at her "sensual" persona in her high school, seemed especially poignant: "I was thinking about what you were saying about feeling alone. There were a lot of years when I didn't want to have anything to do with boys. My energy wasn't there yet. Now I know that. I just wasn't ready. I was . . . too *young.*"

Trina said, "I was too young. Way too young."

Pattie challenged her: "But you said you felt arousal."

"Yeah, but I was too young for intercourse at sixteen. There's a big difference. I was too young for that actual act. But I wasn't too young to feel aroused."

"When it came to men and sex," said Pattie, "I was emotionally immature. Part of me feels like I grew up in a convent—my mother, my sister—my dad not around. Thomas, my first boyfriend, and I loved each other. We would hold each other. But he was always *grop-*

ing. I like I was a piece of candy or something. We'd be in his parents' bed. And me thinking, oh, great."

Trina howled. "In his *parents' bed?*"

"I remember one night at his parents' house," Sandy cut in. "We were all stoned on the water bed, and we had the great revelation that the universe *was* music—you know the kind of insight. I went past that bedroom, and I heard you saying, 'Thomas?' Like you wanted him to stop doing something. And I felt so weird: 'Oh, my friend's in there and she doesn't like what's going on, but I can't intervene.' "

Pattie nodded. "Sometimes I feel like now I am in my thirties, I have a sexuality that is more like a man's. Sometimes I'm at work and I really have to make sure that guys aren't aware I'm checkin' 'em out. I look around and I think, jeez, all these men. If I were single, how much fun it would be just to see what it would be like to experience them sexually. And I guess a lot of women felt that way when they were in high school. But then—I just didn't *want to* do that much.

"My parents let us go to Alaska alone one summer. I didn't want to. We went off to visit the hippie mother of one of Thomas's friends on her commune. They had a tank of nitrous oxide outside this tent bedroom. And an outdoor shower. A guy says, 'You kids want to take a shower?' And he photographs us, these young nubile bodies, taking a shower. I was so naïve, it didn't feel like an invasion to me. Later we went hiking to a meadow, and that's where the deed happened. I remember thinking, I'm with someone I care about and who cares about me, and it was in a really beautiful setting. But I remember feeling alone. I would have loved to have called up one of my girlfriends to say, 'Something must be wrong with me because this feels *funny.*' "

Trina was lying flat on the floor now, with her angular body parallel to the cold fireplace. "A year after I lost my virginity, I took a trip to Venezuela with my mom and sister," she said, picking up her story. "My mom left early. After she left, we met guys. And when I had another experience, it was so much nicer and I was so much more open to being with this man in bed, communicating and talking to him. I didn't want to have sex because I was afraid of getting pregnant. So he didn't penetrate me all the way." As sophisticated as we thought we were, this idea—that "going in partway" must be safe— was a naïveté that many of us shared.

"It didn't hurt—he was so kind and gentle, and I could see his face. The first time, I couldn't see a face. And I thought, maybe it has something to do with who you're with and how they feel about sex and how they are able to connect with you. This was the first experience in which I really figured out pleasure with a man. It wasn't a revelation—I knew it was possible. But this time I could relax."

"The sexual revolution did not have my name on it," Pattie said. "I knew all about the plumbing, but . . . the technology alone isn't the answer. And compared with my women friends, I didn't sleep with a lot of men."

"I remember feeling really weird because I hadn't slept with more guys than were on my two hands," said Trina.

The women agreed that girls we knew were expected to have slept with anywhere from ten to thirty guys by the time we were in college. If you hadn't at least made a start, you were repressed or geeky or "inexperienced," a real pejorative. Sandy said she had slept with thirty, "and you know, out of thirty guys maybe there were three or four where I feel now, looking back, that it was a nurturing experience. The other twenty-six can go to hell," she said with her deadpan laugh.

"Even with all the freedom," she continued, "I remember that the pickings were *slim* for getting rid of my virginity. The guys were either gay guys or jocks that I couldn't relate to, or they were Asians who didn't date white girls.

"The guy I lost it with and I had a courtship of one or two weeks. We hung out together and flirted. A friend had one of those parties in the country. No chaperones. I was ashamed to admit that I had zero sexual experience. I pretended I was one of those girls I looked up to who was so suave and knew what she was doing. I don't think the guy knew until the very last minute that I was a virgin. He said, 'Do you want to make love?' And I said, 'Yes.' And we did . . . very badly.

"It was a letdown—very unexciting. The intercourse part wasn't much fun, but the stuff that led up to it I *loved*. He wore Brut cologne, and I still have this fetish for it. My clothes smelled of it—I didn't want to wash them. I liked the kissing and the touching and the erotic feelings—very sensual and exciting.

"And I was surprised at how easy it was to be aroused." Sandy started, uncharacteristically, to crack up so much that she had to put down her cup. "From all those books the older feminists would give us, you'd think you'd need a master's degree in it. You'd have to study your own anatomy and *train* your partner, or you'd be this fifties frigid housewife. The books just gave me so much anxiety; they made it seem so complicated. How had the species ever reproduced itself?

"I didn't expect the warm human connection that I felt just by touching, even in a relationship that had no history or community or sanction. No one told me to expect this human bond.

"And then immediately after that it was over—he had a girlfriend. I was just a conquest.

"Once again, we were changing, they were the same. To him it was a case of 'I got her cherry.' The expression was, actually, 'popped her cherry.' We didn't get to make up the slang for it. To him it was something he could brag about to his male friends. But I was very hurt. In fact, I was sort of ashamed of being hurt, like I was just supposed to blow it off and go find another guy."

There was a long pause.

"There's something I think people still can't hear, even today," Pattie said, drawing her legs up in the chair. "It's that people come into their sexuality at different times. And people think that as soon as you get a woman's body, or something remotely resembling one, you're a sexual person."

She thought some more. "Today," she said, "the more powerful and in control I feel in my life and at work, the more sexual I feel. We didn't have that."

"*Yes*," Sandy agreed. "The rest of our lives was missing. It's not like we had wonderful social and community activities that were making us feel powerful—"

"Yeah. That was not going on," said Pattie.

"We were having sex, but we didn't have much power. So you feel it was not always empowering sex?" I asked.

"Yeah," said Pattie, "though I had empowering . . . cuddling." She laughed. "And empowering companionship in my boyfriend. But we weren't ready for adult sex."

Suddenly Sandy said, "There was no initiation process. No rituals." We had not been talking at all about rituals, and I was interested that she had expressed the lack in the same terms that I was wondering about.

Pattie elaborated on this: "You don't become a woman through sex. Ideally, you become a person first, and then you become a sexual person. You know, it was as if men were supposed to hold the key to our 'becoming women.' And men shouldn't get to decide how girls become women. Now," she went on, "I feel a lot more comfortable sexually. And I enjoy being a woman, and I enjoy being a sexual woman. But still—back then—I was a girl. I didn't know how to make my way in the world—"

"We were *girls*."

"We were girls."

"We were total girls."

EVEN THOUGH WE had had intercourse, we were girls. We knew what was expected of us sexually by boys and men better than we knew our own strengths in the world—better even than we knew our own bodies. But we knew, though we could not have expressed it, that intercourse in itself was not enough to "make us women." It's not as if we didn't search for alternative places—our dieting, our various manias, the anorexia I've described more fully elsewhere—to stage the female adolescent agon, or struggle, into initiation. But in our sexualized and commodified world, the primary passage that was established and recognized for us as women—the drug activity being more marked as a male rite of passage, and the bar and bat mitzvahs being androgynous—was sexual intercourse.

Anthropologists from Margaret Mead and Bronislaw Malinowski to M. F. Ashley-Montagu to Mircea Eliade and Anne Cameron have recorded the rites of passage that mark many organized social systems. In contemporary North American and European societies, such rituals are the exception rather than the rule. Other cultures are not so impoverished in this respect. Girls in South and Central American countries have the *quinceañera* festival at fifteen, when they dress up in magnificent gowns, are consecrated at a special mass, and announce themselves to the community, with great formality, to be nubile. Girls in the Trobriand Islands of northwestern Melanesia at the turn of the century moved to a separate unmarried girls' house, paid close attention to their skill in weaving clothing, and spent several years in casual, safe erotic play before the serious business of settling down.

Other cultures have also had wisdom we have lost about the psychic need to incorporate girls into womanhood through ritual and public transformation. Mircea Eliade sums up the commonalities of girls' initiation rites in tribal societies: they are based on the first menarche, which signals the time to take the girl out of her customary surroundings; she is isolated in a faraway place (for the Swahili, the forest; for North American Indian and some African tribes, a sacred cabin) for between three days to twenty months; she may observe taboos ranging from not touching the ground to wearing a special costume. During the time of living separately from the tribe, the girl learns "ritual songs and dances and also certain specifically feminine skills, especially spinning"—skills her society considers so important that they help maintain the order in the universe. In Tierra del Fuego, in South America, girls, at least until the 1920s, were initiated through "a course of moral, social and religious instruction" along with boys, but they received separate teaching from old women of the community about applying that wisdom to womanhood. The novices were taken from their mothers and endured "physical and moral discipline"; a group was formed, which was finally given teaching about "the secrets of sexuality and fertility" by these older women, who also instructed them in the female customs of the group. Most important is the larger aim of this process of helping girls to "become women": "The education thus given is general, but its essence is religious; it consists of a revelation of the sacrality of women. The girl is ritually prepared to assume her specific mode of being, that is, to become a creatress, and at the same time taught her responsibilities in society and in the cosmos." The girl in these tribal societies is taught what it means to be sexual. But, unlike us, she was also taught that "sexuality, like all the other functions of life, is fraught with sacredness."

The drive of girls to mark the transformation into womanhood is so strong that it can overcome the most extreme brutality of the initiatory rites. In parts of Africa, girls clamor to undergo excruciating, dangerous, and sexually deadening clitoridectomies, because the procedure is a rite of passage that turns the girl into a socially acceptable woman. Those who remain ritually uncircumcised are often ashamed.

In northern Australia, during the first decades of this century, coastal tribes used to separate the pubescent girl from the community for three days. During this time she observed dietary restrictions; then the older women of her tribe would take her among themselves, paint her with ocher, decorate her magnificently, escort her at first light to "a fresh water stream or lagoon" for a ritual bath, and then lead her, surrounding her in a joyous procession, into the camp to be seen by her family and friends: "Amid a certain amount of acclamation, [the girl is] socially accepted as a woman." In other tribes, a girl's passage into womanhood is celebrated with collective dancing and gift giving. Marks of a girl's new womanhood include the tattooing of her body or the blackening of her teeth.

For another example of a female rite of passage, we can look to Anne Cameron's classic, *Daughters of Copper Woman*, a retelling of Northwest Coast Indian myths, that describes the way in which society can publicly rejoice in a young girl's "sacred time." In Cameron's book, one account describes women who "taught [the girls] with jokes and with songs, with legends and with examples, how to care for and enjoy their bodies, how to respect themselves and their bodily functions, they explained to them all they would ever need to know about pregnancy, childbirth, and child care." As one of Cameron's storytellers says:

> [A]nd every day we had to get our bodies ready. So that when the time came to go from bein' a girl to bein' a woman, we'd be ready.
> Swimmin'. We did a lot of swimmin'. Winter and summer. Sometimes we'd get a rope around our waists and get tied to a log and have to swim and swim and swim without ever gettin' anywhere, just swimmin' until we were so tired we ached, but our muscles got strong and our bodies grew straight. And we'd run. Didn't matter if you ran fast or not, you ran, up and down the beach in your bare feet until your feet were tough and it didn't matter if you stepped on a shell or a barnacle or a sharp stick. Up and down, up and down, and just when we thought we were gettin' good at it they told us we had to learn to run without kickin' any sand. . . . And you had to learn or you weren't a woman. It isn't easy becomin' a woman, it's not somethin' that just happens because you've been standing around in one place for a long time, or because your body's started doin' certain things. . . .
> When you'd learned everythin' you had to learn, and the Time was right, and you'd had your first bleedin' time and been to the waitin' house, there was a big party. You were a woman. . . . And people would come from other places, uncles and aunts and

cousins and friends, and there'd be singin' and dancin' and lots of food. Then they'd take you in a special dugout, all decorated with water-bird down, the finest feathers off the breast of the bird, and you'd have on all your best clothes and all your crests, and you'd stand up there so proud and happy . . . [After having dived in] you'd be out there in the water all by yourself, and you had to swim back to the village. The people would watch for you, and they'd light fires on the beach, and when finally they saw you they'd start to sing a victory song about how a girl went for a swim and a woman came home, and you'd make it to the beach and your legs would feel like they were made of rocks or somethin'. . . . And then the old woman, she'd come up and put her cape over you, and you'd feel just fine. And after that, you were a woman.

Let us contrast Anne Cameron's story of the Native American initiation ritual, with its rigorous tests, its generational continuity, and its public acclaim, with the shame of contemporary First World industrial coming-of-age moments: contemporary second-wave Western women often remember a furtive conversation with a mother about blood and the danger of pregnancy. Such memories of shameful or secretive initiations are common in the memoirs of feminists who came of age before the sexual revolution.

In our case, there was not shame so much as silence. Just silence: all that energy we were inclined to devote to mastering the tasks of "becoming a woman" went undirected. No older women who mattered to us personally took us on retreat, away from our families and from men and boys, into the forests or onto the hilltops of our local parklands, to teach us about the skills of seduction and sexuality, the responsibilities of both preventing and preparing for fecundity, the pleasures of adornment and of caring for our health, the arts of balancing work and motherhood, and the sacredness of femininity, or to test us rigorously in the skills we would need—birth control information, self-defense, math skills, job applications—to survive successfully and conscientiously in our culture "as women." No one was standing by at home, waiting to cheer our arrival, transformed and under our own power, on the new shore.

Eliade has shown that rites of adolescent initiation often involve a quality of danger or pain to signify the symbolic death and rebirth of the initiate. In light of this, how can we wonder at the rituals of girls in our own culture, their vulnerability to the "tests" of starving and grooming that magazines offer, their obsessions, their frustrated pre-occupation with "sacred costumes," their dangerous or drunken sexual adventures? Sex itself is too easy to be a rite of passage; it is indiscriminate. Just about anyone can do it. But rites of passage are, by definition, discriminative. They are meant to weed out the boys from the men—and we females are just as intent on distinguishing the girls from the women. Where else in our culture but in girls' accepting and even colluding in the fact that the passage to womanhood is painful and dangerous is the necessary trial by fire or water to be found?

Simone de Beauvoir wrote in *The Second Sex* that "one is not born a woman, one becomes one." The irony is that our culture does not help "make women" very well. It scarcely notices, let alone values, the tests girls desperately set themselves—the tests of the various fanatical obsessions of ages thirteen and fourteen and fifteen and sixteen. It rarely celebrates them or makes heroine stories of them. No one expects teenage girls to identify with the grandiose struggles for self-creation of male adolescence—to want to forge in the smithies of their souls the uncreated conscience of anything much at all.

In our culture, a girl's passage through tests and rigors into womanhood is marked in the realm of body control such as dieting, but also in the realm of sex acts and the accumulation of material possessions. Our girls move toward womanhood through the demarcations of what they can buy and own or of who wants to sleep with them. The danger to girls is that the culture often makes girls turn into women in ways they do not choose before they are psychologically ready, and it defines their readiness as a passive biological development. It gives them little opportunity to *turn themselves* into women as an active, healthy goal toward which to struggle and to claim at last with pride. "Be a man," the culture says to boys in many ways, both harmful and beneficial. But when we tell girls to "be women," we seldom mean that they must take hold of themselves and overcome their infantile inclinations.

"Become a woman," in our culture, does not mean: show us you can weave, as it did in Melanesia, or even show us you can embroider samplers, direct the servants, and play a harpsichord, as it did in "refined" society in the nineteenth century in the West. No, in our culture, the cliché exclamation to an adolescent girl—"My, how you've grown"—has no cultural echoes whatsoever; the reference is purely physical. In our world, "Demonstrate that you are a woman" means simply "Take off your clothes."

Historians and anthropologists who look at adolescent rites of passage agree that their importance cannot be overstated, not only for the sake of the developing adolescent but for the sake of the coherence of a society. These rituals let young people test their autonomy, learn the mores of the larger culture, and achieve the sense of mastery that alone will let them willingly leave the dependence and aimlessness of childhood behind them.

A paradox of our times and the recent past is that, as in my libertine high school environment, we lost "possession" of our virginity in the sense that it meant very little to others. But at more traditional high schools, in other parts of the country, it seems that girls could not talk about their sexual experience in any authoritative way and so had to struggle to maintain any authority over the experience itself. One long-term study, by sociologist Sharon Thompson, is alarming. This eight-year series of interviews asked four hundred girls to recount their sexual, romantic, and reproductive histories. To the extent that these interviews show what can and cannot be said or owned by girls about sex, some of them are a monument to the silences created by the fear of entering the Slut's Dominion and to how even the grammar of consciousness breaks down in the face of a strong social taboo. Asked simply to think about and articulate their experience, the subjects exhibit the "drawing a blank" behavior, in relation to sexual narrative, that Mary McCarthy described in her memoir, and which I mentioned earlier. "Asked to describe the circumstances of first coitus, many girls blink and freeze, dropping predicates and leaving passive sentences dangling as if under a post-hypnotic suggestion to repress," writes Thompson. " 'It was something that just happened,' they say finally. They don't know how it happened."

(Whether or not they know how it happened, I would caution, they know they are not supposed to tell.)

"I tell you, I don't know why or how I did it. Maybe I just did it unconsciously." . . .

"I don't know what came over me that night. I really don't. I mean, I can't really answer it. But it happened."

"I had no idea. I had no idea at all. I knew I would be taking off my clothes, and I knew he'd be taking off his clothes. But as far as what would happen, I didn't know. . . ."

"I didn't really know what I was doing. I knew what I was doing but I didn't actually *know* what I was doing."

That last sentence is the code girls must speak in a world where they are expected to be sexually available but not sexually in charge of themselves. On many high school and college campuses I've visited, girls explain that you aren't called promiscuous if you have sex when you are drunk or overpowered or "swept away." You are called promiscuous if you have sex *when you are aware of what's going on and are able to talk about it.* It's not the sex but the consciousness of what you are doing of your own volition that makes you a slut.

"Drawing a blank"—lack of consciousness—absolves you. Let me restate this for emphasis: in our culture, girls' sexual availability has a positive value to boys—and girls' lack of consciousness in relation to their own sexual choices *also* has a positive value to society. A girl's setting sexual boundaries that are comfortable to her has a negative value to boys (and to society—remember the derision aimed at the Antioch Rules, the policy at Antioch College that asks students to give a partner consent to sex), and the erotic consciousness, feistiness, and acceptance of her own sexuality that she requires in order to set and explore her own sexual boundaries also have negative value. The results of this perverse value system are predictably disastrous for girls. It is not surprising that, according to *The Washington Post* in 1994, alcohol is a factor in 90 percent of campus rapes and in 60 percent of STD transmissions to women.

Besides the sheer physical danger of this enforced lack of consciousness, there is the philosophical problem that girls and young women face: if you mustn't acknowledge an awareness of your choice to lose your virginity, how can you take responsibility for it or the consequences; how can you know you have "become a woman" at all?

The rites of passage that girls create for themselves in contemporary Western culture out of this frustrated drive to *know themselves* and *prove themselves* women in turn produce many of the social ills that concern our communities. Sex, as I noted, is easy. Getting pregnant is easy and it is better proof you are a woman than simply having sex. Being pregnant and deciding what to do about it—now, that is hard.

Some of the girls of our age were also getting pregnant. Difficult as it is to assimilate such numbers, according to several national studies compiled by the Alan Guttmacher Institute, before they are eighteen, 23.9 percent of sexually active American girls, or almost one such girl in four, has been pregnant. (Each year, almost one million girls become pregnant: 8 percent of fourteen-year-olds, 18 percent of fifteen- to seventeen-year-olds, and 22 percent of eighteen- to nineteen-year-olds, for a total of one sexually active girl in five.) Half of the more than one million pregnancies among teenage women each year end in birth; 35 percent end in abortion, accounting for one fifth of all abortions. Eighty-five percent of teenage pregnancies are unintended.

Social commentators wrestle with this problem, which seems intractable and difficult to fathom. But perhaps Eliade's explanation of the rite of passage sheds some needed light. Since every girl who ever grew has needed to know she has made a successful transition from girlhood to womanhood within the value system of her own culture, why should we be surprised that our levels of teenage motherhood and teenage abortion are so high—that so many teenage girls see their impregnation not as a derailing of their journey to adulthood but as its fulfillment?

As Cameron's interviewee said of a culture very different from ours, "It isn't easy becomin' a woman, it's not somethin' that just happens because you've been standin' around in one place for a long time, or because your body's started doin' certain things." Yet this inert definition of what "becoming a woman" means is precisely what our culture teaches its girls.

Losing our virginity was supposed to pass for attaining sexual maturity. But it was too easy, what we did, and it didn't matter enough to satisfy us more than physically. The end of our virginity passed unmarked, neither mourned nor celebrated: the worldview we inherited told us that what we gained by becoming fully sexual was infinitely valuable and what we lost by leaving behind our virgin state was less than negligible. In other cultures I have looked at, older women, who upheld the values of femaleness, decided when a girl could join them in womanhood. Their decision was based on whether the girl had attained the level of wisdom and self-discipline that would benefit her, her family, and the society. Those older women alone, through their deliberations, had the power to bestow womanhood on the initiates.

In our culture, men were deciding for us if we were women. Heck: *teenage boys* were deciding for us if we were women.

Unhealthily for us and, I gather, fairly atypically in the general history of private life, the power to define our entering womanhood was bestowed upon boys and men. And they, unlike the older women in the tribes, were bound by no tradition or social pressure to consider our "becoming women" in relation to our well-being or that of the community.

By elevating the loss of virginity while stereotyping the state of being a virgin, we tell girls that what boys do with them is more significant to their maturing than what they themselves choose to do. Instead we should be telling girls what they already know but rarely see affirmed: that the lives they lead inside their own self-contained bodies, the skills they attain through their own concentration and rigor, and the unique phase in their lives during which they may explore boys and eroticism at their own pace—these are magical. And they constitute the entrance point to a life cycle of a sexuality that should be held sacred.

13

Skipped Homework: Our Bodies

The pituitary gland at the base of your brain is primarily responsible [for sexual maturation]. Although it's only as big as a pea, it . . . sends out messages of growth and maturation to every part of your body. These messages take the form of hormones. Hormones help girls look radiant.
—Kimberly-Clark, *The Miracle of You*, 1968, 1973

Oh she's a brick house
She's mighty mighty just lettin' it all hang out . . .
How can she lose with the stuff she use?
36-24-36. Oh what a winning hand.
—THE COMMODORES, "Brick House," 1977

We were untaught or mistaught culturally; we also were untaught or mistaught physiologically. Though the experience of losing our virginity was not what most of us had hoped it would be, we went right on into physically adult sexual relationships. And the first "womanly" phase of our lives was infinitely complicated because we were given neither the time nor the information even to begin to understand our physical selves. Indeed, today, almost half of fifteen- to nineteen-year-olds, according to the Guttmacher Institute, "think the average young person . . . does not have enough accurate information about sex and reproduction."

Sexual pioneers of our mothers' generation placed great stock in the saving power of female anatomical knowledge. We were certainly grateful for the information; but we were also proof that sexual technology alone cannot solve a problem that is inherently social. Thanks to *Our Bodies, Ourselves; The Sensuous Woman;* and later

The Hite Report, we knew the rudiments pretty well. But there was a lot more we didn't know.

"Did we know about plumbing?" I double-checked with Pattie.

"We knew about plumbing," she said. "Eventually by ourselves, talking to other girls, we found out that if you pushed this spot it would feel good. Put tab A in slot B. But we didn't get even that in sex ed class when we were thirteen or fourteen. That was all about the least sexy things. Fallopian tubes. Luteinizing hormone. Contraception—sure. And slides of women's organs in a cross section. For weeks. They didn't give us a lot of slides of guys to laugh at when everyone was laughing at the women's stuff. And no one, no teacher, said, 'Don't laugh at the girls' sexuality.' But it wasn't about love or pleasure. I bet fallopian tubes get so much attention in sex ed classes because they are so unerotic looking."

"Sex ed revolved around boys' pleasure," Tonya confirmed. Though she went to a more conservative public school, her curriculum was in some ways like mine. "We were taught about 'blue balls' and shown little cartoons about gonorrhea and syphilis, and how syphilis causes brain disease. Abstinence was what was preached. The message was pretty much: you have to be careful with what you do with boys 'cause they'll get excited and want to have sex with you. Never: *I'll* want to have sex with *them.* More like: they're the enemy that I have to beware of. Female pleasure was not even on the agenda. It was assumed we would want to be with boys because that would give us status—not because we wanted to know what sex was like or if it would give us satisfaction. No whys—why we would date or seek intimacy or crave affection. It was presumed that girls would want to have sex with boys basically because boys pressured them into having sex. Almost the assumption that sex, as the girl experienced it, was always coercive sex. The hormonal changes they talked about were related to menstruation, not to female desire. I never got the feeling that it was condoned or even acknowledged that girls would want to explore their sexuality the same way boys did. All the books are about you're supposed to want to be afraid of boys."

"So you weren't taught about female orgasms or the clitoris in sex ed?" I continued, knowing it was an academic question.

"Clitoris?" she yelled. "What's a clitoris? Labia? Who knew? Only about boys' orgasms. The girls' thing was where they talked about menstruation. Then the boys' thing was where they talked about wet dreams. Then they brought everyone together for the horror stories about STDs. We didn't have *Our Bodies, Ourselves* in *our* house."

My memories echo some of hers: we read textbooks for health class and saw "The Life Cycle Library" materials developed by Tambrands and the Kimberly-Clark Corporation, from which I have been quoting throughout. Our schools used these elliptical materials, designed to slip anxieties about menstrual odor in between sex ed information, because the tampon manufacturers provided them to our impoverished schools cheaply or for free. We heard about male desire: that it was so intense for boys that they dreamt about it and that, nonetheless, it was okay to say no to them. Boys' desire was characterized almost respectfully: "They won't die of it," we were told. It was acknowledged; it was described, there, in public, in the room. But this is what *The Miracle of You*, in use in schools in the mid-1970s, and the text I seem to recall from my own sex education, has to say about female desire:

> You have probably discovered that, besides being very interesting to look at in the mirror, [your body] can produce very pleasant sensations. . . . Later on, each young woman shares her own pride and pleasure with others—with the man she marries and even with the children they create. There is pleasure and pride in the kisses and caresses a mother gives her child. There is pleasure and pride in the kisses a wife and her husband share. So it is completely natural that . . . you should become aware of your body, respectful of it, and of your good healthy physical feelings.

If there could be a more mystifying and sentimental description of emerging female sexual desire, I can't imagine it. We were depicted as civilized, rational beings compared to boys, who were so deranged by their sex drive that it was up to us to fight them off. No one said to us, "Your dreams are so intense; your impulses are so profound; but you won't die of it." Actually, the message was just the reverse: your impulses are not especially noticeable, and yet, if you act on them you might die. The boys were physical, it was understood; we were emotional. So, because the dominant sexual story was teaching us to feel the opposite of what we felt, the intensity of our physical wishes made us fear, on an unacknowledged level, that we must be sluts. "It is important to acknowledge that you, as a young woman, have a very special responsibility to the young men in your life," our sex ed materials warned us. "Male sexual feelings are aroused, in general, much more quickly and easily than your own. A sweater that seems merely fashionable to you may appear sexually provocative to your date. . . . Obviously, the best way to cope with this unwanted state of affairs is to avoid setting the stage for it or irresponsibly provoking it."

That message, which was presented to us as if it were an eternal truth, was part of an ideology that is not very old. In fact, the sexual information we had access to presented us with three genuine myths. The first was that boys want it more. The second was that the sexual revolution had for the first time allowed women in general to be perceived as sexual beings. The third was that twentieth-century science, in conjunction with the renascent feminist movement, had newly bestowed upon us the location and purpose of the clitoris.

What none of us knew—what came as a surprise to me even as an adult—was that the story of female sexuality in the West is not only far more complicated than this, it points to very different conclusions than those to which our sexual culture would lead us. We did not know that women had been considered more carnal than men for most of the record of Judeo-Christian history; that the belief that women want sex less than men was only a little over two centuries old; or that, for that matter, the clitoris had been discovered over and over again for centuries. We did not know how serious was the problem of what was going on inside our bodies in relation to the world around us, nor was it acknowledged how tight was the cultural straitjacket into which we would spend the next few years trying to fit our unequivocating bodies.

But we felt wild anyway. Though *The Kinsey Report* asserted that "at the onset of adolescence there is no upsurge of sexual responsiveness in the female which parallels the dramatic rise in the level of her estrogens. It is the male who suddenly becomes sexually active at adolescence," that conclusion would have been big news to us. We all felt demented. The activation of the pituitary gland—the estrogen coursing through our bodies, stimulated by our woken-up pituitary glands, fattening our hips, curving in our waists, making us sulk and giggle and lash out and giving us complexion problems—was part of the same process that was turning us, with its magic, into guardians of a sexuality intended by nature to be at least as intense as that of the boys. Their sex drive was considered normative, but ours, if it paralleled theirs, was deviant; we did not know what a big cultural fib that premise was. We did not know when we felt wild and danced to Patti Smith's *Horses* with our hair flying and could not stand ourselves for one more minute and wanted to tear the world open, we were not incipient sluts, but normal girls becoming women.

What the well-meaning Mrs. Chong, the extremely uncomfortable hygiene teacher who wore perfectly white sneakers every day, did not convey to the rapt girls waiting for the information of their lives was the objective, scientific fact that we were becoming, physiologically speaking, transformed with desire.

In health class, we heard only the yawn-inducing history of the identification of the fallopian tubes, and we had to memorize lists of such sensuous words as "follicles." In our sex ed material, Tambrands identified the clitoris as "a structure containing sensitive nerve endings" and left it out of the anatomical map altogether. Kimberly-Clark glossed it as a "small organ at the upper part of the vulva" that is "especially sensitive." (The more informative *Our Bodies, Ourselves* was, beginning soon after its 1973 publication, the center of a furor to get it off library shelves where high school girls might find it.) The Kimberly-Clark version now current, "Julie's Story" (1983), defines the clitoris as "the small sensitive organ above the urethral opening." Nowhere in any of this material is there a discussion of how the anatomy of female sexual pleasure actually *works*.

There is no better story to illustrate what we didn't learn in school about female sexuality than a brief history of that socially vexing organ, the clitoris. Here, with the aid of the research of cultural historian Thomas Laqueur, in his pioneering *Making Sex*, and other sources, is the education not given in health class or in any other. We were taught "The Story of Menstruation." Here's the lecture we never got.

LOST AND FOUND: THE STORY OF THE CLITORIS

The Clitoris Identified, 1559

In 1559, Venetian scientist Renaldus Columbus identified a small organ that was "preeminently the seat of woman's delight." Like a penis, he said, "if you touch it, you will find it rendered a little harder and oblong to such a degree that it shows itself as a sort of male member. . . . Since no one has discerned these projections and their workings, if it is permissible to give names to things discovered by me, it should be called," he asserted endearingly, "the love or sweetness of Venus." Columbus went on to explain, "If you rub it vigorously with a penis, or touch it even with a little finger, semen swifter than air flies this way and that on account of the pleasure. . . . Without these protuberances, women would neither experience delight in venereal embraces nor conceive any fetuses."

Still in Its Place, 1671

Jane Sharp, a seventeenth-century London midwife, referred to the clitoris as being like the male penis: "it will stand and fall as the yard doth and makes women lustful and take delight in copulation," she wrote. The Danish physician Caspar Bartholin's *Anatomy*, published in 1611, explained that the clitoris is "the female yard or prick . . . [which] resembles a man's yard in situation, substance, composition, repletion with spirits, and erection." The Dutch physician Regner de Graaf reasoned, with bracing common sense, "If those parts of the pudendum [the clitoris and labia] had not been supplied with such delightful sensation of pleasure and of such great love, no woman would be willing to undertake for herself such a troublesome pregnancy of nine months."

English surgeon William Cowper's textbook of anatomy *The Anatomy of Humane Bodies* (1697) actually shows the clitoris as an organ distinct in itself. An even earlier French medical reference book cited by Laqueur remarks that the organ "enjoys an exquisite sensibility" and refers to a Latin term for "clitoris" (*oestrus veneris*) that translates as "a frenzy of sexual passion." A seventeenth-century French obstetrician observed that the little organ in question is "where the Author of Nature has placed the seat of voluptuousness—as he has in the glans penis—where the most exquisite sensibility is located, and where he placed the origins of lasciviousness in women."

Not Going Anywhere, 1740

In the eighteenth century, it was still widely believed that orgasms helped women to conceive. In the 1740s, when the Princess Maria Theresa asked her physician why, though married, she was not pregnant, she was given this wisdom: "I think the vulva of Her Most Holy Majesty should be titillated before intercourse."

Just Where They Left It, 1750s
Another "discovery" of the clitoris took place in the 1750s when Swiss biologist Albrecht von Haller noted that women's erotic feelings were localized "in the entrance of the pudendum" rather than in the uterus. "When a woman, invited either by moral love, or a lustful desire of pleasure, admits the embraces of the male, it excites a convulsive constriction and attrition of the very sensible [that is, sensitive] and tender parts, which lie within the contiguity of the external opening of the vagina, after the same manner as we observed before of the male." When the clitoris grows erect and the blood is flushed into the woman's external and internal genitalia, the purpose is to "raise the pleasure to the highest pitch." Haller informed his readers that the egg's expulsion "is not performed without great pleasure to the mother, nor without an exquisite unrelatable sensation of the internal parts . . . threatening a swoon or fainting fit to the future mother."

The Great Forgetting
The idea that women's sexuality is less intense than men's dates from the end of the eighteenth century. With the ascent of the Industrial Revolution, Europe and America articulated a new view: women were no longer the more animal sex but the more angelic; their desires focused not on lust but on tender affection and domesticity; increasingly they were seen as so sexually alien from men that they were men's opposite.

There are many theories of what brought about this shift. One centers on the political ferment of that democratizing age: with the triumph of secularism and the emerging nineteenth-century centrality of Darwinism, science had to be used to defend a hierarchy based on gender, for appeals to God and tradition were increasingly too contested to do so.

Other historians look to economics: Linda Gordon, in *Woman's Body, Woman's Right*, argues that sexuality became threatening to the developing "capitalist character structure," which required people to look to the future and defer gratification. Industrialization had the effect not of loosening the "bonds on women and on human sexual expression" but of secularizing them; and it then applied them much more tightly to women than to men.

I am inclined with Laqueur to see the need for the new ideology at the intersection of three developments. The first was the secularization and democratization mentioned above: the social revolutions of 1789 in France and then of 1848 throughout Europe created an atmosphere in which the unquestionable was up for rethinking. If men were to demand liberty and equality, women, too, if not checked by a strong, new belief system to the contrary, might clamor for their own right to liberty and equality in all areas, including the sexual. I agree with Gordon that the shift was also due to economics, but would add the insights to hers of those historians who see middle-class Victorian women's roles as derived from the need to display the husbands' wealth. Economic expansion had created a class of educated women who could enjoy the leisure that would permit them to threaten the stability of the sexual double standard.

The new ideology claimed that, biologically speaking, women were far better equipped than men to control the impulsive and carnal drive of desire. In the nineteenth century, the sex drive became ascribed to the masculine realm, and theories began to deny that it even existed biologically in women.

As a result, middle-class women took on sexual "purity" as their chief virtue, even while prostitution boomed. A further result is just what we inherited: as sexlessness became the feminine ideal, female lust became increasingly pathologized by the rising profession of male gynecologists: "In the sexual evolution . . . strange thoughts, extraordinary feelings, unseasonable appetites, criminal impulses, may haunt a mind at other times unviolent and pure," stated gynecologist Isaac Ray in 1866. "It was women's sexuality that made her mad," concludes the historian G. J. Barker-Benfield of this development in thinking. Eventually, standards for this "purity" became so rigid that all sexual activity outside of motherhood became identified with (and often in fact led to) prostitution, and the notion arose that "the female analog to the male sex drive was the maternal instinct."

We have seen how Judaism and, to a more complicated extent, Christianity sanctioned eroticism between married couples. Before the nineteenth century, young girls could look forward to some marital pleasure after a long virginal wait. But in the nineteenth century even that consolation was stripped from them. Marriage no longer liberated female desire—wives were supposed to be willing but passionless sexual partners (though revisionist historians such as Peter Gay and Michel Foucault have shown that public ideology did not always dictate private experience). Clergy, journalists, and teachers joined the public chorus. Good wives were expected to want sex only in order to have children—and to please their mates.

Many in the medical profession joined forces with the social commentators in dictating this new morality—though the profession always sheltered some heretics. Doctors began to stress the debilitating effects of female sexual indulgence: a woman's erotic appetite, some claimed, could damage her reproductive organs. Uterine problems such as adhesions and hypertrophy were attributed to sexual excitement.

We can date the male-centered notion of intercourse that our mothers inherited at least to the nineteenth century, when doctors "defined normal sexual intercourse as that leading most directly to male orgasm." Linda Gordon notes that at this time women were expected to remain clothed during sex, and for many women, "Intercourse was reduced to such a quick act of penetration that they never had the time to become aroused." "People never exposed to sexual stimulation," Gordon concludes, "may indeed have had truncated, underdeveloped sexual drives."

Ill health, too, helped shut down female desire. The enforced lack of exercise and the constant indoor confinement that were considered ladylike (just as robust health in women was now seen as vulgar) depleted the sexual energy of middle-class women, and the attitudes toward pregnancy that kept "respectable" women passive on the couch throughout their "confinement" may have made childbirth more painful than before, further depressing women's sexual interest. For poorer women, bad food and living conditions, exacerbated by urban overcrowding, tended to make poor health commonplace. Fashion for both rich and poor seems to have been unconsciously designed to hurt female desire: corsets were laced so tightly that they sometimes caused internal damage, further lowering women's vital energy and, as a consequence, their libido.

By the mid–nineteenth century, the passionate nature of women, taken for granted for millennia, had become a mystery: no one was sure anymore how normative the orgasmic woman was.

Dr. William Acton is one of the physicians whom historians most often quote to illustrate the Victorian ideal of female sexlessness. He wrote, "Many of the best mothers, wives and managers of households, know little of or are careless about sexual indulgences. Love of home, children, and of domestic duties are the only passions they feel. . . . As a general rule," he continued, "a modest woman seldom desires any sexual gratification for herself. She submits to her husband's embraces, but principally to gratify him. . . . The married woman has no desire to be placed on the footing of a mistress."

In 1850 the influential English periodical *The Westminster Review* asserted in a debate about women's sexual feelings: "In men in general the sexual desire is inherent and spontaneous and belongs to the condition of puberty. In the other sex, the desire is dormant, if not non-existent, till excited by actual intercourse. . . . If the passions of women were ready, strong and spontaneous in a degree even remotely approaching the form they assume in the coarser sex, there can be little doubt that sexual irregularities would reach a height, at which, at present, we have happily no conception." But once seduced, the young woman's downfall was expected to be swift and irrevocable: "Literally every woman who yields to her passions and loses her virtue is a prostitute," declared Bracebridge Hemynge in Henry Mayhew's *London Labour and the London Poor* (1851).

In the sex ed class discussions about men's "blue balls," in the Kimberly-Clark teaching material about women's responsibility to put the brakes on male lust, the teacher was presenting a belief system that had descended directly from Dr. Acton and his colleagues more than a century before.

Another legacy to us from this time, alive and well in sex ed classes today, too, is the male corrupter/female innocent scenario. The historian Peter Cominos, in *Suffer and Be Still*, argues that the one model for illicit sexual relations that young Victorian girls witnessed was that of female innocence yielding to male aggression. "[T]he responsibility for seduction," as the scenario appeared by the 1850s and 1860s, he writes, "never rested with the innocent, angelic, non-seductive, non-cooperative, naïve, helpless victim whose famous last words were 'I didn't mean to do it.' "

Still There, but Doesn't Matter, Mid-Nineteenth Century

As middle-class women were increasingly represented in public debate as sexless, there were convoluted efforts to explain away the sensitivity of the clitoris.

This led to the assertion that women may *have* orgasms, but they certainly cannot *feel* them. An 1836 handbook acknowledges that "the lower part of the vagina and the clitoris are possessed of a high degree of sensibility." But then it cautions that while in *"some* women, but not in all,"* these parts of the body are "the seat of venereal feelings from excitement," still, "in many women such feelings are altogether absent." Many commentators at the time admitted that the clitoris and internal organs of women underwent erection, arousal, and even ejaculation, just as men's tissues did. But they still insisted that "many women could somehow undergo all this physiological upheaval without having any inappropriate feelings."

Made Suspect, 1886

German neurologist Richard von Krafft-Ebing's *Psychopathia Sexualis* appeared in 1886; based on case histories of those who deviated, in ways both commonplace and extreme, from the Victorian erotic norm, it had the effect of casting all sexual variation as a form of illness. Women who exhibited "excessive" sexual desire were placed in his category of nymphomaniacs. Krafft-Ebing inadvertently revealed the widespread anxiety about the intensity of female desire: "If [a woman] is normally developed mentally," he wrote, "and well-bred, her sexual desire is small. If this were not so, the whole world would become a brothel and marriage and a family impossible."

Clitoris Celebrated, 1899

English physician Henry Havelock Ellis's seven-volume *Studies in the Psychology of Sex*, published between 1899 and 1928, revolutionized thinking about female sexuality. As a version brought out later for students summarizes, "Every woman has her own system of manifest or latent erogenic zones, and it is the lover's part in courtship to discover these zones and to develop them in order to achieve that tumescence which is naturally and properly the first stage in the sexual union." Ellis claimed that the presumed sexlessness of women was a Victorian falsehood. He held that men's and women's orgasms are strikingly alike but that women are naturally inclined, if given the chance, to have more of them, and that multiple orgasm is frequently possible among women.

Celebrated Again, 1902

The pioneering American physician Dr. Elizabeth Blackwell proclaimed in her 1902 collection, *Essays in Medical Sociology*, that "the unbridled impulse of physical lust is as remarkable in the latter [women] as in the former [men]." She made note of women's orgasms, which she called "sexual spasms," and explained that it is not coitus itself that women crave so much as "the profound attraction of one nature to the other which marks passion, and delight in kisses and caresses—the love touch." This "love touch," which could well be a euphemism for sexual gratification by hand and by tongue, was, she insisted, women's version of "physical sexual expression."

Demoted, 1905

Sigmund Freud's contribution to the early modern view of female sexual desire included his assertion that little girls start life centering their erotic feelings on the clitoris and do not ever mature into healthy, integrated women if such feelings are not subordinated; for the developing girl must direct her clitoral eroticism and her alleged penis envy into feelings of longing for a child. He asserted that clitoral and vaginal eroticism were distinct and that successful feminine adjustment involved successfully transferring sensation from the immature clitoris to the mature vagina. Clitoral eroticism eventually leads, he held, to self-loathing and frigidity.

In *Three Essays on the Theory of Sexuality* (1905), Freud set forth his theory: "If we are to understand how a little girl turns into a woman, we must follow the vicissitudes of [the] excitability of the clitoris." At puberty, he maintains, when boys feel an intensification of libido, girls feel only "a fresh wave of repression" that affects their clitoral erotic feelings; in an appropriate process of maturation, the "masculine machinery" of the clitoris is abandoned in favor of the more feminine, receptive, passive vagina.

Promoted, 1910

By 1910, clinicians in Margaret Sanger's birth control clinics were hearing about a great deal of sexual discontent from their clients. Doctors Lena Levine and Abraham Stone began to offer marriage counseling using a large sculpted model of the female genital and reproductive system. "Few clients," they found, "knew exactly what or where the clitoris was."

One woman in the Stone-Levine groups said to another who had been making the effort to achieve a vaginal orgasm "that maybe she should not care about it, perhaps not every woman needed to have a vaginal orgasm. . . . Some of the ideas, for some people, were totally new, particularly the sexual importance of the clitoris . . . the discovery of that one small organ, its capacity for feeling so long feared and suppressed, was the main theme of these sessions."

Promoted Again, 1918

In 1918, the English birth control advocate Dr. Marie Carmichael Stopes brought out *Married Love;* it went through many editions worldwide. Stopes noted, "By the majority of 'nice' people woman is supposed to have no spontaneous sex impulses. . . . So widespread in Anglo-Saxon countries is the view that it is only depraved women who have such feelings that most women would rather die than acknowledge that they *do* at times feel a physical yearning indescribable, but as profound as hunger for food." (Almost seventy years later, writer Sallie Tisdale could cause a shocked and excited stir by noting in an eloquent first-person essay, "Talk Dirty to Me," that she had felt sexual sensation as sharply as "hunger.") Stopes minces no words in chastising what would come to be known as "patriarchal scientific and sexual mores," and called quotes such as the following examples of "ridiculous absurdities which go by the name of science": "In the normal woman, especially of the higher social classes, the sexual instinct is acquired, not inborn; when it is inborn, or awakens by itself, there is *abnormality.* Since women do not know this instinct in marriage, they do not miss it when they have no occasion in life to learn it." She insisted that men pay good sexual attention to women:

> The supreme law for husbands is: . . . no union should ever take place unless the woman also desires it and is made physically ready for it. . . . A man does not woo and win a woman once for all when he marries her: *he must woo her before every separate act of coitus.* . . . [He] must himself rouse, charm, and stimulate her. . . . In distressingly many cases the man's climax comes so swiftly that the

woman's reactions are not nearly ready and she is left without it. . . . So complex, so profound, are woman's sex-instincts that in rousing them the man is rousing her whole body and soul. And this takes time. More time indeed than a husband dreams of spending upon it.

And Again, 1926

Dutch gynecologist Theodore Hendrik van de Velde's *Ideal Marriage* (1926), published less than a decade after Stopes's hugely popular best-seller, also succeeded on a grand scale, being reprinted forty-three times in English alone. His was the first modern manual to endorse in an authoritative male voice practices intended primarily to please women, such as cunnilingus and extensive foreplay. Van de Velde believed that women, like men, should be monogamous; the best way to maintain fidelity was for husbands to learn the erotic techniques that could please their wives. He advocated a technique called "maraichinage," "in which the couple, sometimes for hours, mutually explore and caress the inside of each other's mouths with their tongues, as profoundly as possible." "We must clearly understand," he wrote,

> that the sensations caused by stimulation of the vagina are quite distinctive and dissimilar from those due to stimulation of the clitoris. In both cases there is pleasure, and characteristically sexual pleasure, or *voluptas*. But the sensations differ as much between themselves as the flavor and aroma of two fine kinds of wine—or the chromatic glories and subtleties of two quite separate colour schemes. . . . Perfect and *natural* coitus would give the woman a blend of both types of sensation. Such a blend would involve supreme pleasure. . . .

Van de Velde recommended the "genital kiss"—but advises that the man bestow it more often than the woman, since the woman's tempo tends to be slower. The man must "exercise the *greatest gentleness, the most delicate reverence!*" in a kiss that should consist of "gentle and soothing caresses with lip and tongue." He was stern with men: "It is both stupid and grossly selfish," he maintained, of a man to attempt intercourse if the woman is not truly aroused.

And Again, 1930

In 1930, British gynecologist Dr. Helena Wright published *The Sex Factor in Marriage*. This was a how-to guide for women that taught them, in calm, reassuring tones, how to exorcise a lifelong sense of guilt and shame in relation to their own pleasure: "A wife who allows her mind to keep any unworthy ideas about sex lurking in its corners is her own worst enemy. Her body will only yield its fullest joy, will only allow her to know the experience of physical ecstasy, if her mind and soul are in active sympathy with it," she wrote. "Many wives fail to reach the climax because their husbands fail to realize that rhythmic friction is necessary right up to the end of the act."

She also described the importance of the clitoris, insisting that her reader, to find fulfillment, must identify it. She must locate for herself the "small round body, about the size of a pea, movable to a slight extent, and coated with delicate membrane, which is always more or less moist. . . . This little organ is capable of giving the most acute sensations. . . . The only purpose of the clitoris is to provide sensation; a full understanding of its capabilities and place in the sex-act is therefore of supreme importance." In 1947, Wright took up the cause of the clitoris with even greater deliberateness. The earlier instructions, she had realized, were not encouraging enough for women whose socialization had forbidden them from touching themselves at all. "Arrange a good light and take a mirror," she instructs. "The hood can be gently drawn backward by the finger tips and inside will be seen a small, smooth, rounded body . . . which glistens in a good light." Then touch it, she instructed ("Any small, smooth object will do"). She promised that "the instant the clitoris is touched, a peculiar and characteristic sensation is experienced which is different in essence from touches on the labia or anywhere else." Wright compares the eyes' response to the pattern of specific light waves and the ears' response to the pattern of certain sound waves to the clitoris's need for a pattern—a unique pattern for each woman—of "rhythmic friction." If her reader finds her own rhythm, well, the good doctor concludes somewhat abruptly, the sensation "cannot be described in words."

Now, why would it have been so important for us as girls to have been marched at a brisk pace through the main points of a cultural history of actual female sexuality, rather than given the minutiae of reproduction and the history of the discovery of the menstrual cycle? Because the prevailing culture convinced us that the identification and celebration of female desire was revolutionary—so revolutionary that it could not be mentioned on our library shelves. The subtext of such a message? Such knowledge was not our birthright. "Revolutionary" information stands in opposition to the culture and therefore is a fragile legacy.

LISTEN to Dr. Stopes. She explained in 1918 that she developed her theory that good sex must be premised on men's attention to women's distinct erotic needs by having the radical idea of asking women questions about their sexuality and listening to the answers: "Many, many women have shown me the truth of their natures when I have simply and naturally assumed that of course they felt [desire]—being normal women—and asked them only: when? From their replies I have collected facts which are sufficient to overturn many ready-made theories about women." Now look at the very first sentence of Shere Hite's declaration of intent in her *The Hite Report* (1976), the book we searched out while baby-sitting to fill in the blanks in our education, and one that was represented as a daring, transgressive, unprecedented (and thus culturally tenuous) high-water mark of female self-assertion. "Women," she wrote, with the cymbal crash that introduces the absolutely new,

> have never been asked how they felt about sex. Researchers, looking for statistical "norms," have asked all the wrong questions for all the wrong reasons—and all too often wound up *telling* women how they should feel. . . . Female sexuality has been seen essentially as a response to male sexuality and intercourse. . . . This book presents a new theory of female sexuality. . . . What these women have shared (anonymously), with so much love and honesty, comes from the wealth of female experience that is usually hidden, but which foreshadows women's great courage and potential for the future.

Wow, we thought. That's as far as or farther than we're allowed to go. But was it "a new theory of female sexuality"? Hardly. It was essentially the same theory as that of Levine and Stone, and of Drs. Stopes, van de Velde, and Wright, if somewhat less explicit than theirs. It was, in short, less a theory than one more "discovery" of the natural facts—so simple yet so incendiary that they are erased decade after decade—of what women happen to like to do in bed. The seduction and fulfillment of women by men's loving use of hand, of mouth? The notion that men should take their time because women's responses may be slower? The elevation of the notion of sharing with women nonphallocentric sex play? In 1976, these ideas were greeted as a Copernican displacement of male-centered sexual ideology. Little did we know that these ideas could have been found in women's bureau drawers since before the invention of talkies.

Look again at the find-your-clitoris instruction pages—the well-perused pages 169 to 170—in *Our Bodies, Ourselves*. Under the heading "The Role of the Clitoris," it asserts: "Until the mid-1960s, most women didn't know how crucial the clitoris was. . . . Even if we knew it for ourselves, nobody talked about it. . . . Learning about the clitoris increased sexual enjoyment for countless women and freed many of us from years of thinking we were 'frigid.' Our ability to give ourselves orgasms and to show our lovers how to please us has been one of the cornerstones of a new self-respect and autonomy, and has therefore been politically as well as personally important for women." Picking up on our culture's treatment of the subject as a controversial, highly politicized novelty, we thanked heaven for our good luck in having been born after this great secret of the ages—along with the mysteries of penicillin or space travel or eight-track tapes—had been revealed. The ritual of the at-home search for the clitoris among second-wave feminists during my adolescence became virtually a form of political protest; the speculum, which these women were encouraged to use—the more efficient version of Wright's mirror—became practically a totem of the revolution. The rhetoric of discovery in such books as *Our Bodies, Ourselves* was certainly sincere; thank goodness for the Boston Women's Health Book Collective. But the act of searching for one's clitoris was presented as being a challenge to the silence of the past, a dramatic, confrontational rending of old, heavy veils of secrecy and shame. Nowhere, when we were growing up, did we glimpse this more historically accurate insight: here we are, darn it all, on the floor, with our good light and a mirror, *again*.

For her time, Hite was indeed making a brave, transgressive assertion. But all the men and women who had written essentially the same book over the course of the entire preceding century, with the same rhetoric of clouds parting to reveal to grateful women a new day, had also made brave and transgressive assertions. We did not know that generations of men may have received the same "groundbreaking" instructions about exactly what to do to please women, and yet somehow the culture had misplaced its notes when it came time to pass on a legacy of collective wisdom to its sons and daughters. We had no idea what had been well known about us, and thoroughly forgotten again, on our behalf.

14

More Skipped Homework: Our Pleasure

All animals and humans have the urge to mate. This healthy, normal desire has been built into every living creature since the beginning of time. . . . A dog will not mate with a cat; a bear will not mate with a lion; or a horse with a cow.

—Kimberly-Clark, "The Miracle of You," 1968, 1973

T he school board bestowed upon us, as the special female information was conveyed in sex ed class, little personal grooming kits supplied by the menstrual products manufacturers that also contained needle-and-thread packets, a little tube of Woolite, as I recollect, and some Kotex pads. There was no way to escape the connection: the first message about sexual maturity for girls was that it was something you needed new skills and products to clean up. We got the official message that for us sex necessitated information about cleaning dirt ("Suddenly, you don't smell like a little girl any longer . . .") and protecting against disease; and from the larger culture came the message that sex was entirely about sensation. We were left disastrously to ourselves to try to piece together the answers to our questions about where sex met with need, love, vulnerability, and passion.

We saw in the last chapter that young American girls are taught little enough about the "where" of female desire. We were taught just as inadequately about the question *"What* is female desire?" We certainly had no idea that sex researchers were confirming what earlier cultures had never questioned—that female sexuality has the potential to unfold without limits.

OVERWHELMING PASSION: THE MISSING MIDTERM

In Greek mythology, the seer Tiresias, who had experienced life as both a man and a woman, was asked who had more pleasure in bed, women or men; women, he replied. Physiology may bear him out.

In 1973, Dr. Mary Jane Sherfey, an anatomist, cited Masters and Johnson's finding that "the average female" with "optimal arousal" is generally satiated by three to five climaxes brought about by hand. Kinsey et al. believed that men's and women's responses are similar but noted that "the labia minora and the vestibule of the vagina provide more extensive sensitive areas in the female than are to be found in any homologous structure of the male." Dr. Sherfey, whose scientific text *The Nature and Evolution of Female Sexuality* forms the basis of some of the following anatomical discussion, also explains that, because of the way women are made, it is wrong to expect them to be fully satiated with one strong orgasm: "The more orgasms a woman has, the stronger they become; the more orgasms she has, the more she *can* have."

In the first phase of arousal, when even a slight distraction such as a sudden noise can subdue an erection, women's response shows no such distractability, and the contractions of women's orgasms last longer. As for the intensity of orgasm, men's most intense pleasure lies in the first few contractions, but the female orgasm can be more prolonged.

This capacity for pleasure comes from the structure of the woman's pelvis. Sherfey sees the whole lower pelvis of women as an extensive "erotic network," in which not only the clitoris but the labia, perineum, the lower vagina, and anal region—the entire "sexual skin," inside and outside—is responsive. In this view, the vagina, clitoris, and "G spot" are not separate organs. (She also makes the point that the network of blood vessels that creates the extreme potential for responsiveness in women becomes more complex after each birth, which suggests—contrary to contemporary culture's view that women lose sexuality with motherhood and with age—that mothers, and older mothers in particular, are the real sex goddesses.)

In our "liberated" culture, foreplay is often seen by both partners as a special gift to the woman rather than being nothing less than her natural due. Even though *The Hite Report* confirmed (again) that most women like extensive foreplay—and even though well-intentioned sexologists and feminists have announced that women are entitled to ask for this "gift"—there still lingers a general sense that women, due to their creakier makeup, demand "extra" warming up, working as they do like an old hand-cranked Model T rather than a brand-new Porsche.

But it turns out that some anatomists believe that on an *evolutionary* level, women need long, drawn-out foreplay leading to plenty of orgasms. Dr. Sherfey maintains that women's need for elaborate foreplay is *biologically ordained*. Since women don't go into heat, they require caressing to stimulate and release the blood flow to the pelvis. Nature, in her view, may have determined that women must be adored and lingered upon and lavished with sensuous attention for the survival of the species. Some theorists, such as Elaine Morgan in *The Descent of Woman*, hold that women's capacity for orgasm, as well as their need to be touched, facilitated evolutionary success. (This would suggest that there is nothing "vestigial" about the friendly neighborliness of the clitoral system to the structures of reproduction.) In other words, it may well be that women's asking for pleasure is Nature's commandment. Helen E. Fisher confirms this view of female sexuality in her book *The Sex Contract*:

> [T]he human female is capable of constant sexual arousal. . . . She can make love whenever she pleases. This is extraordinary. No females of any other sexually reproducing species make love with such frequency. . . .
>
> Because a woman has no obvious period of heat, a couple that wishes to have a child cannot tell when the woman is ready to conceive. So they must make love regularly. . . . [T]he human female is particularly designed to do so.
>
> It was not until the 1950s that investigators documented a second extraordinary human female endowment. Not only can she

make love with impressive regularity . . . but her sex organs generate intense sexual pleasure—even more pleasure than the human
male derives from intercourse. For nature has provided the human
female with a clitoris, a bundle of nerves designed solely for sex.
Furthermore, about four or five dense masses of veins and nerves
congregate in the muscles of her genitals—and during intercourse
these sensitive aggregates sharply distinguish her sexual performance from that of her mate.

For a man, she writes, there are three or four major contractions, a
few minor ones, localized in the genital area, and sex is done. But
"the female pattern is different, for women feel five to eight major
contractions and then nine to fifteen minor ones. They diffuse
throughout the pelvic area. For women, sex may have just begun.
Unlike her mate, her genitals have not expelled the blood, and if she
knows how, she can climax again and again if she wants to." Still
another theorist, David Buss, makes the argument that women's
unique sexual availability is useful for evolutionary success because
of the delayed development of human children compared to other
primates. Since the brain keeps growing, among humans, into adolescence, a child's chance of survival is best helped by a large social
group sustaining him or her. Women's capacity for sexual pleasure,
Buss speculates, strengthens a woman's bond with her mate and this
in turn maximizes her offspring's success.

It is irresistible to speculate on this idea that women's sexual pleasure has an inherent evolutionary boon. Perhaps its function is to
give females a physical incentive to seek out mates who are attentive
and a disincentive to stay with a selfish partner. A man who gives his
partner pleasure is not only more likely to take a role in rearing the
young, he also benefits himself in the genetic sweepstakes. Making
women feel good helps men with the Darwinian struggle. Could
Nature's "real" men be those who are the best lovers to women?

Sexuality is located in the mind as much as the body. Even psychologically, it appears, women are as erotically preoccupied as men.
Research into female erotic fantasy indicates that women's desire is a
resilient force.

Harold Leitenberg and Kris Henning, in their overview "Sexual
Fantasy," summarized a quarter century of research on female sexual
longing. What they found is that women's preoccupation with their

own desire manages to surmount cultural taboos, life circumstances, even their own inner censors.

It is hard to establish accurately how many women fantasize erotically: the studies on female solitary sexual fantasy included in the Leitenberg-Henning summary show that the range of women who say they have such fantasies extends from a low of 26 percent to a high of 100 percent—though the authors point out, as many others have done, that self-reporting of this kind is unreliable.

Do modern men want sex more than women do? Superficially, it is easy to conclude that the answer is yes. Virtually all the studies cited show that men think about sex—or report that they do—more than women. But Ellis and Symons in 1990 found almost no gender difference when subjects reported that fantasizing felt good to them. Knoth et al. also showed no difference when it came to rating such experiences "exciting" or "involving," and researchers Sue (1979) and Cado and Leitenberg (1990) discovered that both sexes had just about equally positive feelings about their fantasies during intercourse. Carlson and Coleman (1977) found it was women who described a higher level of sexual arousal when they were writing down their fantasies. Of course, what women fantasize about may or may not shed light on what they want in real life.

The evidence, taken together, points to the striking vitality of the female erotic imagination. One 1990 study asked male and female college students to record externally triggered fantasies as opposed to internally generated ones. The women had fewer than half the number of externally generated fantasies than the men did—about 2 versus 4.5—but the frequency of their internally generated fantasies was nearly identical—2.5 for the women versus 2.7 for the men. Since there are far more external erotic cues for men in the media than there are for women, this finding could suggest a highly creative use of the female imagination.

Just consider what some acknowledgment of our own dreams and fantasies could have meant to us, at fourteen, at fifteen, as we were becoming hyperattuned to the fantasies of boys, and through that deafening static somehow trying to learn about ourselves.

15

Babies

I was sixteen, he was twenty-one . . .
Pa woulda shot him if he knew what he'd done. . . .
I never had schoolin' but he taught me well with his smooth, southern
style.
But three months later I'm a gal in trouble, and I haven't seen him for a
while . . .
Gypsys, tramps and thieves,
We'd hear it from the people of the town. They called us
Gypsys, tramps and thieves. . . .
and ev'ry night all the men would come around
and lay their money down.
—CHER, "Gypsys, Tramps and Thieves," 1971

Sure of what boys wanted, unsure of what we wanted, with children's hearts and mature reproductive systems, we moved into the world. Our vulnerability was heightened by the way that sex became sui generis as the seventies progressed. Increasingly, we lived in a moral vacuum in which sex and its pleasure had become so detached from both consciousness and reproduction that it was easy to think of sexual pleasure also as detached, not only technologically but morally and philosophically, from any consequence at all. It was a worldview that may have led to more unplanned pregnancies rather than fewer.

The teen birthrate in the United States is the highest of any industrialized country, nearly twice as high as that of Great Britain, which has the second-highest rate. Of the girls who give birth, more than 80 percent end up in poverty. Teenage mothers are less than half as likely as their counterparts who are not mothers to graduate from high school. The children of these adolescent mothers are 50 percent more likely to be of low birth weight, with all its health problems; two to three times more likely to run away from home; and more than twice as likely to suffer abuse and neglect; in addition, they have a harder time learning. The cost to society of this devastation is estimated at $29 billion a year. The way we fail to teach girls not only about the nature of their sexuality but about the sacredness of their sex in relation to their potential fertility must have something to do with these grotesque numbers.

The "feminine sexuality" we first learned, as I've noted, was the sexuality of Barbie. No matter how she metamorphosed with time— from Barbie into the James Bond girls into Playmate of the Month into Disco Queen—she was *not even potentially maternal.* Maternalism, in our world, signified the end of being a "sexy girl." If you were sleeping casually with someone, you were supposed to take care of all birth control arrangements. Our initiation tasks as teenagers really were sex-segregated, just as in any tribe that sets up functional rather than dysfunctional initiation rituals. The task of acquiring and distributing drugs "belonged" to the boys. While boys had sports and, very far in the distance, the possibility of military service, it was the risk, ritual, and secrecy of drug acquisition and abuse for these middle-class boys, just as it was gang initiations for the working-class and poor boys across the bay in Oakland, that served many of the purposes of manhood rites. Birth control and abortions "belonged" to the girls.

Martin was anomalous. Most boys didn't like it if you dragooned them into helping with contraception. It wasn't the mess or the delay or the feel of rubber alone. It was the mere thought that we could become pregnant that would turn boys off.

By extension, we understood, we should dispose of our potential maternity the same way we were supposed to "go on" the Pill: efficiently, without revealing any distasteful hint of it to boys. The mere biological fact of our ability to become pregnant was, for women our age, the secret to be discreetly "dealt with" that menstruation had been to our mothers' generation. Though a pregnancy was considered by some girls to be a rite of passage, it was considered by boys, like a stain on your skirt, to be your own antisocial faux pas. Girls made plenty of room for the drama of the unplanned pregnancy and the abortion; but in the boys' eyes you were even more gauche if you made a big thing about "taking care of it."

Our difficulty in "becoming women" was intensified by the way that babies and sexual pleasure were unnaturally presented as opposite ends of a spectrum marked "Sex." The benefits of having control of our reproduction were obvious, but the compartmentalization that was demanded was damaging for us. It meant that we could not even begin to think of the two aspects of ourselves holistically.

Among the events described by the women I interviewed, it was only the accounts of their teenage abortions that they wanted to confide anonymously, compartmentalized from the rest of their stories. Out of all the difficult sexual events the women I spoke to experienced, it was the abortions alone that seemed, even twenty years later, just too painful to integrate. By and large, they did not regret the choice to have the abortion, but they did bitterly regret the circumstances that had led to the need to make the choice.

The compartmentalizing lingered, corrosively. One woman who spoke to me for this book told me about her abortion at seventeen but asked that I separate it even from her pseudonymous account of her life—a double distancing: "I did get pregnant. I really wanted to have the baby, but I was so in love with my boyfriend that to protect him I had an abortion. It really devastated me. We were so young.

"The abortion was okay. It was just really weird because we were both so fucked up about it. You're not supposed to have sex for two weeks after it—and right after we had to have sex because it was like we were trying to put it back. That's the thing I feel worst about. I wish I'd had that baby. I did it for him, even though he said, 'It's up to you.' Logically, I thought, Okay, this is what you do in this situation. I had no idea what the emotional ramifications would be. It was the strong, smart, emancipated thing to do. We had no idea of the enormity of it. We were just kids."

"At nineteen I had my first abortion," another woman who spoke to me remembered. "The feminist party line was that it was just a medical procedure. I had very mixed emotions about it. But I will say that I am absolutely one thousand percent grateful abortions were available. A society that practically *requires* young women to be sexual had damned well better have that available. My boyfriend and I had this conversation about it, and he said, 'I couldn't go with you to the clinic because it would be like looking death in the face.'

"By their twenties, almost all my friends had had abortions," she said. The reason one friend of ours got pregnant was that by then she was living according to conservative religious values, and she was not supposed to be having sex, so of course she was not going to be using contraception because that would be acknowledging she had sex. With other friends it was lousy contraceptive innovations—the cervical cap that fell off or the sponge that didn't work very well—innovations that have been taken off the market since.

"An insight I had in my mid-twenties," this woman continued, "was that my body wanted to produce children and I could not do so. Emotionally, financially, partnershipwise—all these things I needed, I could not get. And I thought, This society does not support motherhood."

No one told us that for much of recorded history sexiness and potential maternity in women may have actually been considered *the same thing*. For the belief had intermittently endured throughout Europe until at least the late eighteenth century, as Thomas Laqueur documents, that women had to have sexual pleasure in order to conceive.

Today, pleasing women sexually has some renewed cultural value. Clinicians and men's magazines tell men that pleasing women sexually will give them better relationships, happier sex lives, and the knowledge that they are decent guys. But in the not-too-distant past some European men were taught that everything worth having—children and posterity—depended on men's attention to pleasing their wives erotically.

The right partner and the right technique were also thought to mean the difference between barrenness and fertility. (Aristotle knew that women could conceive without pleasure, but he thought this an aberration.) The ancients paid such close attention to women's desire that they noted what they thought was the best way to time the female orgasm. The scientist known as "the Hippocratic writer" believed that if a woman is too excited before intercourse, she will "ejaculate prematurely"—and then her womb will close and she will not conceive. "Like a flame that flares when wine is sprinkled on it, the woman's heat blazes most brilliantly when the male sperm is sprayed on it. . . . She shivers. The womb seals itself. And the combined elements for a new life are safely contained within."

Pliny's recipe for contraception involved diminishing women's desire for sexual intercourse. Since his concoction included advising a passionate woman to apply mouse droppings and swallow snail excrement, and to rub on herself "blood taken from the ticks on a wild black bull," his recipe probably did manage to quench not only the woman's but also the man's lust, and thus prevent conception.

Avicenna, the influential Arabic philosopher and physician, writing in the eleventh century, also thought that women had sperm and that it instigated "a specifically genital itch . . . in the male's spermatic vessels and in the mouth of the womb . . . which is relieved only by the chafing of intercourse or its equivalent." Avicenna warned that female sexual frustration cannot be suppressed and that dire consequences can follow from leaving women unsatisfied. Not only will they be barren, but they will "have recourse to rubbing, with other women, in order to achieve amongst themselves the fullness of their pleasures." The first-century B.C.E. Roman poet and philosopher Lucretius believed that children resembled their parents because "at their making the seeds . . . were dashed together by the collusion of mutual passion in which neither party was master or mastered." In Christian Byzantium it was felt that the quality of a woman's erotic pleasure would determine her baby's gender and health, even its temperament. According to Laqueur, the "babies-through-female-lust" paradigm dominated the West until the nineteenth century, when the Great Forgetting took hold.

It is impossible from the fragmentary accounts in the historical sources to be sure how widespread the belief was. One obvious caveat is that brutish oafs were doubtless impregnating their wives all over Europe. But it is tempting to speculate upon this glimmer of a possibility that may have existed at moments in the past: that in certain communities, female lust has been valued by both men and women, in contexts in which children were welcome. A young married man who wanted a legitimate child would have seen mastering the techniques that would bring pleasure to his wife as being a fundamental task of manhood. A married woman may well have felt her sexual self-discovery to be a sacred and legitimate development, part of the dowry she brought to her husband and a precursor of the family itself. Any lack of sexual interest a woman may have felt toward her husband would not have been cast as a lonely misfortune or a personal failure, as it often is today, but as a shared challenge. Cultivating female satisfaction within marriage would have been considered by the whole community, as it still is in observant Jewish communities, to be a family value.

When the boyfriend of the woman who told me about her abortion at nineteen explained to her that she would have to go alone to the abortionist's because he could not "look death in the face," he left her emotionally isolated. She went through that trauma and bitter disillusionment partly because the culture that praised her boyfriend was prepared neither to eroticize nor to take responsibility for girls' and women's ability to give life.

To heal this wound we have a past we can learn from. Looking back, even the sex education textbooks of the twenties, thirties, forties, fifties, and sixties were sometimes more successful in talking about the connection of teenage sex to responsibility and pleasure than was our curriculum of the recent past. In those earlier guides to adolescence, "love" and "pleasure" are ubiquitous terms. Sexual gradualism, or "petting," was taken for granted.

Though petting was warned against as something difficult to control—"petting is dynamite"—there is a fascinating, barely subtextual message offered up under the routine denunciations; that secondary message explains exactly how to pet and how to find a safe, comfortable level of petting. According to a manual from 1946, "necking and petting" refer to "a wide range of activities. . . . At one extreme, petting may be no more than kissing and semiplatonic caressing; at the other, it may be an intimate fondling only just stopping short of actual sexual intercourse."

Twenty years later, petting itself, apart from warnings about what it could lead to, is described in positive terms in this guide for teens, *Consecrated Unto Me*, put out by a conservative Jewish educator: "Petting serves an important purpose in nature's scheme of things. It is meant to be a prelude and preparation for intercourse. One of the tragedies of our culture is that so much petting occurs before marriage and so little occurs afterward. For petting is nature's preface to full sexual relations." The most common conclusion was that though teenage couples should be careful and the girl should provide the "stoplight," the best course was for the couple together to make an informed, mutually negotiated decision about "how far is enough" or, failing that, that "it is . . . the individual who must finally decide how far to go." *Consecrated Unto Me* signals the same safe ground:

> A variety of definitions of petting have been offered. One of the oldest is that necking refers to anything above the neck, petting to everything below. Most of us, when we use the word petting, refer to any fondling by boys and girls of those portions of their respective bodies which are sexually exciting. . . . Some unmarried couples have fallen into the habit of petting to the point where each has an orgasm without actual coitus.

Another guide, while condemning the practice of "petting," also explains it in easy-to-follow detail: "Moreover, even if the mutual masturbation (for that is what 'necking and petting' often amount to) proceeds to the climax, things are still unsatisfactory" (one reason being that petting can lead the woman in later life "to an overconcentration on the clitoris").

In *Hands and Hearts: A History of Courtship in America,* Ellen K. Rothman writes that close dancing, movies, and cars influenced the small-town culture of petting from the 1920s onward. She documents the universality of petting, and notes that the culture of petting was supported by parents and schools. Commentators in 1928 and 1930 conceded that "what is vulgarly known as 'petting' is the rule rather than the exception in all classes of society" and "could refer to 'the universal convention of petting' with little risk of understatement." "Petting," the author explains, "included all forms of erotic behavior short of intercourse." Petting parties were a standard part of life for high school students: a 1936 study by Phyllis Blanchard and Carlyn Manasses confirmed this distinction, which accepted advanced petting but prohibited intercourse. "Many girls," it found, "draw a distinct line between the exploratory activities of the petting party and complete yielding of sexual favors to men." The petting party was "a self-limiting form of experimentation. . . . Here sexual activity was manifestly regulated by the group. . . . To maintain one's position with peers . . . petting was permitted but intercourse was not."

Considering today's furor over Dr. Joycelyn Elders's circumspect comment that "masturbation . . . perhaps should be taught" in schools, and over the "Antioch Rules," which recommend explicit sexual negotiation between young people, it is astonishing how ahistorical we are, to our detriment: for these mainstream, middle American, socially conservative manuals from mid-century were, with wide parental approval, teaching youth in schools about passion, masturbation, mutual masturbation, and explicit sexual negotiation. From the twenties through the fifties, many "respectable" kids didn't abstain from sexual *activity*; sexual activity was tolerated and even tacitly encouraged. They abstained from sexual *intercourse*, which was, their elders knew, where the greatest risk lay.

With the sexual revolution of the late 1960s, this system broke down. How did early sex educators get away with a frankness that is so controversial today? Because intercourse was not yet then, as it has become for kids since the sexual revolution, the definition of teen sex. When "petting" rather than intercourse was the peer-sanctioned and peer-enforced code of teenage behavior (enforced, of course, to girls' disadvantage relative to boys'), 1920s-to-1960s sex educators could talk more freely about lust, both female and male ("Every individual in the world—with no exception!—has his or her point of no return,") as well as about how to address it realistically, because doing so did not make them accountable for opening the door to unwanted babies, rape, and disease.

The reason for this tacit acceptance and between-the-lines encouragement of some level of nonintercourse sex play among adolescents should be clear in retrospect: this approach essentially taught teenagers how to stay securely within the area of the "bases"; they were given information that would keep them safe from major life disasters.

Today, as in my day, among teenagers, the base system has collapsed. "Girls are getting pregnant," one Washington, D.C., Planned Parenthood sex educator told me, "who haven't even taken their clothes off." And ironically, the social sanction for adult instruction about the base system has collapsed as well. This is the worst possible situation, for kids are prohibited from learning from their teachers what they used to learn from their peers as well as their teachers—but no longer do. This leaves girls, especially, at profound risk: in a world without bases, girls risk everything intercourse can bring when they are simply trying to begin the natural process of exploring their bodies and learning about their own desire.

As for today's curriculum: of course it is important to teach girls about the consequences and dangers of sexual intercourse. But not in the absence of positive information about what to try instead. These girls, denied ownership of what they physically feel, are instructed by the culture to be passive or silent just at the moment when they, like their partners, should be the most sexually responsible and expressive.

The phenomenon of date rape and the tragedies of sexual mis-communication have been well documented. The majority of teenage girls do not use reliable contraception for their first act of lovemaking. Only one in three subsequently always uses contraception during sex. Their lives are submerged under a silence about female sexual desire that converges with the desire itself.

Solutions from the Left include sex ed film footage about menstrual cycles and prescriptions for condoms. Solutions from the Right define "abstinence" in a way that rules out even the kind of sexual touching that was taken for granted in the fifties, as in this "Focus on the Family" brochure promoting abstinence: "Some sex educators have tried to redefine abstinence to mean non-penetration, thus allowing for oral sex, mutual masturbation, etc. But this . . . misses the purpose of abstinence education, which is best defined as preserving sexual intimacy . . . for the commitment of marriage." But neither approach comes close to easing the human longing in these girls to know, their need to be curious, to take risks, to be close, to feel good, and to be safe.

We should address the teen abortion and unwanted pregnancy rate by doing what Dr. Elders lost her job as surgeon general simply for mentioning: we should teach petting—"sexual gradualism"—and let our kids know that there are many ways of having pleasure and intimacy that don't involve intercourse. This is an agenda both the Left and the center can agree on, for it is hardly a radical notion. Mutual masturbation: history shows it's the old-fashioned, Main Street, American way.

If we teach kids about other kinds of sexual exploration that help them wait for intercourse until they are really ready, we let girls find out about their desire, give them back power in erotic negotiation, and let kids have an option not to go immediately "from zero to sixty." Teaching sexual gradualism is as sensible as teaching kids to drive. We as a society would be in a better moral state if we handed fifteen-year-old girls a copy of *Our Bodies, Ourselves* and gave them a detailed discussion of how safely to explore their sexuality than we are when we maintain a hypocritical silence about teenage girls' natural desire, and tolerate the highest teen pregnancy and abortion rate in the industrialized world. So many girls should not have to suffer this trauma or else lose their young hopes—even risk their lives—in simply trying to find who they are, and what a sensible Nature has granted them.

16

Cheap or Precious?

This is the secret of really vulgar and of pornographical people: . . . sex is
dirty and dirt is sex, and sexual excitement becomes playing with dirt,
and any sign of sex in a woman becomes a show of her dirt.
— D. H. LAWRENCE, *Pornography and Obscenity*, 1929

A s the decade wore on, and we became more personally
ready for it, it seemed sex grew always dirtier. It seemed day
by day as if the sex industry was breathing harder down our
necks. Again and again, young girls in our middle and high school
classes would be accosted by older men who hung around at street
fairs and in cafés who offered to "turn them into models." More often
than not the girls would agree. These men were sometimes "real"
photographers, but most of the time they were old-fashioned per-
verts to whom the culture had suddenly granted unforeseen access to
create sexualized images of us.

I recall a genre of romanticized, eroticized photographs of what
looked like barely adolescent girls, posing with summer hats and
wearing sheer muslin dresses, their thighs just slipping out of the
petticoats or their nipples just showing through the chemises. The
photographer was named David Hamilton. These images had so
much cultural currency that he had become something of a celebrity.
The photos were everywhere—gift shops, even the local Woolworth's. They were of us—of children—being objects of desire.
They scared and intimidated us, and they also became the benchmark of our aspiration.

A girl we knew, the frequent winner of the local Asian beauty con-
tests, at sixteen, had already built up a portfolio of modeling photographs. One of them showed her done up in heavy makeup, her
bone-thin arms clenched at her sides, her chest visible under the
fashionable muslin, impersonating a sexuality she had not yet experienced. She posed for a photographer on the side of a hill in the
Castro District, the wind whipping the thin shirt against her chest
and, at one point, actually lifting it. "Don't get uncomfortable," the
photographer said. "This is great. This is beautiful." In the pictures—
which got her jobs and the envy of all of us—she looks into the camera with defensive eyes.

"Here's what I remember from the culture when we were sixteen,"
said Sandy, and she began talking about leather bustiers and fishnet
stockings. During this conversation, which took place a few days
after Trina, Pattie, Sandy, and I were all together so late at night,
Sandy and I were alone, in the middle of the day, in her orderly
home. Without talking about it, we left her place. Finally we reset-
tled ourselves in an anonymous hotel room downtown. It was not
easy to talk about our experiences in view of a patio littered with
toddler's toys.

So, on the hotel room balcony, with beer and nachos from room
service, we talked. It was easier, for the junk food, drinks, and transient space marked familiar territory for the girls we were trying to
summon up again: party territory. These girls would not have
reemerged in her domestic backyard (or mine, for that matter) without more of a fight.

We went on to album covers, for the music industry mirrored the
way the value of sex had deteriorated in our teens. Nineteen seventy-
seven: The Tubes. The cover of the album showed a woman stuffed
into latex and cut off at the eyes. She looked like an amputee.
"Mondo Bondage" was one song. We recalled the scene in the band's
show where the lead singer plays a student and the student ties the
teacher, a woman wearing a short, tight skirt and horn-rimmed
glasses, to the chalkboard.

The Ohio Players' *Honey* album cover also came back to us. It had
been famous in the teen subculture. The model was shot in profile,
naked and covered with what looked like real honey. Her mouth was
open, and she was licking up a stick dripping with honey. The urban

myth that went around was that the model had gotten a skin disease from the honey. The story was that she had confronted the record's producers while they were recording "Love Roller Coaster." Afraid of being sued, the producers had killed her, and the screams on the song were of her being murdered. We would play the album, look at one another, and say, "Listen to the screams!"

"Boys' rock and roll was all about sex," said Sandy. "They used to call it 'cock rock.' " Foreigner, Rick Derringer, AC/DC, Van Halen, Aerosmith, and songs like "Christine Sixteen" and "Walk This Way," about sex with hot high school girls, were what the guys listened to.

Girls were into punk rock, disco, Blondie. All of these were highly sexualized, too. The message was that the sexier you are, the more powerful you'll be. It wasn't romantic. You were supposed to be wearing a Lurex halter top and screwing men in Guccis. "The sheer number of men was important," Sandy observed. "The variety of sexual acts and behaviors was important; the drugs you did."

There was another, if dated, cultural image still around for girls: the Grateful Dead "Sugar Magnolia" ideal, where you were supposed to be the good hippie wife. "That always made me gag: 'She takes the wheel when I'm seeing double and pays my tickets when I speed,' " said Sandy.

By contrast, if you were a disco babe, you didn't have responsibility for anyone else or their feelings, and they didn't have responsibility for you or your feelings. The only responsibility you had was to keep up a chic façade. This image of female sexuality was empowering to a degree, we agreed, but ultimately terribly distorted; loveless, soulless. "You weren't paying the man's tickets—if he speeded or passed out from drugs, you'd go find someone else," said Sandy.

"I remember seeing a picture in *Time* of Uncle Sam in fishnet stockings and a corset. The headline was THE FASCINATION OF DECADENCE. That said to me, as a sixteen-year-old, that it was normal for adults to be sadomasochistic and that that was fun and exciting. They probably had President Carter the week before and now they had Uncle Sam in fishnets. It made me feel that by doing kinky sex I belonged to something that was important—important enough to make the cover of a national newsmagazine," said Sandy.

Then memories surfaced of the *The Rocky Horror Picture Show*, which was a midnight cult film when we were in high school. "That's when all the freaks came out, and we were freaks," she said. The kids who went were kids who were questioning their sexuality. It was a safe place to get together with others who were doing the same thing.

"I saw that movie again recently," said Sandy, "and I was taken aback at the message. It's about a nice couple just engaged to be married, and when they are going to share the good news, they get waylaid by a castle full of freaks. Before that, they are singing about how glad they are to be engaged. It was total satire. It was making fun of the idea of heterosexual marriage. What a total candy-ass fifties thing to do, to get engaged with a diamond ring and be excited about it. It was saying: this is completely outdated and will *never* be a part of our lives again. We've moved beyond that. It made me feel ashamed of the part of me that wanted to grow up and get married."

In general, we got the message that being a monogamous heterosexual was worse than being boring and stupid. It was more freakish than being a middle-class fifteen-year-old girl waiting to see *The Rocky Horror Picture Show*, wearing a garter belt on Market Street in the middle of the night.

In the movie's last scene, everyone's swimming around in a swimming pool in corsets and fishnet stockings. They are all kissing and touching and singing, "Don't dream it, be it." The message is that you should do anything sexual that you can possibly think of. It was our anthem. "Personally," said Sandy, "I took it as marching orders.

"At the hundredth midnight performance of the show, there was a celebration in Berkeley at the U.C. Theater. I remember sitting on the hood of my friend's car on University Avenue, in the middle of town, like the parade queen. I was sixteen. I was sitting there dressed in a black garter belt, maybe with a red ribbon, black panties, and a black corset, and black fishnets and a red feather boa, with a lot of makeup on. I made my face white with red lips and lots of blush because, in the movie, that's how they look. I was driving past the crowd, and I was spitting at the crowd and waving. People loved it. They were asking, 'Boy or girl? Are you a boy or girl?' And it didn't matter, because 'Whatever you are, I want to get kinky with you.'

"I was walking past a car window wearing black bikini underwear when someone pinched my butt, and I slammed their hand against the window and I heard this muffled groan. Was it empowering? I was putting myself at risk for this, obviously; I felt justified in defending myself. I was doing it for a lark. The way my parents in the fifties would swallow goldfish.

"This was my tribal coming-of-age ritual. You put on the costume the adults have, you do something dangerous, and then you belong to the tribe.

"What did the image of female sexuality in the movie say to me? I had a sense that when the Susan Sarandon character slept with the hero, the transvestite Count Frank N. Furter, and became transformed by it—when she came out in her corset instead of her dorky virginal fifties underwear—that that was a possibility for us as girls. If I just found the right kinky sex partner, I would—gosh, it would be like winning the lottery. I would be the coolest person on the planet. You'd leap right over all that adolescent insecurity without even having to feel all the doubts and fears that go along with growing up and becoming sexual. Kinky sex was safe—it was safe because it was numb. Very focused. Forget about your family dynamics, your career wishes, your education—we're just doing *sex*. It felt very controlled compared to all the other things in my life. The script was written, the costumes were set, the roles were there—and you could just step into it and know what to expect. Whereas all that other stuff was breaking down. There was a direction. I didn't get that anywhere else—that sense of movement toward something. My parents didn't tell me to get married or date nice boys or go to the prom. Mainstream culture seemed stagnant—not going anywhere new, just decaying, in comparison."

During my junior year, the last year of my brief hippie idyll, in which I was able to associate sex with the "purity" of the natural world, came to an end. As the meaner 1970s erased the vestiges of the 1960s, the growing understanding that embracing adult female sexuality meant walking into "dirtiness" as well as into pleasure intensified still further.

Martin went across the bay to college. For reasons that only a gentle and slightly self-conscious boy in a new place can fully understand, he joined a fraternity, where I had to visit him. There, walking up the deep streets to the old wooden mansion, I would see, perhaps more clearly and strongly than ever before, what the world thought sex was and what it thought women were. As I made my way up Fraternity Row, groups of young men stood on balconies with placards marked "1" to "10," grading each woman as she passed. I hated that they did that, hated looking to see what number they held up for me, and hated caring.

That world was so much dirtier, in how it saw women and their desire, than the safe place Martin and I had created. The discovery was a shock to me.

Some fraternities had a designated urinal above which the guys were supposed to put individual pubic hairs of girls they had seduced. There were no women's rooms. So a strange little row of unidentifiable, carefully lined-up hairs was arrayed within the eye-sight of the carefully dressed sorority women who applied their makeup at the bathroom mirrors during parties. "What was that?" someone would ask with a grimace, and the frat boys would answer evasively and smirk. Part of the fun was making fools of the puzzled women who walked out of there. Martin's own house, though not considered particularly outrageous, had such a collection. The guys in Martin's fraternity were rumored to peer into a "brother's" room as he made a conquest.

Martin did not become a "regular guy" in this way. His loyalty remained with me. But as time went on, he grew sadder and sadder, surrounded by male joviality but never fully part of it. We could both feel that some of the guys were ready to ostracize him for his qualms. His friendship with me, which had been free and simple, had a price now that we were turning into men and women. Though he never said so, he must have felt resentful. Knowing it was irrational, some-times I felt guilty.

One night a young woman from one of the sororities came to a keg party, during the initiation of a pledge class, and got drunk. She passed out on the couch in the downstairs common room of the fine, shabby old Arts and Crafts house. I heard that someone had lifted her by the arms, and someone else by the legs, and they had taken her into a room. By morning all the guys in the house knew that a number of the guys had—"felt her up"? molested her? The details were imprecise. Martin remembers that "People were drunk and rowdy and assaulted a woman. It wasn't date rape; she was not on a date. They jumped on her, groped her, dry-humped her. Somewhere between six and twelve guys were part of the scene—two involved directly."

When the woman came to, she fled. The joke, as I recall (and my memory of this episode fades in and out of focus), was that she had escaped so fast that her shoes remained. Someone had put her red high-heeled pumps on the wood mantel of the fireplace, next to the collection of beer cans from around the world, like a trophy.

The guys and I were friends. Over breakfast, they did not hide the story from me or from the other girlfriends who had stayed the night. I remember all the guys having their morning coffee were laughing about the episode, which was hinted at but not fully described, and glancing now and again at the girlfriends, watching their reactions. We were, it was understood, nice girls because we were in relationships; we would understand that what had happened to her had nothing to do with us.

I sat quietly throughout that breakfast. Later I heard about another girlfriend's act of dissension. I remember her as a quiet, small girl, not presumed by any of us to have a lot of personal power. But she eventually went over to the mantel and, without saying a word, took the shoes, walked across the street to the sorority house, and, in full view of the "brothers," lined them up carefully and sat down beside them.

I wish I could write that I had done something remotely like that. I would like to imagine that both Martin and I walked out. But my eyes widened, and I said nothing. I knew the words I was applying to the actions of these laughing, confident young men—friends of mine—in my head, words such as "sexual assault," would have no social meaning if I spoke them. Only the wildest-eyed of "lesbos," in their terms, would, in 1979, have called it a sexual assault. I stayed inside. So did Martin. We finished our expertly cooked breakfast.

Later, Martin told me how appalled he had been by what his "brothers" had shown themselves to be. We circled and circled around what we could have done differently. I said, probably rationalizing my cowardice, that I hadn't wanted him to bear the brunt of my making a scene. He wondered, perhaps rationalizing too, if maybe it was better for him to be a quiet example to the contrary from within. His kind face was twisted with the effort of explaining something to me that went against his own sense of decency, and my own cowardice made me ashamed of myself. I remember the mood of that conversation clearly: we were in his room with the shutters closed, feeling as if we were in enemy territory and holding on to each other. Our shared equivocations and our capitulations to a gender script that we both hated were, for the moment, drawing us together; but I could sense how they might also in the long term start pushing us apart.

For I understood that he was being expected to choose, just as I had been expected to choose. He faced a great risk in following his own good heart and good sense—a risk that is too often downplayed. He was not sure he would be considered a man if he did not choose the other men, and that fear was realistic. There was so much at stake—his current life, really. The way those boys punished dissenters—I had seen this—was with a paranoia-inducing social withdrawal that culminated in the subtle, perpetual taunt of thirty men's collective homophobia.

I had been worried I would no longer be considered a real woman if I spoke out, either—that I would no longer be invited to the *parties*—but the world had changed enough so that there would be other places I could go if the frat boys rejected me. But for Martin the situation was serious. Throughout high school Martin, the close observer of invertebrates, a Dungeons and Dragons enthusiast, had been a self-described "nerd." This designation had given him freedom, in a way: nerd guys in Martin's teenage circle had shared value systems vastly different from those that made the frat boys "men." But now, because Martin had been "accepted" by "real men," his eccentric and charming and truly egalitarian real self was at risk. Martin was being silently, powerfully pressured to abandon his outsider status, with all the freedom and integrity that went with it.

The girl with the high-heeled shoes, we heard, underwent a psychological crisis and dropped out. He and I stayed together until I went away to college a year later. But I had lost something with him. My English textbook that year, in a discussion about contemporary poetry, had explained that the word "ecstasy" had derived from the Greek *ekstasis*: "standing outside" oneself, displacement or trance. Not too long after our relationship first began, I had felt that way about Martin. But at that frat house, I could never "lose" myself that way again. There was no longer any room for Martin to be simply my lover and friend. No matter how intimate we were, I could never again feel that we were entirely alone. We had entered the alien space of the "real" world, where men and women were wary of each other.

The most difficult aspect of what I had learned in Martin's fraternity house was the way in which the brothers' view of women and their sexuality was a more accurate reflection of "the real world"—the adult world—than Martin's and my experience was. We were made to feel that we were wrong and childish and that "they"—with their *Penthouse* magazines, their Budweiser girlie posters, and their adversarial attitude toward the women they courted in the evening and derided the following noon—were sophisticated and in sync with the world. Their certainty made me doubt myself. If "sex" is *Penthouse*, I thought, well then, *Penthouse* must be the measure of my life. If I am to have love and admiration, I must pay attention to its rules.

Seventeen was the overture to the central drama of *Penthouse*. We watched boys look at *Penthouse* in front of us, and we felt sad, jealous, intrigued, and challenged. These magazines were our instructions in negotiating what we understood to be the only sex there was in the only possible world.

Had we known that alternative historical views existed, we would have had a way of thinking beyond our own experience. Had we known at sixteen and seventeen that once upon a time, somewhere on this earth, there had been other ways of looking at female sexuality and desire, the frat boys' culture that was closing in on us, defining what sex was for girls and what could happen to girls who were sexual, might not have seemed so powerful, or the walls protecting it, so strong.

EROTICA HAS NOT always been insulting to or even objectifying of women. Let us look, for instance, at ancient Chinese civilization. In a poem written by Chang Heng around 100 C.E., a young woman describes the awakening of her desire on her wedding night through the use of an erotic manual:

> *Let us now lock the double door with its golden lock*
> *And light the lamp to fill our room with its brilliance,*
> *I shed my robes and remove my paint and powder,*
> *And roll out the picture scroll by the side of the pillow,*
> The Plain Girl *[a guidebook] I shall take as my instructress,*

So that we can practice all the variegated postures,
Those that an ordinary husband has but rarely seen,
No joy shall equal the delights of this first night,
These shall never be forgotten, however old we may grow.

Chang also described a novel, *Jou P'u T'uan*, which recounts the marriage of a scholar to a prudish, beautiful, and aristocratic young girl. She refuses to experiment sexually or to make love with lights burning. The young husband tries to show her an expensive erotic album. Initially she rejects it, but she is soon perusing it with enthusiasm. Jade Perfume's "passion becomes greatly aroused" from this tutorial, and her sexuality is awakened.

One way the ancient Chinese conveyed sound sexual techniques was through erotic scrolls, novels, and pictures. These were studied by young women as part of their education in finding the erotic ambience that would best release their own beneficial yin. This use of what we in the modern West might call pornography—imagery that in our world has become a debased and degrading male-centered genre—often can be seen in the context of ancient Chinese texts as having been helpful to young women on their own terms. From this material, the inexperienced bride could learn various erotic patterns and scenarios that best expressed her own personal longings but without taking the social and physical risks entailed by promiscuity.

In this literature, the awakening of girls to erotic fulfillment is not a trashy and titillating cliché of material aimed at objectifying women for the consumption of thoughtless men, but a poignant tale of female coming of age that, if negotiated successfully, brings well-being to all.

In the Han Dynasty of ancient China, from 206 B.C.E. to 221 C.E., female desire was not treated with fear, nor with contempt and ridicule. It was regarded as a powerful elemental force, a force that, properly directed, would bestow health and well-being on men as well as women. Female desire was studied with the care that we now focus on the ecosystems that keep us alive and well.

At least two thousand years ago, philosopher-sexologists in China were studying human sexual response as part of their larger philosophical vision, the Tao, or "Way." They saw the sexual union of men and women as fundamental to the health of both sexes. The earliest sex manuals we know of were produced in this environment in China. These guides instructed practitioners in the art of making love so as to attain the ideal of harmony in what the Tao masters called "the yin-yang relation." In their view, the passive force of life—the feminine—is yin, and the active, or masculine force, is yang. According to R. H. van Gulik, author of *Sexual Life in Ancient China*, "[sex] was never associated with a feeling of sin or moral guilt."

Of the three tenets of the Tao of Loving, the last is "the importance of female satisfaction." In the ancient Chinese view of the different erotic capacity of the sexes, the male may be "more volatile, more active and quicker" than the female, like fire, but, while women are superficially calmer, the force of their desire is deeper and stronger, like water. This ancient Chinese wisdom embodied one historical moment among many in which women were assumed to be far more carnal than men. Women's yin essence was seen as inexhaustible, while men's yang—embodied in semen—was rare and precious.

The men of ancient China who followed the Tao were intent on learning how to give their lovers as many orgasms as possible. It was believed that the precious yin essence that women yielded to men, to men's benefit, was most intense, concentrated, and powerful at the peak of the female climax. Ancient Chinese manuals paid close attention to foreplay, because foreplay was believed to stir this yin essence.

The Tao view of the preciousness of female desire and all actions that generate and satisfy it is clear in the very language the Taoists used to describe women's anatomy. Every day, one of us adolescent girls might hear in conversation in the schoolyard, or on the street, these words: "cunt," "fuck," "pussy," "whore," "bitch," and of course "slut." We shrugged them off again and again but always felt as if a small stain from them clung to us, a show, as Lawrence put it, of dirt. Of course we knew the words were about us, our bodies, our wishes. If we consider the slang terms that describe female sexual anatomy, the veil of ugliness through which our culture sees women's sexuality is all too obvious. Many have noted that the words tend to connote, at their worst, wounds; at best, receptacles. Not one slang sexual term—or formal term, for that matter—about women that we girls heard encoded the idea of value or preciousness.

Consequently, when I read, as an adult, the ancient Chinese erotic texts in translation, I felt oddly embarrassed. The terms the Taoists used to describe women's genitals were metaphors of beauty, sweetness, artistry, rareness, and fragrance. In ancient China, the poetic synonyms for the woman's sexual parts included "the Open Peony Blossom," "the Golden Lotus," "the Receptive Vase," "the Cinnabar (or Vermilion) Gate," and "the Golden Cleft." This was such a reversal that the incongruity seemed over the top. To appreciate women so much! To my ears, so accustomed to the dirtying of women's sexuality, the Han Dynasty affection for women's genitals seemed, at first reading, hilarious, but also enchanting—like a life-enhancing comedy. Other Western women to whom I showed the Chinese translations had the same reaction.

We should look at that response. Just imagine how differently a young girl today might feel about her developing womanhood if every routine slang description she heard of female genitalia used metaphors of preciousness and beauty, and every account of sex was centered on *her* pleasure—pleasure on which the general harmony depended.

The frat boys' education about female sexuality included movies such as *Deep Throat,* which treat women as sexual objects whose main satisfaction derives from skillfully catering to male desire. In contrast, the Tao of Loving taught men about women as sexual subjects and guided them carefully to minister to female desire. (The ancient Chinese also believed that, no matter how young or old the woman, sex with orgasm was always healthful. It was sexual frustration, they held, that was the health threat for women.) Confucius, in his *Book of Rites,* held that wives and concubines had sexual rights and that it was a husband's duty to take care of his wife or concubine sexually as well as financially and emotionally. A woman under fifty, he believed, should be satisfied by her husband at least "once every five days."

Among seven Tao instructions to men about good sex, four involve teaching the male student how to kiss, appreciate, and arouse his female partner:

(2) He must know how to feel his woman's nine erotic zones.

(3) He must know how to appreciate his woman's five beautiful qualities.

(4) He must know how to arouse her so he can benefit from her flooding secretions.

(5) He should drink her saliva and then his ching [semen] and her chi [breath] will be in harmony.

Another suggestion is that the penis, or Jade Stalk, should linger around the Cinnabar Gate while the male partner gazes at, strokes, and kisses his lover. Not until the Golden Cleft is "in flood" should the Vigorous Peak thrust forward.

If he does these things and more, the Tao proclaims, "his five organs will be regulated and his health protected and no disease will stay with him." The converse is implicit: if he *fails* to do these things, he risks throwing the energies of his body out of balance and harmony, which in the Chinese scientific schema is an invitation to fatigue and illness.

Deep Throat put skillful (in fact, anatomically nearly impossible) fellatio at the center of the sexual universe we inherited. In contrast, again, skillful cunnilingus was considered by practitioners of the Tao of Loving to be a cherished art, for it made the woman ready while generating yin essence for the benefit of her mate.

To think in Tao terms is to imagine a world in which feminist commentators could not possibly equate heterosexuality with a set of assumptions that are innately degrading to women. Our view of our own sexuality and the meaning of sex with men would change completely if we were really to use the past to "think beyond" our own paradigm. What if the male triple-X adult bookstores that now give men a vision of women's desire that often seems so threatening and cold to women themselves were dispensing to men a way of thinking about female desire that looked like this?

In Han China, the belief existed that rape would harm the rapist. The equivalents of the young men in the fraternity who assaulted that young woman would have believed they were bringing ill fortune upon themselves. The Han manuals told men that it was a serious mistake to urge a woman to have sex against her will or even when she was willing for his sake but not really in the mood herself. For men who followed the Tao of Loving, our modern debate about "date rape" might seem bizarre: a man would be ambivalent about forcing sex on a woman when, her desire absent, he would receive none of her all-important yin essence. Any such sex is, the Tao held, *destructive to the man* as well: "If the man moves and the woman does not respond . . . then the sexual act will not only injure the man but harm the woman."

Let us ask the question again, this time not of Western anatomists or psychologists but of Chinese philosophers: What is female desire?

Modern sexologists take as a given a four-stage model of female desire and satisfaction—arousal, plateau, climax, and resolution. The Tao, in comparison, contains descriptions of female desire with nuances so carefully observed that they make twentieth-century sexologists' descriptions seem crudely impressionistic. The difference in subtlety between ancient Chinese and modern Western views bring to mind the aphorism about the many different Inuit words for "snow": "There are ten indications [of women's desire]. A man must observe and know what should be done." This, of course, is advice that many women would cheer in our own culture and time. In case the male reader has not yet gotten the point, the milestones of female desire are demarcated in explicit terms:

(a) She holds the man tight with both her hands. It indicates that she wishes closer body contact.

(b) She raises her legs. It indicates that she wishes closer friction of her clitoris.

(c) She extends her abdomen. It indicates that she wishes shallower thrusts.

(d) Her thighs are moving. It indicates that she is greatly pleased.

(e) She uses her feet . . . to pull the man. It indicates that she wishes deeper thrusts.

(f) She crosses her legs over his back. It indicates that she is anxious for more.

(g) She is shaking from side to side. It indicates that she wishes deep thrusts on both the left and right.

(h) She lifts her body, pressing him. It indicates that she is enjoying it extremely.

(i) She relaxes her body. It indicates that the body and limbs are pacified.

(j) Her vulva is flooding. Her tide of Yin has come. The man can see for himself that his woman is happy.

Other detailed lists of this nature were part of the literature. Clearly the ancient Chinese noticed women's desire. In this sort of atmosphere, a woman would have no need to "fake it" and a young man could scarcely think that "yes means no."

The positive view of women's desire was not restricted to ancient China. For the Zuni Indians of New Mexico, before the nineteenth century, baby girls started out by being blessed in a formal ceremony that celebrated the lucky fact of their gender. The tribe's women would place a seed-filled gourd over a baby girl's vulva. They would then pray that when the time came and the girl became a woman, that part of her body would become big and its fruit plentiful. Through these rites, women reminded the community that "their life-bearing capacity was immense in comparison to that of men." Zuni men argued that they were as important as women, that their sexuality too was valuable, and that they too, through their semen, could make the earth fertile. The men would don immense false penises and would support their claims for equality with boastful songs about how happy their members could make the women.

In their world, it made sense for Zuni men to make claims for equality with women based on the assertion that they were effective ministers to female desire. Ramon Gutierrez writes, in his study of shifts of sexual mores and power in New Mexico between 1500 and 1846, that "After feeding, the activity of greatest cultural import to Pueblo women was sexual intercourse." Through sex, he explains, women drew husbands into their family structures, benefited from the labor and respect their children offered them, and tamed wild spirits into domestic deities. For this community, nothing less than "the peaceful continuation of life" depended on female sexuality. Through "libidinous" female desire, Pueblo society was integrated and the bonds of community were affirmed.

Indeed, it was understood that men's abuse of women's sexuality did men no good. A Zuni man who sexually abused women believed he would be weakened economically: "For a man to enjoy a woman's body without giving her a gift in return was for him to become indebted to her in a bond of obligation." It was stealing, and he had to pay her back.

Among Zuni women, sexual practices spanned the spectrum from heterosexual to homosexual, and age was no barrier to eroticism.

Among the Hopi pueblos of northern Arizona befor[e]
the Europeans, female desire was literally the engine t[he]
woman-led rite celebrating "female fecundity, sexua[l]
duction," would bring about the symbolic re-creation
mony: after four days of songs and prayer, pubescent Hopi girls who
had just had their first periods would have their hair washed as a
form of initiation into all-female sacred societies. Then, for two
days, all the women would dance together naked, caressing clay
phalluses and singing erotic songs. They would incite men to passion and then to lovemaking, thus securing the semen that was analogous to the rain and lightning that would help the fields yield food.
"If the Indians sang of sex, copulated openly, staged orgiastic rituals,
and named landmarks 'Clitoris Spring,' 'Girl's Breast Point,' 'Buttocks-
Vagina,' and 'Shove Penis,' it was because the natural world around
them was full of sexuality," writes Gutierrez. Peruvian drinking vessels, made by women potters, were crafted in the shape of vulvas,
thus allowing the drinker to simulate cunnilingus (at least one pot
showed "a most realistic" depiction of a woman being kissed geni-
tally by a lover of indeterminate sex).

Europeans who witnessed native women's assertion of their sexuality saw not divinity but depravity. According to the colonizers,
Pueblo women could not even conceive of modesty or shame in relation to their bodies. Since, in the Western tradition, human beings in
Eden were redeemed by shame and particularly, as Christian theol-
ogy evolved, by feminine shame, Europeans were inclined to see
Hell where the Pueblos saw everyday pleasure. The Spanish friars
saw "naked," "promiscuous," and "lascivious" Pueblo women—"those
heinous females, those wells of the devil, who celebrated the pleasures of the flesh"—where the Pueblos themselves had seen the
human embodiment of holy natural cycles.

By the early eighteenth century, in the same landscape but under
a colonial social order, the term specific to women's genitals was
partes vergonzozas, or "shameful parts." Shame was synonymous with
feminine sexuality.

The Conquest is the story not only of Europeans' laying claim to
the culture of the Indians but of patriarchal values superseding matri-
lineal ones: Pueblo women lost their ancient control over land,
crops, and their sons and daughters. Their orgiastic fertility rites

were eliminated, and the erotic symbols around which they had danced, naked and singing, were banished forever.

But the old ways were not easily relinquished. Gutierrez describes a European cleric, Fray Tomás Carrasco, preaching to the Indians. He railed against their indigenous "promiscuity" and exhorted them to embrace monogamy. An Indian woman stood up in the crowd and raised her own voice. She preached against the new European ways that advocated male-dominated marriage and female sexual shame. As she spoke in defense of the older world's ways, a bolt of lightning descended from a blue sky and the woman was killed.

The friar interpreted this event as God striking down a witch. But to the Indians in the audience, those struck down by the sacred force of lightning were understood to have been turned into "cloud spirits." To these witnesses, the lightning was proof that the woman's defense of the older ways was pleasing to the Divine Spirit.

Even within the Judeo-Christian tradition, there are systems of belief in which female desire is valued more highly than we can imagine. The Zohar, the Jewish European mystical tradition, charges, "When the wife is purified [that is, after her ritual bath when she is finished menstruating], the man is in duty bound to rejoice her, in the joyful fulfillment of a religious obligation. . . . It is his duty, once back home [from a journey], to give his wife pleasure, inasmuch as she obtained for him the heavenly union [of male and female aspects of the Divine Presence]." A man should also please his wife because "this pleasure is a religious one, giving joy also to the Divine Presence, and it is an instrument for peace in the world." Like the Taoists, the Jewish mystics believed that sexual satisfaction given by men to women helped to please the Maker and created balance, order, and harmony on a cosmic scale.

Islam, too, has a tradition of valuing female desire. Today, of course, the Koran and the commentaries, the Shari'a, are used to condone the most egregious abuses of women, from murders of teenage girls who lose their virginity before marriage and of married women accused of adultery to clitoridectomy and infibulation. The widespread practice of clitoridectomy in some Muslim countries is performed on the basis of the belief that "without it a woman wouldn't be able to control herself, she would end up a prostitute." But the journalist Geraldine Brooks points out in *Nine Parts of Desire,* her study of women in Islam, that "the lessening of women's sexual pleasure directly contradicts the teaching of Mohammed." Islam held, and still holds, according to Brooks, that "almighty God created sexual desires in ten parts; then he gave nine parts to women and one to men." There is a large body of commentary on the Koran that maintains that Mohammed and his disciples praised female sexuality and upheld women's entitlement to sexual pleasure within marriage. In one story, Mohammed chastises a follower for being too busy praying to make love to his wife. Mohammed encouraged husbands to be sexually attentive: "When any one of you has sex with his wife, then he should not go to her like birds [quickly]; instead you should be slow and delaying." In another passage, Mohammed refers to intercourse without foreplay as a manifestation of cruelty.

Among the sacred books of Hinduism, the Kama Sutra and the Tantric literature, women's sexuality is also seen as sacred, and women's desire as slow to kindle but more sustained than that of men. They, too, view women's erotic "essence" as beneficial to men and consider the act of forcing women against their will to be destructive. In these systems, women's sense of safety, confidence, and long-drawn-out fulfillment is central to the sexual act: "For Tantra, each and every woman incarnates the Goddess, is the Goddess, Absolute Woman, the Cosmic Mother . . . the concrete perception of the divine aspect of each woman is a precondition to maithuna [lovemaking] and the Tantric ritual preceding the sacred sexual union aims at making one perceive this reality." "A Tantrist worships the cosmic [goddess] Shakti in all women." In all women: fat or thin, young or old, able-bodied or disabled.

> The Tantrist is able to "feminize" his sexual experience. To the ordinary male, sex is a convergent experience both in time and space—revolving around his sex organs and becoming progressively narrower in space and time. When the spasm is over, they claim, men's desire vanishes and men turn away from women, wounding their self-esteem.
>
> [In contrast, the Tantrist] . . . does not make love to a vagina, but to a human being as a whole, i.e., the physical, psychic and cosmic woman, the incarnation of the cosmic Shakti. . . . He intensely shares the Shakti's ultimate sexual emotion when she experiences a deep orgasm. This makes him aware of the sacred

part of the woman, without trying to appropriate her body or her sex life. He does not think nor say, "This is my wife, her vagina is my property, I own her sensuality." He perceives sex as the manifestation of cosmic creative power, which is suprapersonal.

The Kama Sutra, the ancient Sanskrit text on erotic pleasure, also shows respect for women's sexuality in ways that would be foreign to the frat-boy culture: "In Hinduism, sex is almost sacramental—essential to life and therefore worthy of serious study. [Its] pleasures are as necessary for the well-being of the body as food. . . . How different from the all-too-frequent association of sin and guilt with sex as in the Judaeo-Christian tradition." The advice it gives men focuses their attention on female pleasure. "For a man to be successful with women he must pay them marked attention. . . . Do not unite with a woman until you have excited her with playful caresses, and then the pleasure will be mutual." Seduction of a virgin on a wedding night includes the man's gently shampooing the woman's limbs, one by one, as she gives him her consent to do so, and it involves not just talking to her but *asking her questions and listening to her*. The love manual warns men against rape: "A girl forcibly enjoyed by one who does not understand the hearts of girls becomes nervous, uneasy and dejected, and suddenly begins to hate the man who has taken advantage of her." Forcing sex upon a woman was strongly to be discouraged also because such aggression could interfere with her desire in the future.

"Pornography," as we understand it, was not a concept that would have made sense to the audiences of the Kama Sutra. "Even young maids should study the Kama Sutra before marriage," elders believed. Imaginative lovemaking is important because it generates "love, friendship, and respect in the hearts of women."

These varying cultural interpretations give the lie to the message in *Penthouse*, the primary teaching text for the teenage boys we know, that female nakedness and sexuality are cheap, as well as those of some second-wave feminists whose wish to restrict images of female nudity is argued on the grounds that they are inherently "objectifying." Both assumptions are historically shortsighted, and both derive from a poisoned well of sensibility in which the naked female body is far more profane than the male body, and not, because of its eroticism and generative capacity, if anything, more sacred.

But as girls, we weren't told there had ever been alternatives to the double image of sex on the only card we were being handed—an image that showed us a *Penthouse* Pet ("degraded," according to feminists; "our ideal," according to the frat boys) on the one hand and, on the other, the chaos that had beset the girl in the upstairs room, whose red shoes would end up on the mantelpiece of the frat house. In California in 1979, sex was not the wild, powerful, magnetic goddess Shakti giving herself willingly to a carefully thought-out seduction. Sex was a disco babe in a spandex halter top who could still take the blame for giving the boys wet dreams.

17

Adults

Hot child in the city
Runnin' wild and looking pretty . . .
So young to be loose and on her own.
Young boys they all want to take her home. . . .
Hot child in the city.
—NICK GILDER, "Hot Child in the City," 1978

With some exceptions, adults were feckless, or they were buddies, or else they were suppliers of drugs, or else they were predators.

In our junior year, at sixteen and seventeen, we all, independently of our school reading list, read *Lolita*. We could not get over the narrator's delusional view of Lolita and of girlhood, and the frightening implications of the way great art seemed to make what happened to her, if not good, at least completely understandable. We could not believe where most of the sympathies in the story lay. Once again, reading had betrayed us. Humbert's eloquence and Lolita's silence urged us to abandon our sympathies for her and, by extension, for ourselves.

The book scared us in several ways. Humbert's physical revulsion with the grown woman, Lolita's mother, and his fascination with the child's body gave us a sense of foreboding. Was this how grown men really felt? Was this book perverse or merely honest? "Her looks had faded" at sixteen, when her story ends, *because* she is married and pregnant. Were we already, at sixteen, in decline?

Our sessions of literary criticism usually took place in Sandy's bathroom. As the water hissed and the bathroom grew comfortably steamy, we would talk about what we'd been reading. Sometimes we'd pass the book back and forth. In the case of *Lolita*, we read the more lurid lines out loud:

" 'There would have been a sultan, his face expressing great agony (belied, as it were, by his molding caress), helping a callypygean slave child to climb a column of onyx. . . . There would have been a fire opal dissolving within a ripple-ringed pool, a last throb, a last dab of color, stinging red, smarting pink, a sigh, a wincing child,' " I intoned. Sandy howled. The revolting quality of the image, for us, was reinforced by the photograph on the back of the book of Vladimir Nabokov, the bald and, in our eyes, ancient man. The revulsion we felt for the narrator also had a quality of revenge.

To us, the older men who were continually trying to get at us were not the dreamy movie stars that Humbert sees himself as. They were wattled, hairy-backed, "skanky," "halitoid," black-socked. We imagine the scene: The poor girl! we thought. Here she is, orphaned and at this guy's mercy. And he's . . . her father figure. And here she's stuck in some god-awful tourist motel—some *sweat lodge*—with him, in Wisconsin or somewhere, and he's got all the traveler's checks. . . . Comedy and horror battled in us.

" 'Pubescent Lo swooned to Humbert's charm as she did to hiccuppy music.' " We wanted to get into the story, knock on the door when Humbert was out, and slip Lolita a bus ticket to get out of there.

It was only years later that my eye caught a line that Lolita speaks at the very end of the book. For once the words are unmediated by Humbert Humbert's desire: "[Y]es, this world was just one gag after another, if somebody wrote up her life nobody would ever believe it."

I believed it. Adult men were continually encroaching upon us. There was always some fortyish fellow at the bar trying to look studly in our direction or some unemployed guy in his thirties trying to convince one of us that he was David Bowie's stage manager. There is an invisible subculture of adult men who make a concerted effort to lie to teenage girls and try to get them into bed. When it works, a man who cannot get respect in the eyes of an adult woman can impress a young girl easily enough with his paycheck, his car, his very adulthood. Through the attentions of the grown-up men always hovering on the horizon, we went from being little girls—the most powerless of categories—to beings with power over grown middle- and upper-class white males—the most influential ones. When it was fun, it was great fun; but it was also nauseating and scary. "Two sixteen-year-olds . . . twins," as the Tony Roberts character in Woody Allen's *Annie Hall*, a movie that came out when we were teenagers too, joked salaciously. The audience laughed with him. The adult world was out to prey upon us, not to protect us, and to foist upon us a power beyond our years.

In *Male and Female*, the anthropologist Margaret Mead makes the point that many preindustrial cultures keep girls and adult men who are not their fathers apart. These cultures take for granted adult men's sexual interest in teenage girls, as well as the damage of this interest expressed to girls while they are still too young. In 1996, sociological studies have finally proved that two out of three teenage pregnancies are the results of adult men—"often much older men"—impregnating adolescents. When we were in junior high, there were rumors about a teacher; on a high school trip, one of the teacher's aides groped a student. "What are you afraid of?" I remember one businessman sneering when I declined to go for a ride. "Think your mom will mind?" To other girls in our circle, some of these men said, "It's good for you to learn." Others said simply—but effectively—"I love you."

Sandy observed, when we talked about this later, "Men have always had that sexualization of their daughters or stepdaughters but were forced to hold it back. Now, when we were growing up, they could express it. A lot of women I know have fathers who simply didn't notice them until they grew breasts. And then it was not physical contact but inappropriate comments. These fathers or stepfathers would always be making comments like 'I know men must love to look at your breasts.' Or, 'Gosh, your friend sure is a knockout, I bet the guys want to go after her.' And you wonder, if they're thinking that about your friends, what are they thinking about *you*?" As she recounted this, I thought again of how tenuous the fathers' presence in so many of those homes had been and how vulnerable daughters were to accepting sexualized love from father figures to take the place of fatherly love.

"They would always say then, 'Isn't it beautiful that I can share this with you?' As if it had been bad to repress those feelings in the past.

Over and over again, I would hear, 'Isn't this beautiful?' when an adult was making inappropriate touches.

"The massage thing was big. When we were fourteen, camp counselors and friends' older sisters' adult boyfriends would give girls massages. There was a camp counselor who used to French-kiss us all good night. He was twenty and we were ten. I thought it would make me cool if I did it. It was a hazing thing."

"Why didn't you tell the adults?" I asked.

"They knew. Our counselor knew. She was dating him. She was sharing him with us. She said, 'It's good for his ego.' And then it was hard to tell adults because it was couched in these terms of being beautiful, so what could you complain about?

"The encroachment by adult men got worse once we got our adult bodies in high school. I remember not being able to walk down the street, by sixteen, without being hit on by adult men.

"There was an old man in our neighborhood who offered money to women and couples to walk around naked in his house while he sketched them. If you resisted, he was like, What's wrong with you? It's beautiful, it's artistic. A girl in our neighborhood took him up on it. She was fifteen. I thought of that girl as being slutty. Engaging in that was like crossing a line. That was cheap and trashy, whereas giving a blow job to a twenty-year-old when you were thirteen wasn't."

The world that adults created for themselves was sometimes corrosive to their children because the adults failed to set up boundaries that would keep that very grown-up world from being imposed too soon upon those too fragile to bear the weight of its freedoms. In the most literal manifestation of this, children were for sale on its street corners.

"No kid I knew," Sandy went on, "ever said, 'I can't stay overnight in a mixed-sex group because I'm not allowed.' I remember being so surprised when a friend's mother kicked me out when her brother came home from the Navy. 'Family time?' It didn't compute. My mouth dropped open. What's 'family time'? I was a little pissed off, but also I had a little bit of respect, which was something I very rarely had for adults."

I knew what she meant by that disillusionment, though for me it had happened later. When I left San Francisco to pursue my education, I was still full of respect for adults who read perceptively and wrote beautifully. When, some years later, one "encroached," the source of my respect was poisoned.

I once had a professor whom, since I am still afraid of him, I will call Dr. Johnson. Let us imagine him as a visiting philologist from New Zealand who taught Colonial and post-Colonial literature at one of the institutions at which I studied as a young adult. Let us imagine that he had red hair, freckles, and bifocals—that he was gaunt, wild-haired, rawboned, hawk-faced, loose-jointed, with the light, inflamed eyes and reptilian skin of a heavy smoker. This man, with his histrionic teaching syle, was a locus of campus worship.

He would lean over the desk, grasp a gingery forelock, and fling it out of his eyes. "The Unfettered Wilderness," he'd say. "You are a Victorian writer drenched in fantasies of empire. Exotic fictions are your food and drink. You wake in rainy Stoke Newington, stare at your toast, and retire to your library to limn the contours of the paradisiacal Orient. Your preconceptions are about the Noble Savage and the unregenerate Primitive; you situate the Garden of Eden at the base of the Blue Nile. But the unregenerate Primitive you dream of is not a *natural* man in contrast to your own fantasy of effete, elite Britannia; oh no! It is rather a way for you—*civic* man, *bourgeois* man, mid-nineteenth-century *urban* man—to find an amateur enthusiast's delight in creating one's own idea of nature as an organizing force of mind. By inventing nature, in effect, Kipling, W. E. Henley, and Joseph Banks, the botanist who represented Tahitians as ancient Greeks, artificially created what became the industrial ideal of 'nature.' "

With his fingers, Dr. Johnson made the quotation marks that were beginning to be so fashionable. "Through their *own* artifice, imperial literary loyalists invented nature as what nature so 'naturally' appears to be to us today. So now, as we will see, we inherit this idea. God died. Nature was manufactured. Now our world is only mind, superimposed with travel posters. This began with a claque of tubercular Londoners reading explorer accounts beside their gas fires."

Dr. Johnson suddenly ducked his head and worried his forelock. He bit at a nail. "The massive vistas—" he pounded out suddenly, his hand whacking time on the podium "—the Patagonians of titanic size—the great Lake Victoria, the source of the holy river—shipwreck, treasure, travelers' routes—even the dream of the grassland itself endlessly outward flowing—toil, bustle, the romance of cartography—all this, the idea of Empire itself, derived its symbolic power ultimately from little more than the fantasists' self-delusion. It was not nature, never nature, to which they turned; but to the 'nature' "—those gestures again—"that was merely the scrim onto which they projected the mid-Victorian conquerer imagination."

He was a genius. He stopped, took a crumpled handkerchief from his pocket, and wiped the pale brow that had started to sweat. He patted the forelock back into place. Then he rose and went to the window, turning his back on the hypnotized class. He leaned on the windowsill. We waited a minute, then two. He seemed to have forgotten all about us. A thrill went through the room.

I looked around. Judging from the other students' expressions, I was not alone in my admiring attitude: half the young men looked as if they longed to produce for him some consolation by becoming brilliant young protégés, and half the young women looked as if they were waiting to be chosen as votaries.

I had heard rumors about his way of relating to certain of his female students, but there were rumors about half a dozen teachers on campus. Sometimes, when one young woman who had taken the professor's course was introduced to another, she would say, in a deep, slow, ironic voice, "You have the aura of election upon you." It was the code.

Several weeks into the term, Dr. Johnson handed back my first essay. The pages were covered with comments in his neurasthenic hand. As I reached for the essay, he grasped my wrist.

"Come and see me," he said. I was sick with excitement.

In our higher education, my girlfriends and I were learning about being sluts in a different way than we had in high school. I remember conversations with other ambitious young women about this powerful man on the faculty or that one; how this or that Shakespearean will want to flirt but won't actually ever touch, but a certain medievalist likes an awestruck silence, and an eighteenth-century scholar likes a good sparky quarrel. We knew that the smart young men, our peers, were mentored to take these elders' places and the smart young women were either chosen to be handmaidens or overlooked altogether. The role of intellectual handmaiden was heavily eroticized—though the eroticism expected of us was usually sublimated and very seldom explicit.

Mostly our professors just wanted our fresh and nubile *emotional* submission. Some women became proficient at playing this game; one wrote all her papers on perfumed, colored paper; another had a talent for medieval bawdry that skirted the line but never crossed it. We acknowledged to one another that one of the things we were learning was how to gaze dewy-eyed at the men who would write our recommendations.

In spite of the gossip about him, I gave this man my manuscript of fifty-four poems. To me, at the time, it was the most important gift I had ever given any man.

Not long thereafter, Dr. Johnson called and invited himself over for "a glass of Amontillado." The professor sometimes went drinking with students. Of course, it was only male students with whom he drank, but I ignored that distinction. He appeared at seven on a Saturday night at the door of the run-down student housing I was sharing with two other girls who were, as he had established in advance, out for the evening. The manuscript was under one arm, a bottle under the other.

I had felt serious and private, preparing for his visit. ("You allowed him over to your apartment?" "Yes." "In the evening?" "Yes.") I cleaned up the ratty apartment and put out a pot of chrysanthemums. I spent a long time choosing what to wear: a maroon leotard, jeans, and the small opal earrings my mother had given me when I turned thirteen.

Those details damned me into blaming myself in part for what happened. I wanted him to think I was someone whose work was worthy of mentoring, but I was also a teenager from a middle-class home in a West Coast city about to face a brilliant man from far away. I also wanted him to think I was attractive. That fact made me feel like enough of a slut never to discuss what he did then.

I sat on the battered couch. There was a less battered chair facing it, but he too sat on the couch. We made awkward chat about the local landscape, how hard it was to find a good cup of coffee. Then his tone changed. "You seem so cheerful . . . externally," he murmured, sliding closer, "but—perhaps I am projecting just as the Europeans projected—I see sadness in your eyes."

I sat up straighter. Was this true? No one had ever said so. No one had ever looked that hard, perhaps. I did not want to remember that one of my closest friends had reported a similar exchange last term.

She had loved it too. He poured each of us a glass of the reddish Amontillado, and he toasted me. "Drink up," he said, refilling my glass. "This was the downfall of many a Georgian poet. Hard to find. Not too bad."

I did as he said. ("Did you drink what he gave you?" "Yes.") He was my teacher. Young men I knew thought it an honor to be asked to drink with him. I felt my body relax and thought pleasantly about my interesting sadness.

I turned to the manuscript. He had, as I understood him, praised me. I wanted more of this. ("So you responded to his flattery?" "Yes.") The manuscript lay beside the open bottle of wine. I lifted it off the table. Odd: The pages seemed as pristine as when I had carried them over from the photocopy shop. I flipped through. There were no notes. Not a dog-ear.

"Ah, yes, your poems—" he said. "I'll get to that. In good time." He slid closer. Huskily, he said, "You have the aura of election upon you."

Something warm spread over my thigh. I felt like I was blushing down to the level of my bones. It was the dry heat from his hand, wedging itself between my knees.

I sprang backward. "Oh no," I said. I held my hands out and stepped backward toward the kitchen area. Dr. Johnson advanced. Finally my back was against the sink and there was nowhere else to go. "This is not what I meant," I said.

My professor was trying to stroke my hair. His nose loomed. All at once my carefully chosen leotard—chosen, goddamn it, because I had thought it looked nice—seemed to cling too closely. My consciousness narrowed to the indentation just visible between my breasts. What had seemed that afternoon to be only a hint felt now like a deep, lewd shadow. I "remembered" on the level of my skin that Ben had first hit me while I was wearing a leotard. It was not a coincidence—it was my fault that I had not learned the first time. My whole body, my whole self-image, once again, *again,* burned with culpability. It felt so familiar: this sense of being exposed as if in a slow-moving dream of shame. I could practically hear my own pulse: What had I done, done, done?

Disgust and drunkenness fused together. I doubled over the kitchen sink, heaving the red liquid from the pit of my stomach. Dr.

Johnson released me roughly. He looked at his hands, which had almost been spattered with vomit, and turned away without a word. I washed my face and rinsed out my mouth. In the bathroom at the rear of the apartment, I could hear the great man flushing.

He came back into the room where I stood, threw his overcoat over his arm, and—in the same tone of voice he had used in class to say "read *The Settlers in Canada* by Monday"—said, "You are a deeply troubled girl." My professor pushed the front door open and stepped out. Then he glanced back and stepped inside again. He picked up the bottle. It was half full. He looked for the cork, found it under the table, and took it with him out the door.

My manuscript lay dead on the table. I felt emptier than I ever had been, and sore—even more sore than I would be when I found, at the end of term, that he'd lowered my grade. I was sore in exactly the place where my creative self-regard, still so new, had just begun to seed.

ONCE WE COULD BE sexualized by older men, it seemed as if that fact was permitted to corrupt any responsibility they had for our development. At any moment the groping hand could come through the greenhouse pane. We girls and young women seemed to be valuable to these grown-ups not because we were our growing selves but because they could use us to teach them to play and to stanch their own middle-aged insecurities. Touching our youth like a fetish, they could convince themselves that it was okay that they wanted so much to do so.

18

A Virus

I remember exactly where I was when the window closed on that anomalous era between the Pill and the Plague. I was living in New York, after I had graduated from college, and working at my first adult job. It was midsummer. I had a new friend, Paul, a molecular biologist. We were sitting on the floor of the living room in an apartment I shared, and I was listening to his excitement about the research he had done the year before in a laboratory in Paris.

"We're trying to isolate the makeup of the virus that is causing a new illness, mostly among gay men—it's being called the 'gay cancer.' It has the research team spooked. We think it could be linked with STDs—especially with hepatitis; that is, hepatitis B. Now, that's a nasty illness.

"But it's going to be hard to deal with this outside the lab, too. Back in San Francisco, where we are gathering some of our data, there's a feeling among some that hepatitis is the price you pay for sexual activity—and most STDs need a course of antibiotics to cure them. A lot of people don't think anything much of getting an infection, going to a clinic, and going right back out to the bathhouses or the bars. There's some talk out there about closing down the bathhouses."

This news startled me, because I knew those bathhouses were thought of as outposts of personal freedom. My hometown had always prided itself on its refusal to intervene in any way in private pleasures—especially those that the rest of America saw as deviant. For San Franciscans, our tolerance was a kind of citywide boosterism.

The glimpses of that world, which was represented as being one of pure flesh and pure fantasy, made the more mainstream dating culture of the city seem repressive and old-fashioned in contrast. That the city might even think of shutting the bathhouses seemed to signal an extreme change in the weather.

"I didn't know you could get cancer from a virus."

"There is a lot about this disease that would surprise most people," Paul said. "This one is definitely a strange one. There's conjecture among some doctors that it can be passed through different kinds of intimate contact."

"Intimate contact." That phrase had a medieval echo. I had taken a course on the bubonic plague in college. The way that disease had led to mass hysteria, to neighbors' fearing neighbors, to physicians' walking away from the stricken, and to family members' abandoning one another seemed to me the definition of an archaic response. To harbor a terror of another human body seemed like a superstition from a world long dead.

"Like touching?" I asked. "Hugging—kissing?"

"They haven't necessarily come to that conclusion," said Paul with the precision of his scientific training. I knew from the tone of his voice—that low, understated timbre that is unique to scientists or physicians when they are describing an interesting physical phenomenon that will bring human suffering in its train—that he was more serious than I wanted to understand.

"It's more likely to be something that's getting passed between partners during sex itself. They're looking at drug use too—the disease seems to go along with some drugs. Poppers, for example. Poppers are a heart medicine that makes the heart race; some people use the ampoules to get a better rush during sex—"

"They're saying that something in poppers causes this cancer?"

"They don't know yet. But if that's true, there is every epidemiological reason to believe it can leapfrog populations. That the factor to look at is not something biologically unique to a particular kind of gay sex but something about all sex."

"You mean that a man could pass it to a woman and a woman could pass it to a man?"

"Maybe—in fact, probably. There's a lag time with this stuff, so much we don't know—I wouldn't be surprised if that's what's happening already."

I looked through the dark apartment to the bright window and the passersby on the sidewalk in the summer sunlight. Halters, short shorts, sundresses; bare arms, legs, throats, the heat glancing off the flesh; men and women, men and men, women and women—it was the everyday cornucopia. But already it seemed to be fading, a record of a lost time caught in the gaudy chemical colors of a snapshot.

"I don't understand what you're saying. What does that mean?"

"It means—" He shifted uncomfortably. I remember how he hitched up his knees and looked full into my face. "That you would do well to think twice before you sleep with anyone—anyone at all. You should be really careful."

"I'm not careless."

His inflection was no longer conversational. "It means . . . for everyone . . . I don't even know how to say this. Not to make love to anyone at all until we know more."

I almost laughed out loud. This was as preposterous as a sentence could be.

"The party's over," he said.

The room felt even darker. I recalled my earliest childhood memory of what dread felt like. It was from a Countee Cullen book, *The Lost Zoo*. It described the Flood of the Bible and all the beautiful and mysterious animals that we would never know, that had not made it onto Noah's ark.

Paul knew, and I suspected, he had given me something that was at that time inside information, but would soon become the folk wisdom of a new world.

I ignored his warning for many weeks, not worrying about what he had said. Then some details of a casual affair I had had began to surface into my thoughts, and soon I was obsessed with them.

In the early 1980s, the ethic in Manhattan was that girls could do what boys did. That summer I was taking that to heart. At a party I had met a likable young man, Marlon, a high school dropout from a Baptist family in Wisconsin who now made a living on the fringes of the movie industry.

Marlon introduced me to his friends. His brother and sister-in-law, Thomas and Amy, and their twin toddlers lived in an expensive apartment, paid for by Thomas's job as a male model.

On the walls there were photographs of the couple's wedding. She had posed for her wedding pictures like "a model": pouting and looking sideways, her hair waving in what looked like a wind machine. Somewhere in that room, too, was the image of female sexuality that epitomized to me, in retrospect, the hardness and sexual cruelty of the early eighties: Avedon's picture of the "perfect" Nastassia Kinski, naked, wrapped by an enormous serpent. Playing underneath these images were their twin boys, who thumped around in a circle in the one open room, and in and out of the gritty yard.

One night we stayed late. Two friends of theirs came over, bearing a chunk of cocaine. I had sampled cocaine only once, in high school, and never wanted to go near it again because it gave me that feeling: if I start with this, I won't ever want to stop. But that night, I thought, as I often did that summer, What the hell.

The woman friend, Denise, wore a deep-cut T-shirt and a fringed leather vest and jeans. She too said she was a model, and it soon became clear that "model" and "film actor" were designations for a whole subculture of people who made all-cash livings in one way or another out of their sexuality or their drug connections. Her boyfriend was the dealer or intermediary. He was a light brown–haired, balding, mustachioed bumbler wanting to impress.

When the conversation flagged, the dealer asked, "Want a treat?" I thought people spoke that way only in the movies. The man unfolded the thin white paper and drew six lines in the powder on the glass of a mirror. I discovered that there was an etiquette to drug abuse. When I was done with my line, Amy showed me how to lick my finger and dab up the crumbs scattered around the glass and then rub this on my gums.

The dealer was self-conscious in the long silence that followed the end of the buzz from the single lines. He chipped off one more crumb and then another. Finally there was a moment of no return when he reached into his inner pocket, produced the whole rock once again, and laid it on the mirror.

We stayed together, taking turns putting a rolled-up hundred-dollar bill to our nostrils, all night long—a night that had darkness but no time. The casual connections between us seemed to thicken into heavy bonds.

By dawn things started to get bad. We crumbled into ordinariness. My mouth tasted like a shovel. Our faces were pale. One of the babies was clambering for his high chair, beating the countertop with a long-handled spoon. The other was still sleeping. Amy began feeding the child floppy slices of white bread and pudding from a plastic container. At the time I paid little attention to the baby. Now, as a mother myself, out of all the events of the night, the memory of that breakfast shames me the most.

At length I found myself with Marlon, standing outside in the morning. I was exhausted and repelled by my own complaisance. Down the street, clubs released their patrons: "Yeow!" cried a group of adolescents leaving one of them. My eyes rested on trash cans, brickwork, and concrete.

By then, it was a few months after my conversation with Paul. After that night, there was no way I could pretend to myself that just because Marlon was strong and worked out and liked girls, it did not mean he was not, as some were beginning to say, "risky." His whole life environment was one extended risk factor. I did not even know where to begin to look for the evidence of risk, there were so many places to start. But, as Paul had instructed me to, I asked Marlon one day, "Were you ever with guys?" And "Were you ever with women who had been with gay or bisexual guys?" He bridled. I had hurt his somewhat homophobic pride.

But I noted that his protests that I had offended him did not give me an answer. In spite of my fondness for him, I broke off seeing him soon afterward.

At about this time, I donated blood to the Red Cross. I would be notified if there was anything wrong. No envelope came after that hellish two weeks' wait, so I took it for granted that I was healthy. But for years thereafter I did not get officially tested. That refusal meant that over the course of the following decade, as the consequences of intercourse acquired heavier reverberations with every infection and every death, I would lie awake on nights when my brave-girl, my *entitled*-girl demeanor was shaken—and listen to the sound of my own blood.

"Have you been promiscuous?" was one risk-factor question that began to appear in the popular literature. Again: What did that mean? AIDS, of course, was beginning to devastate the gay community and inflame a demonic wave of punitiveness toward homosexuality. Less obvious was a much more muted, but still far-reaching evil: the renewal of punitive hostility toward active, assertive female heterosexuality. AIDS gave elements in our culture tacit license to regard every sexually active woman as a slut once more.

With the epidemic, there were no longer any "good girls" who were not virgins. One safe-sex commercial I saw a little later presented a message something like this: "In every bed there is your partner; and all of his partners; and all of their partners; and all of their partners." When the camera panned back, as I recall it, there were multitudes of people in the shot. It was a horrible parody of that realization you have as a kid that if you trace your family tree far enough back, you're related to everyone in the world. Now, though, the message was: if you've had sex with him, you've had sex with them all.

This new variant on the definition of promiscuity has a harshness that is distinct from the definition that prevailed in our grandmothers' time. Now, once you are "exposed" to one, you are not simply fair game for possession by the many; you have, metaphorically, actually *been* possessed by the many.

As the science was filled in over time, it seemed that the question once again—"Have you been promiscuous?"—meant, for girls, what it always had. It meant: Have you willingly done *anything*? I would lie awake and think of what I had done, and that I had liked it. In spite of all the information I had and the liberalism of my upbringing, the stubborn and irrational thought interjected itself: if I had not liked it, I would have no reason to be scared now. *If you don't enjoy the sex, you need not be punished.* I would bring onto my own self the full weight of womanly guilt and certainty of punishment that my times had, up to that point, failed or forgotten to impose upon me.

By the mid-1980s, *The New York Times* gave gentle coverage to an HIV infection in a young, affluent, college-educated woman. She was going public, she said, to warn others—specifically, other young women like herself: "nice girls." The treatment of the story and her own language made the subtext clear: if I can get it—and I look like you, readers of the *Times*—you can get it too. Her language was charged—understandably, given the courage it still took for her to do what she was doing—with defensiveness: she met a nice guy, they did not engage in any high-risk practices; she did what any nice, modern girl might do. It was as if she were pleading: "I am not a slut."

If an infected woman had said, "I had a one-night stand with an attractive loser and we did everything we could think of," there would have been no story—or the portrait would not have been painted with such sympathetic delicacy. She probably would not even have come forward to offer herself as an object lesson. We know the reason without even thinking: if someone is going to die of sex, it is the homosexual and the whore, both of whom are understood to have been asking for it.

For all of us young women, a door closed just as we reached full adulthood. Most of the sexual dangers we had faced until that point had been man-made. Even though this one was biological and, in that sense, impersonal, the irrational meaning we ascribed to it was personal. Gay men have written about how many suffer guilt about the possibility of infection because they have internalized the message that gay sex is decadent and transgressive. I think many straight women have a set of feelings about sexual pleasure in the age of AIDS that is closer on the spectrum to gay men's guilt than it is to straight men's fear, because sexually active straight women too have internalized some suspicion that their sexuality is decadent and transgressive.

Before, when mainstream culture was saying to us, "Go for it!," we had worked hard to imagine the punishments of the slut as abberrations left over from a bad old world that was, we hoped, passing away. But now it seemed that nature itself was out to confirm the inevitability of the punishment our sexuality could elicit. It wasn't true, what they'd promised us—that we could go where we wanted to go and lie down and yield our bodies to strangers, take our pleasure and put on our lipstick in the morning and call a cab. It was not true. It had been one long, inveigling dream. The sluts got nailed, just as they'd always been; just as we'd always, beneath our bravado, feared.

19

An Hypocrisy

That existential crisis of finding out what sexual danger meant—one I thought I had left behind with adolescence—resurfaced when, a few years later, I volunteered to work with survivors of sexual abuse and assault.

The volunteer trainer, Lucy, sat me down at a phone bank and started to describe the different kinds of silence I would have to familiarize myself with.

"There are all kinds," she said. "You just have to learn how to read them." I told her I didn't understand. How could there be different kinds of silence?

"Say the phone rings," she explained. "You answer, and there is nothing on the other end. What is your guess?"

"Someone is harassing us?"

"No; it's someone who has made it as far as dialing us but can't make it any further. It's up to you to talk then. You can start very quietly: 'Do you want to tell me who did it?' "

"Then what?" I asked.

"Then you wait," she said. "After a while, say, 'Was it someone you knew?' "

"And then?"

" 'Someone you trusted?' "

I thought I knew what the last question would be: "A relative?" I ventured, and Lucy said, "Good girl. By that time, the caller will either have answered, or she will have hung up. Sometimes all you will get is the sound of crying. You just have to listen to her cry until she hangs up. It's hard on you, but it helps her. The crying calls are not the worst; the worst are screams and the line going dead. That happened twice." Lucy was chain-smoking. "Do you smoke?" she asked.

"No," I told her.

"You will."

Mandy, who worked there, had been gang-raped just as she had been due to graduate with an M.A. in mathematics from her local university. She had sat her exams but had not been able to write a coherent paragraph; she'd known the facts, but they simply hadn't made sense to her on the page.

"Why didn't you tell your instructor?" I asked. And she explained the nature of the profound silence in which most survivors of the more unbelievable narratives of sexual assault live. "You know," she said, "you can say, 'The cat ate my homework' or 'I broke up with my boyfriend.' But you can't really say to people, 'Two weeks ago Thursday I was gang-raped. Can I have an extension?' It is so beyond the pale that it would affect the way the instructor would read my exam. No one believes that things like this happen. Or if they do, no matter how hard they try not to, the strangeness and horror of it—they project that not onto the rapist but onto me. And always, then, I would be: that girl who got gang-raped. That Martian. It's not worth it. I'd rather fail and keep being a person."

She had kept silent, and she had failed.

Sexual violence is often like a surrealist painting: a normative scene in which a few key details are weirdly wrong. There was the young woman so frightened of her stalker that she slept on the floor of her student center for three nights, her books open beside her. There was the pile of tear-soaked tissues on the table in the room where we saw clients; you'd clear it away, and it would be replenished by the fresh crying of the next client. There was the vocabulary of fear that I never quite mastered. I was often a beat or two behind conversations between survivors of sexual assault. For a long time, for instance, I was aware that many of the volunteers and clients were extremely concerned with something I heard as "the celadors." Conversations would be full of legal terms, and I imagined this was one such term, maybe Latin. I kept hearing worried discussion about these "celadors": something would have to be done about them.

"Why is everyone so upset about 'the celadors'?" I asked Lucy. She looked at me as if I were living on another planet and wordlessly guided me to the front gate. She opened it and gestured. Just off the passageway to the center, beside the stone steps that led down to it, were two gaping, rust-stained, half-open cellar doors. I saw that each led into an alcove big enough to hide from view one woman and one assailant.

I doubted I would have been able to recall seeing them if I had been under oath. I had never noticed them at all. I had misheard the words that were obvious to all the other women—women who had been raped—because my perceptions had taken in a selective view. I was not as fully conscious as they were about myself as prey.

Over the course of several months, I became increasingly depressed. I grew miserable at hearing the same questions, often years after the attack: "When will I be over this? When will this be behind me?"

My experiences began to affect my social life. At parties, when I mentioned my volunteer work, there would be, at the most unexpected moments, an asocial beat in the conversation. Then the stories would spill out, alarmingly, unasked for. A woman would pass her beer or her cigarette to her other hand, look at my feet or over behind my head, and say, "I was raped after my sixteenth birthday party." Or "From the time I was eight until I went off to boarding school, my uncle abused me." Or "When I went to sports camp for a summer after my junior year, the trip leader had me swim with him away from the group and he took down my suit in the water before I understood what was happening." Or "When I was baby-sitting, the kids' father tried to have sex with me when he drove me home and almost really hurt me." Or "When I was in junior high, this guy forced my head down into his lap on our first date. It was my first date ever."

It was beyond heartbreaking, it was spiritually confusing, because each story involved the most benign situations. There were no dark alleys. There were no monsters. There was no way to tell the safe afternoon from the dangerous one, the trustworthy tour guide or music teacher from the treacherous one. And there was no closure. Almost none of these girls had ever confronted her attacker in a court of law. And what the hell am I supposed to do, I asked myself as the narratives poured out at me and I felt wholly unequipped to deal with them, offer to get her another drink?

One afternoon, a raw, wet December day, we were all sitting in the living area on the shabby couch, listening to the local public radio station. On it, two male legal scholars were debating, in very abstract terms, what was to them—and, it seemed, to the law—the nebulous idea of female sexual consent. In the Quiet Room, the small counseling area off the main room, a twelve-year-old girl and her mother had been meeting with a volunteer for nearly three hours. On their way out, I saw the girl clinging to her mother's hand, and I thought how most girls that age would never be caught dead holding on to their mothers in public.

I needed to go back to being a clueless young woman, able to make mistakes without being paralyzed with the fear that came of knowing too much. Eventually, I told Lucy I was quitting.

My last night was a Friday night, when business was always brisk. We were open late. The various lamps in the place always looked incandescent during those hours, the increasingly serious darkness of a city getting down to its Friday-night moves. I thought about the young women who were at that moment emerging hopeful, blow-dried, and smelling nice into the night. And of the young men who were testing the cut of the sleeves of their new jackets. And how before the night was over, in the places where these women and men would encounter one another, there was bound to be some violence done; and none of the women knew to whom it would be. For once, I was the first to arrive. I checked the machine for the last time and switched it to PLAY. On the tape were two silent calls, one call that consisted only of sobbing, one rent reminder, and a woman who wanted to thank the center for existing. The volume of the answering machine was at maximum. I could hear the sounds clearly as I walked from room to room, turning on the coffee machine, pulling out chairs.

Even after I left the center, the scenes and stories I had seen there began to influence the way I looked at men, including my boyfriend at the time, Andrew. When I lay beside him on the fresh-smelling sheets of his narrow bed, I would think again about the violence I had heard about in such detail all afternoon. Gazing at the model ships he so meticulously painted and his endearingly big white sneakers lined up beside the bed, I would ask myself about the sense of security I felt after we made love. Was I deluding myself? I would try to understand how this affectionate creature could be the enemy and how this tender act could, in other times and places, be the medium of terror and humiliation.

Andrew was warmhearted and thoughtful. Like Martin, he was fundamentally a good guy, and his intention was to be my friend. But, as with each of my earlier relationships, the foundation of the friendship itself and the caring feelings we had for each other were undermined in critical and sometimes devastating ways by the way men and women were supposed to behave toward each other in our world. The construction of sex, and of "women" and "men," made it harder, not easier, for affection and empathy to prevail.

Andrew was gentle, but he was also tall and broad-boned. I would consider, as my head was cradled against his neck, that without too much effort he could encircle my neck with his hands or pin me down in a struggle. Physically speaking, we were so unmatched in strength that I had to face the fact that when I played with him and caressed him as if we were equals, I was doing so with his tacit consent. Weaker men, as I was seeing every week, had hurt stronger women. He was thirteen inches taller than I and half again as heavy.

I was beginning to wonder how it could be that some men were violent and others could never be. There appeared to be two different species, and on the street they looked the same.

I had begun to be troubled by the thinking of some of the women who were active in the antiviolence community—that all men were capable of raping, of liking rape, that it was a natural progression of the natural inclination of male sexuality. There was Andrew. Where did he fit into that theory?

"Andrew?" I asked one evening as we lay in bed. "Could you ever imagine forcing a woman to do something sexually that she does not want to do?"

He was so insulted that he refused to answer.

And I was piqued and angry that he would not swear an oath to me—for that was the nature of the feminism I was learning at the time. I wanted him to make a blood vow to me—something, perhaps, like D. H. Lawrence's *Blutbrüderschaft*—not only that he was not a rapist but that he harbored no aggression, not a shade of response, that could be counted as misogynist. He, of course, balked at my inquisition. Finally I let it go—for the moment. I thought, Yes, I believe you, but how can you be so sure, when the tormentors of women I'm counseling are just as sure that they're entitled to humiliate them for pleasure? What makes the difference, I wondered and wondered again, between the two masculine ideas of pleasure and excitement?

The feminist analysis of male sexuality that swirled around us in the seventies and eighties made some of the young men our age feel that they could not move forward sexually without hurting women; feel as guilty about and ashamed of their biological responses as their great-grandfathers had done in the days when "autoeroticism" was singled out as a weakener of character. As one woman—a bleached blond political activist from Oregon—confided to me years later, when I told her I was writing about adolescent girls and sex, "Hey: I'm thirty-six. I remember at nineteen desperately trying to give my virginity away to anyone who would take it. But all the guys were nice sons of feminists—'Are you okay? I don't want to hurt you,' they'd say. I needed to find one asshole in the Zip code to take care of it. And," she said, flipping her hair and sticking out a hip, "I'm not a *troll*. Finally I had to find a twenty-three-year-old scumbag to do it. He was from New York. *He* didn't care!"

I understood what she was describing—that postfeminist erotic polarization in "sensitive" men. The stereotypes for men attentive to feminism were two: Eunuch or Beast.

I had failed entirely, during my time at the rape crisis center, to draw a workable line between my work and my personal life. Besides, the dark lessons I was learning there were so real that I felt it would be craven of me even to try to draw that line.

But that austere position was not without its price. Once, as we were dressing to go out for the evening, Andrew complimented me on a short black denim skirt I had put on. For so many women of my generation, such a comment would be met, for good enough reasons, with both pleasure and anxiety.

"Do you think you like the way women look in short skirts and high heels," I asked, "because you've been socially conditioned?"

"Maybe I do!" he snapped, losing patience at last after more than two years of this kind of inquiry. "Maybe I don't. Maybe I just like women, period; maybe I just like women's legs in high heels. I'm sure I have been socially conditioned. Maybe I'm a pig. Maybe we all are! Maybe I just agree with your theories so I can get you into bed. Who cares, after a certain point? Forget I said anything." And out he went for a walk to the neighborhood bar, where he could have a drink with other young women who were wearing short skirts and high heels, or not, but either way not, possibly, arguing so much about it.

I challenged him, and challenged him again. But hypocrite that I was, my own desire, with its blinders and its greedy self-deceptions, went unchallenged. The world had language to describe, evaluate, and even condemn what he felt for me and my black skirt, but few words indeed—scarcely any acknowledgment, evaluative or not—for the speechless atavism of the emotions I felt for him.

This man made me feel split at the very center of my identity. Did I love him? Sure—I suppose. His droll cynicism made me laugh; I respected him: his politics were those of an unreconstructed Marxist, so I admired his fervor even as I thought his worldview sometimes simplistic (as he, no doubt, thought mine).

But I would be lying if I pretended that it was his belief system or his sense of humor that held me to him for four years, in some ways inexplicably, through exorbitant phone bills, cultural misunder-standings, and the seven-hour standby flights across the Atlantic that separated us.

My taste was just as culturally conditioned as his was, but I was allowed to judge him and remain free of being judged myself. The appeal he held for me was hardly original. The external symbols of his maleness were as codified as the symbols of masculinity in a leather bar: his motorcycle; the tough blunt cut of his fair hair; the boots; the single earring; the combination of vulnerability and bravado. I had accused him of being indoctrinated. But there is no doubt my own emotions were reflexes of cultural indoctrination.

Those symbols may have been clichés of a cultural ideal of mas-culinity, but they were also codes of a genuine personal masculinity. There has been a feminist "deconstruction" of masculinity but very little reconstruction. Perhaps it is time to recognize that all cultures codify maleness and femaleness within sexual symbolism and that we can create a new world in which those categories need not be fixed or oppressive, but neither do they need to be dismissed or devalued. Something beautiful—a mostly benevolent manhood—was being symbolized, however reductively, by the leather, the taciturnity, the entirely unwomanly aura about him. Precious little feminist language of the last century and a half, let alone the last two decades, has done justice to this quality and what it means to so many women.

Following Walt Whitman, who probably still is the one to have said it best: How can I value femaleness if I do not value maleness equally? How can I ask a man to celebrate my difference, and the way I choose to express it, if I do not celebrate his?

Andrew's appeal for me wasn't primarily about my mind or his. It was purely about attraction within nature. Did I feel that my obsession with his masculinity was a secret weakness that undermined my strength as a feminist? Sometimes I did.

"What do women want?" asked Sigmund Freud. "I want to hold you close to me, I want to touch your body, I want. I want," wrote the feminist and socialist Emma Goldman at about the same time.

Years after my affair with Andrew, I was startled by a question from a young woman in a college audience: "Okay," she challenged me, "Madonna: Feminist or Slut?"

I laughed in spite of myself, because the stark, worried choice she offered me was so current in popular debate at the time, so personally familiar, and so inadequate. ("Feminist or Slut?" was also the female mirror-image stereotype of the male "Eunuch or Beast?")

I knew by that time, too, from my own life and my reading, how old this question was and how mistakenly phrased. Just about all of us, I tried to say, still laughing—Mary Wollstonecraft, Emma Goldman, Djuna Barnes, Josephine Baker, Gloria Steinem, Erica Jong, Victoria Woodhull, Madonna, the student, her friends, her mom, her teachers—were always struggling to integrate what both stereotypes split off from us. And we always tended to think that we were alone in that struggle.

A longing for the male body is often read in our culture, even by women themselves, as being a flaw, a debilitating weakness. Very little language available to us echoes the feelings of Jeanne, the woman who had experienced, unexpectedly, the male body as a "gorgeous trick" or casts female heterosexual desire as a manifestation of female power.

This split—"Feminist or Slut?"—has antecedents. Feminists of the past contributed to the debate about female desire, though in two contradictory ways.

Most Victorian feminists believed that the feminist was the arch-enemy of the slut in herself and the rescuer of the slut in the street. This, for instance, was antiprostitution activist Josephine Butler's crusade. The early feminists campaigned not for women to have more sexual expression, but for a single sexual standard in which men had less. Many feminists of the time opposed birth control on the grounds that it would make pure women even more vulnerable to male sexuality. Feminists with a more retiring view of female sexuality highlighted male sexual brutality, which was, realistically enough, associated with exhausting pregnancies, disease, forced prostitution, and debility.

But others, a minority, believed that the feminist must integrate the slut. Elizabeth Cady Stanton, referring to a Whitman poem, wrote, "He speaks as if the female must be forced to the creative act, apparently ignorant of the fact that a healthy woman has as much passion as a man, that she needs nothing stronger than the law of attraction to draw her to the male."

Eventually, free-lovers and many suffragists united in stressing women's right to sexual refusal. A Victorian activist named Elmina Slenker, though counted among the "sex-haters," as they were called by contemporaries, still revealed in her writing a more complex erotic reality: it was not sexuality itself that these women hated but their husbands' hurried, insensitive style of lovemaking: "We want the sexes to love more than they do," she wrote. "We want them to love openly, frankly, earnestly; to enjoy the caress, the embrace, the glance, the voice, the presence and the very step of the beloved. . . . Fill the world as full of genuine sex love as you can . . . but forbear to rush in where generations yet unborn may suffer for your un-thinking, uncaring, unheeding actions." Dora Forster, writing in the 1890s in a journal of the free-love movement, described a similarly complex erotic consciousness: she charged that "the jealousy and tyranny of men have operated to suppress amativeness in women, by constantly sweeping strongly sexual women from the paths of life into infamy and sterility and death."

Finally, in the wake of the free lovers and the suffragettes, in the dusk of Edwardianism and the dawn of modernity, the birth control movement insisted upon a recognition of female desire. Under Margaret Sanger it did so in what amounted to a public relations triumph. In 1912, Sanger wrote the series of articles in the New York

Call titled "What Every Girl Should Know." Here Sanger spoke frankly about the female sexual and reproductive system and called "the procreative act" natural, clean, and healthful. Sanger and the sex radicals turned the Victorian notion of sex as animal passion around—sex became spiritualized. In Sanger's sex manual, she called intercourse "sex communion": "At the flight, body, mind and soul are brought together into the closest unity . . . the sexual embrace not only satisfies but elevates both participants."

Though attempts were made to silence Sanger—she was refused permission to address audiences in Akron and Chicago; arrested and jailed in Portland, Oregon; censored by the Comstock Laws; locked out of her hall in St. Louis—she eventually succeeded in making the birth control movement socially acceptable and rehabilitating female desire, if in "respectable" dress. The charge that her cohorts were "free-lovers" was always a stumbling block, and Sanger tried to distance herself from it. But the fact remains that the origin of the birth control movement, decades before, had been with the utopian "free-lovers."

Anarchist Emma Goldman, in contrast, never felt the need to repudiate the radical nature of her vision of sexual expression for women. But no matter how bravely she faced controversy in her public life, even this visionary firebrand, who stirred audiences to riot and individuals to acts of violence, was tormented by the private thought that she loved too much.

Though a radical egalitarian decades ahead of her time, Goldman believed what my young questioner about Madonna probably believed: that there must be a conflict between "weakness in love and strength in politics." Goldman's letters show that she felt her identity was torn in half by her own sexual desire.

Typically enough for a respectable young girl in the early years of the century, Goldman's erotic coming of age was unhappy: her sexual initiation in Russia by a young peasant was savage, and she found little more sexual happiness in marriage. It was Ben Reitman, her lover and impresario, who eventually "awakened" Goldman sexually. Reitman was a tall, sensuous, mustachioed man who embodied, in Goldman's eyes, exciting contradictions: he was at once vulgar and poetic, a fellow idealist who had a medical degree but consorted with pimps, prostitutes, and hoboes.

When Goldman began writing her autobiography decades later, her old lover sent her the letters she had written to him. Though now elderly and no longer in love, Goldman could not even bear to let her secretary read these private letters. "It is like tearing off my clothes to let them see the mad outpouring of my tortured spirit," she wrote, "the frantic struggle for my love, the all absorbing devotion each letter breathes, I can't do it!"

Though she disowned them in her own lifetime, the letters that chart Goldman's erotic awakening reveal the lineaments of an unusually undistorted female libido. The libido she describes is important to us because, being a product of the Edwardian era, it obviously antedates the modern ideas about the nature of female lust and how it should be expressed.

In Emma Goldman's letters you can hear the metaphors of turbulent landscapes, particularly of wind and water, that women writers often use in reaching for and masking descriptions of female passion. Of her sexual awakening, Goldman wrote to Ben, "You have opened up the prison gates of my womanhood. And all the passion that was unsatisfied in me for so many years, leaped into a wild reckless storm boundless as the sea." She asked him, "Do you think that one who has heard the roar of the ocean, seen the maddening struggle of the waves . . . known all the madness of a wild, barbarian primitive love, can reconcile one's self to any relationship under civilization?"

When they became lovers, the revelation was transformative: "I was caught in the torrent of an elemental passion I had never dreamed any man could rouse in me. I responded shamelessly to its primitive call, its naked beauty, its ecstatic joy."

Goldman has articulated what women intuit to be the transformative nature of their own gratified desire: men who have been stirred deeply by a lover may well feel that they have been given joy, but perhaps it is unique to women to feel that they have been "given life." In another passage she echoes that metaphor, describing herself yet again as "the woman, the woman that lay asleep for 38½ years and that you have awakened into frantic, savage, hungry life."

Finally, Goldman's erotic account is a uniquely unguarded and undistorted template for how a liberated female libido waxes stronger over time: at forty-one she knew herself to be "just in the age of passion's highest expression."

Yet sadly, the duality of female desire made Goldman, like so many women, feel that her passion was at war with her rationality and her dignity. She saw her own anguish at Reitman's infidelities, for instance, not as being a normal human response but as being a betrayal of her free-love principles.

As a revolutionary, Goldman advocated the themes of women's liberation, contraception, and free love as part of the upheaval in sexual mores she believed the world was ready for; and the freedom of woman in relation to man was a fundamental component of her worldview. Much to her own distress, however, her passionate nature led her to a sexual and emotional attachment to the dissolute Reitman that felt to her like a form of enslavement, a weakness at her core, and a lived contradiction to the notion of personal liberty in which she just as passionately believed.

We can see in her conflict the paradigm of the modern woman's relationship to her own passion: Goldman felt deep shame about the intensity of her lust and the way its pressure drove her to behavior she felt to be unworthy of her "higher self"—yet at the same time she sensed that in a way the world was not yet ready for, that same desire was the gateway to a half-remembered, deeper self. Like so many women today, she held self-possession, clarity, and control to be her female ideal. So when she acknowledged the lengths to which desire drove her, she could only view her visionary, analytical self as fraudulent. She preached free love, but her letters show that, though she tried, she could find no way to integrate that intensity with any dignity.

"If ever our correspondence should be published," Goldman wrote to Reitman, "the world would stand aghast that I, Emma Goldman, the strong revolutionist, the daredevil, the one who has defied laws and convention, should have been as helpless as a shipwrecked crew on a foaming ocean. . . . Emma Goldman, the Wollstonecraft of the 20th century, even like her great sister is weak and dependent, clinging to the man. . . . What an irony of fate." (Mary Wollstonecraft, who had proclaimed autonomy for women in a way that was scandalously radical for the end of the eighteenth century, had abased herself in a destructive unwed relationship.) "Yes, I am a woman," Goldman continued, "indeed too much of it. That's my tragedy. The great abyss between my woman nature and the nature of the relentless revolutionist is too great to allow much happiness in my life."

Her most important insight about female desire was expressed nearly a century ahead of her time, in her lecture "Sex: The Great Element for Creative Work." She took issue with Freud's view that creativity emerged from repressing sexual feeling and proclaimed that "the creative spirit is not an antidote to the sex instinct, but a part of its forceful expression. . . . Sex is the source of life. . . . Where sex is missing everything is missing. . . . Love," she declared, "is an art, sex love is likewise an art." And finally, she turned the truisms of the industrial era on their head—reasserting the older worldview that "sexual sensibility [is] greater and more enduring in woman than in man." One of her most popular lectures spoke idealistically of love freed from the economic imbalance between men and women, and she went so far as to proclaim that sexual inhibitions in women led to marital conflict and divorce, just as sexual ignorance, along with economic desperation, led women into prostitution.

"Emma Goldman: Feminist or Slut?" one might ask—just as she was mortally afraid that people would; and just as one might ask the question of the discarded but adoring Wollstonecraft and note the attacks directed at Gloria Steinem for acknowledging passionate feelings. A curious hostility is directed by women as well as men against "feminists who love too much." It is a projection of our own failure to integrate the urgency and even neediness of female sexual passion into the strength of female character that creates this reflex of animosity in us. Goldman was in this way no different from so many women: a feminist with genuine ideals waging an internal war with the "promiscuity" of her sexual and emotional feelings for a man. Or, one might also say, keeping in mind what we've seen of the fierceness of female desire: a woman with a living mind and a living body. Can we make room for so much vitality in ourselves, in the world, in other women?

20

The Technically White Dress

E ventually, dear reader, I would be married. And to my astonishment, as the date drew nearer, I found myself poring over the pages of the bridal magazines. Even though, as a feminist, I had "deconstructed" the institution of marriage and knew perfectly well that a white wedding derives from traditions that value women's virginity as a form of currency and that transfer the woman herself as property from one man to another, still I returned again and again to the visions of white. I began dreaming about a veil, a garter, a rose, a ring. What was it I was longing for?

The magazines were full of details that attested to the naked patriarchal origins of the traditions that still lingered. I learned that bridesmaids were originally dressed in ways similar to the bride so as to confuse marauders intent on abducting and holding the bride for ransom. The tradition of "groomsmen" originated in the old practice in which warriors were needed to help the bridegroom fight off would-be kidnappers and rapists. The cedar chests and the mother-of-the-bride embroidered handkerchiefs—even the beading and the faux pearling and the glitter that spilled down the bodices of many dresses—are all vestigial reminders that brides and their trousseaux were essentially no more than chattel to be bartered. Even the word "honeymoon," I discovered, derived from the Old English custom of sending the new couple away for a month to drink honeyed ale and learn about having intercourse; the alcohol was intended to relax sexual inhibitions and ease the anxieties of teenage virgins who had never before seen the men who now had unreserved access to their bodies—girls whose own attraction, or lack of it, to their mates had counted for nothing in the decision to wed. The alcohol was meant to do the work of female desire.

But the centerpiece of what I began, half ruefully, to think of as "Brideland," this new country of gratified material desire, was of course the dress. I became preoccupied with my need to re-create an image that had lodged in my head long ago, when I was seven or eight and sitting beside my grandmother on the hard black wood of the piano bench in Stockton, as she played melodies. The song she was singing was "The Raggle-taggle Gypsies," an English ballad about a young aristocratic woman who leaves her proper sexual niche—her house, her lands, her "new-wedded lord"—for a life of wanderlust and subversive desire: "to go with the raggle-taggle gypsies, O." The sterility of her sexual life with her designated mate was implicit: "Last night you slept in a goose-feather bed / With the sheets turned down so bravely, O. / Tonight you'll sleep in a cold, open field / Along with the raggle-taggle gypsies, O." And her raw, defiant reply evoked an erotic passion that would compensate for any material privation: "Oh, what care I for my goose-feather bed? . . . Tonight," she gloated, "I'll sleep in a cold, open field, / Along with the raggle-taggle gypsies, O." The illustration showed a dark man, ragged, handsome, smiling.

As I struggled through racks of tulle, I found at last a marked-down, beat-up, yellowing gown with a vast skirt of netting that I immediately gathered around my waist in both fists. The dress now looked as if it had stepped out of the eighteenth century and had been worn by someone who'd been sleeping in a forest.

I realized that I wanted to be married as that renegade bride who would sleep in a different place every night, but with the same man. I wanted the dress I wore to say the opposite of what married love too often says: I wanted it to say that we would keep traveling; that desire would still drive me out of doors; that I would not be domesticated by matrimony.

When I asked around, I gathered that I was not alone in thinking more than cursorily about what might be assumed to be, in times like these, a shallow symbol from an outmoded ritual system. Many modern women who marry, it seems, no matter how independent and how politically self-aware they are, still harbor strong feelings about the dress they wear on their wedding day.

What does this object offer a modern woman that she cannot find in her everyday life? The most common "period" the wedding costume refers to offers a clue. The eternal time of the traditional wedding is Victorian—or, at the latest, Edwardian. There is the bell-shaped crinoline, the corseted bodice, the elaborately piled hair, the bustling to the rear, the hundred cloth-covered buttons down the woman's back. No zippers; no Velcro.

There may be a good reason why the feminine ceremonial attire of the wedding goes back to a time when the fastenings surrounding women's bodies were laborious to undo. On our wedding days, we tend toward the imagery of the Victorian Age more than to that of any other precisely because of our time's denigration of female sexuality and desire. Few of us want the bad old days of enforced virginity to return. But there is a terrible spiritual and emotional hunger among many woman, including myself, for social behavior and ritual that respect and even worship female sexuality and reproductive power. We are no longer—if we ever really were—goddesses, priestesses, or queens of our own sexuality. But we want to be.

Paradoxically, when we are swaddled in the white satin of the formal bridal gown, we take on, for a few rare moments, a lost sexual regality. In Brideland, today, unlike in the "real world" with our boyfriends at the beach, we are hard to unbutton, to get at—even to feel through the stiff corsetry. We are made into treasure again. In white we retrieve our virginity, which symbolizes that sexual access to us is special again. We carry bouquets of roses and other lush flowers, which have always symbolized the female sexual parts and their fruitfulness. Finally, we don a veil, a metonym for the hymen, the veil of the inmost feminine sexual self.

Then, in photo after photo, the bridal magazines show us images of men, those masters of the universe, before us on bended knee, offering us polished gems. The old archetype, banished from the world in the rush of the sexual revolution and the least-common-denominator literalness of *Debbie Does Dallas*, lives briefly again. Sacred virgin, sacred prostitute, the two avatars come briefly into the world again: for a day men worship the goddess of female sexuality.

The dream revealed in those magazines, and in the culture that surrounds the formal wedding in the West, demonstrates just how barren the world has become when female desire is stripped of its aura, its magical power, even its sanctity.

I do not want to return to the values of the prefeminist "sexual mystique." But perhaps the knowledge that we have lost the sense of the value and power of female desire and that we are suffering, collectively, from that loss as if from a physical deficiency, will lead us to find new rituals, new laws, and new lessons for our daughters through which both men and women will recognize that female desire is priceless—and not just for one expensive day. In the meantime, all we have are glimmers of what a culture that venerates female desire might look like. And who wouldn't want to drift in those seductive currents for just a little while? I did.

A college friend helped me prepare for the ceremony. She adjusted the veil and shook out the flounces. I was glad that the tulle had yellowed. It had almost made me laugh, that less-than-pristine quality of the fabric. I remembered, while I held it up under the lights in the room where I was dressing, the way that, at fourteen, we had arched our eyebrows when referring to our virginity. We had always used that qualifier: "technically."

"Technically," the dress was white. The age of the material, its exposure to the air and to the touches of different hands, was beautiful to me, and stood in my eyes for my own coming of age, which I wanted to incorporate into the commitment I was about to make. If my past had not yet made me a woman, whatever that was, it had at least helped provide me with the rudiments of a self to give.

21

The Time and
the Place: 1996

A t thirty-three, I had gone back to check on the past. Could our memories have been as extreme as they sounded to me from the vantage point of the present?

My "adult" life had been left, for this brief journey, three thousand miles away. Mother, wife, writer, mortgage holder, all those conscientious selves were shrugged off. I felt dangerously light; layers of identity and experience peeled away from me like inappropriately heavy garments in the insistent wind. For a moment I was ranging again, starting out, a teenage girl, that fierce, crackling, self-regarding creature. I was edgy with excitement to go home again to adolescence, to the Haight, and to the wind that continually blew in from the ocean, smelling of eucalyptus.

After dropping off my bag, I paced up and down the hills of my old neighborhoods. The night, as I think it is nowhere else, was lit from above like candlelight showing through blue glass.

Everywhere I could see, faintly, something that I thought the tourists did not notice and that made the banal postcard of "everyone's favorite city" into a place that was real, and mine. It was the fine sediment of the city that smudged windowsills and moldings, gathering in corners from that cool wind.

I felt as though I could not stop walking. I wanted to find those girls we had been. I stopped, eventually, in front of the hotel where I had lost my virginity. It had decayed still further. The building's recent history was a history of the times: the baths in the building next door had been closed down by the Department of Health when the AIDS threat had become apparent. I was told by a habitué that in the mid-eighties the hotel had become a crack house. Now, in the lobby, young people with tattooed faces sat smoking. It was a cheap youth hostel and hard-drug scene. I would not have felt safe enough there to do again what I had done.

Over on Valencia Street, I looked in at a New Age gift shop. Now there were vulva effigies, as well as phallus crystals, in a range of settings. The New Age is kinder to women than the hippie subculture was. But the images were still displayed at the height of an eight-year-old's eyes, and two little boys, about that age, stood by the counter trying to pick a crystal that went with their birthday sign. I passed the Good Vibrations store, a clean, well-lit place staffed by dedicated young women with appealing, clean-scrubbed faces. It was doing a thriving business selling profeminist erotic books and sex toys. I had heard that sales were up 200 percent a year and that a new line of sex toys for women had been produced in bright, happy colors and was selling briskly. At a café filled with young people in buzz cuts and boots, I felt again that San Francisco frisson of being in a room where you can be checked out by girls or boys or people whom you can't distinguish by gender.

In a crumbling movie house, I watched *The Summer of Love*, the documentary on the Haight-Ashbury in the sixties. As I ate popcorn and stared at the screen alone in the darkness, I saw, drifting barefoot across Hippie Hill with a crowd from a be-in, wearing a long Bedouin dress and amulets and making a peace sign to the camera, my twenty-five-year-old mother.

Back in my old neighborhood, I saw that the Free Store had become an elegant Pacific Rim–cuisine restaurant. On the "Evolution" mural, the paint was peeling. LIBERATE YOUR DESIRES, read a poster on the window of a medical clinic. Opposite the psychedelic-colored hippie mural was an eighties punk mural in shades of gray, red, and black: WHEN ONCE YOU ENTER PASSION'S DOMINION, it read, YOU ARE FOREVER ENSLAVED. In the window of the framing store next to my hotel was a blown-up cartoon, like the ZAP comics that had so imprinted my generation, showing Jesus having sex with a nun.

An array of young blond heroin addicts was sitting on the sidewalk panhandling. Their lines had changed with the times. "Can I have a quarter to help me get high?" used to be the favorite. Now one young man with a small, sedated-looking dachschund in his lap asked, "Do you want to pet my puppy?" A rangy fellow added, "Give me a quarter so I can be a Nazi jerk." His girlfriend laughed at him and at my expression. On one corner, a thirtyish woman who looked as if she had once been a debutante sat folded up in a shopping cart, gazing calmly at the scene. On another, someone was throwing up. It seemed someone was always throwing up on Haight Street these days. "Heroin," Jeanne, who knows the neighborhood, had said when I had mentioned this. "It makes you barf."

I turned back to the hotel. My room was in a 1904 structure, painted magenta, that had been reclaimed by a smiling, artistic matron who had renamed herself Sami Sunchild. It was now devoted to being a living museum of the sixties. I found it odd to inhabit a tourist attraction essentially committed to re-creating for excited visitors what I thought of as the texture of my childhood.

Each room was decorated according to a different 1960s motif. There was the Summer of Love Room, adorned with Fillmore Street posters and supplied with meditation tapes; the Peace Room, styled after a Japanese garden; and my own room, the Rainbow Room, with its psychedelic canopy over the bed. It was strange to see this self-consciousness about a time that, for me at least, had preceded irony.

I had tried to conjure up for myself, as I checked in and made my selection, a Chicago 1968 Room, a Kent State Room, and so on. But my unspoken joke was inappropriate; the hotel was dedicated to "Peace." "They say that I'm a dreamer, but I'm not the only one" was its newsletter's motto. The guest book was crammed with various messages and good wishes on every page: "Spirit of Woodstock Lives! Love, Bill and Suzanne, Sydney, Australia"; "Amor y Paz desde Puerto Rico"; and one easily overlooked entry written in a tiny, regular hand: "Dear Sir: I have disassembled my room: drawer, table and bedstead." That one had no signature.

From my room, I looked out of the window to see the familiar Haight Street sights, my childhood scenes. Boutiques displayed high heels and latex bondage accessories. BIKER SLUTS, proclaimed the headline of that week's sex magazine, ranged in metal vending machines similar to those that had stood on the corner twenty years before. I watched an alert four-year-old girl in a stroller be pushed down the street.

Evening came, and the fog surrounded the streetlights. By midnight, most of the stores had closed. The center of the action was a young father and a group of his friends who sat on the ground in a shop doorway, having a great time, playing the bongo drums for a ten-year-old boy doing a mad, gleeful variation on the Highland fling. Should I call the police or go and join them? I was home.

IN SPITE OF all the wreckage, I am glad we lived through what we did, where we did. Certainly, there was a real darkness to those times and their legacy, and it's fashionable to look back and say that those were years of chaos and decadence only, that nothing came of it but disease and failed marriages.

We faced grave pressures and risks, just like every cohort of girls who have ever grown. But when I consider on balance our historical good luck, it sometimes dazzles me. Those ten or fifteen years in which we came of age were years that, as far as girls were concerned, the world had never seen before and may never see again. Yes, we too had to learn about abuse, shame, danger, derision, and harmful myths, but in that brief window, female desire, still hedged around by so many warnings and threats, was nonetheless freed in some critical ways. I started by describing how the sexual revolution did not do all the work of "freeing" us as young women. Nonetheless, each of us, in our different ways, took for granted a state of mind about sexuality that was in some respects new. The benefits of the freedom we had were the result not so much of the sexual revolution's technical emancipation as of the feminist revolution's (still-incomplete) efforts at emancipating women's thinking about their right to define and defend their sexuality. For the first generation of young women to come of age after the sexual revolution, then, it seems that the organ that best registered the effects of real social change would turn out to be not the clitoris, though it had been so widely discussed in our youth, but the brain.

What have I learned from going back to our teenage years and considering what we knew in the light of what we did not know? That the old truism "Sex is in the mind" has many more layers of truth than I had ever understood. Sex was, for us, not so much about how we were taught to *do* it but how we were taught to *think* it. The framework available to us determined if, in a given sexual gesture or action, we felt weak or strong, dirty or precious, self-defined or at the mercy of others.

What harmed us was not physical threats so much as psychical degradation; what we gained from our "liberated" age was not so much a technical advantage as a *glimmer* of a better kind of sexual consciousness.

Can we imagine for our own daughters still better information that can shape a better sexual culture? Yes. We can encourage them to believe that the notion that female sexuality participates in the divine image should not remain a curiosity in history books but should be a presumption underpinning their daily lives. We can teach our daughters that shame belongs to the act of abusing or devaluing female sexuality, not to that sexuality itself.

I am conscious that an inquiry such as this ends by raising more questions than it can answer; sexuality is so personal, and the creation of a sexual culture such a subtle, collective undertaking, that any simple prescriptions are too crude a response. But what hints or glimmers of better actions can we take away as grown women?

We can come away with the determination to present our stories. Filling in the sexual subjectivity, curiosity, sensitivity, and humanity of teenage girls is especially important considering that the education of teenage boys is largely, and destructively, based on sexual cartoon imagery of girls. Stories are the magic that can reassemble around a stereotype its humanity. One man my age, a father of a daughter, after he read some of these accounts, said, "I recognize myself. To us, it was just a game; I never really knew in my gut that there were egos involved." He said he wanted a different sexual culture for his daughter to grow up in: "It shouldn't be too much to ask that she can just grow up thinking that the ways she feels and develops is okay."

Making room for our stories will not only help transform the environment for girls growing up now; it will also, I think, strengthen grown women. So many of the women who spoke to me were certain that the events that marked their coming of age were either trivial or shameful. But when one is asked to consider the very essence of one's identity to be something ridiculous or contemptible, one's core dignity is radically compromised. The assertion that an essential characteristic—a skin color, a facial feature, a biological response—is degrading is the same assertion that undergirds racism, anti-Semitism, homophobia. The shaming of girls and women from acknowledging a sexuality on their own terms, or a sexual past, pressures them into a contemporary version of "passing." The need to pass for someone one is not creates a vulnerability to external anxieties about womanhood in one's private life—as well as a vulnerability *about* the fact of one's womanhood in the workplace. In other words, if one is allowed to grow up being proud of one's sexual womanhood as it develops day by day, one may acquire that "sureness" that Margaret Mead spoke of, and be far less susceptible to the blandishments of industries or ideologies that promise to bestow a sexual womanhood, as well as being less susceptible to the pressures that stand ready to stigmatize women for their sexuality.

Obviously, girls need better rites of passage in our culture. Such rituals, we have seen, require rigor, separation from males and from the daily environment, and the exchange of privileged information. It is important, in such rituals, for grown women outside the family to be part of that initiation. I'd like to propose that groups of friends with children sign one another up, upon the birth of a daughter, for the responsibility. Instead or in addition to the familiar role of godparent, someone who signs on for such a task would join with a few other women, and a small cohort of girls, in the girls' thirteenth year, for a retreat if circumstances allow it, such as a hiking or camping trip, organized through the schools, church groups, or through family groups—or at least for a series of informal all-female gatherings. There, the older women would pass on to the younger everything they have learned about womanhood, and answer *every single question* the girls want to ask. According to their culture and religion, the older women would teach the younger skills and techniques, such as self-defense, contraception, sexual pleasure, and parenting, passing on to them an ethic of adulthood as well as an ethic of sexual responsibility—helping them, too, to recognize when they are truly ready to become women.

In addition to this intimate education, a family's friends can commit to being part of a wisdom initiation: transmitting their professional skills to the girl whom they are assigned to guide. I have, for instance, such a commitment of exchange from the scientist parents of a two-year-old girl; as my daughter grows up, they have agreed to teach her about earth sciences, show her experiments, and explain to her the jobs that one can do in that field—something in which I have no expertise—and I in turn have committed to working with their daughter on her writing. In this way, through these commitments of mentoring exchanges, girls feel valued not only by their families but by the extended community, the locus of initiation tensions; and the possibilities of what they might love and become good at expands.

As for our own sexual consciousness, those of us who are adult women: this is the area in which one can merely disclose possibilities. Sexuality is so very personal; every woman has her own pattern, to use van de Velde's metaphor. Découpage is an old art form, a feminine one, in which images are cut out in a bright, unstructured display and reassembled to make a unique pattern. I hope the gathering-together of so many mixed diverse—"promiscuous"— images and scenes of female sexuality and desire will serve as an array of new choices for those tired of the old monochromatic scenes and the old flat characters; I trust that women will use them as they wish, individually, to re-create and reassemble mental landscapes more pleasing to their own unique patterns. And I hope they will serve, too, for men who would like to learn more about what women really want, and confirm the intuition that many men have— that the sexual selves of girls and women are more complicated, compelling, and subtle than we as a culture have been allowed to know.

For despite the centuries' severe constraints on female desire, the history of women's sexuality did not submit to a straight line of oppression. Joy, nature, and love have continually subverted it. In generation after generation, women—perhaps many women—in spite of whatever cultural obstacles have been placed in their paths, have remembered themselves.

Does the resilience of the intensity of female desire—this golden thread of eros that insists on surfacing throughout the dense weave of history—help to explain why women's passion has been and still is viewed with fear? If women's sexuality weren't in fact subversive in some way, why should those who have sought to control women have had to work so very hard for so very long? Perhaps men have intuited in women a potential for wildness that, if neither repressed nor integrated into society, threatens to lure women—as it did those bored, undervalued Roman matrons—away from familiar hearths, toward fire and rivers and the arms of strangers.

The long, rigorous record of masculine efforts to punish the slut seems to rest upon an intuition of women's actual erotic nature and its actual magical potential. It seems premised on the suspicion that women can, like sorceresses, shape-shift, and escape erotically to a place where no man can follow. Anatomically, as we've seen, that may well be true. Women *are* the more carnal sex. Tiresias was right. The nature of female desire can in fact lead women into a "fugue state," a level of pleasure that must seem otherworldly to an observer whose body cannot take him into this state of consciousness. Traditional feminist theory has taught that the male fear of female sexuality is merely a projection of male lust and misogyny. But what if the struggle to contain women's passion has been a struggle against a powerful, potentially disruptive force that inheres in women themselves?

This possibility must never excuse misogyny; it could explain, though, the enduring belief, found in many unrelated cultures, that women's desire renders them, sexually, powerfully magical beings. Maybe women really *are*, sexually, powerfully magical beings.

What might we learn from finally accepting that? Not to repress female desire, as it has been repressed in the past; nor to devalue it as a joke at women's expense, as we often do today; but to integrate it fully into our civilization. Our resistance to dealing with the true nature of female desire is destructive to us as a society. Half of marriages today end in divorce; most of the divorces are initiated by women. At least some of these are initiated by women who are worn down by feeling starved in their senses, erotically lonely.

What would happen to our divorce rate if we accepted that, when women long to be attentively touched, gazed at, caressed, deeply kissed, and surrounded with sensuality—when they long to be given a kind of sexual adoration or devotion, and an "extreme" abundance of pleasure—it is not because they are neurotic, possessive, or pathologically needy, but because, as other cultures have better understood, *that is how women are made*, and their erotic nature brought into balance? What would our culture—and our divorce rate—look like if we dared to teach men the skills that could keep women's promiscuously responsive bodies happy in monogamous lives? What would male adolescent sexual behavior look like if boys were taught to treat teenage girls neither like prudes nor sluts but like nascent sexual goddesses, and respect their sexuality and reproductive potential accordingly? What would our violent landscape look like if men believed that true masculinity meant becoming an extraordinary lover to a life partner?

What would we get if we let women's passion truly enter and dwell in our social world?

Above all else that would accrue to us, we would have our girls enter into womanhood fully alive.

FOR ALL its excesses, I am grateful to my hometown for the glimmers of hope that it granted. The Bay Area of the 1970s was a place where we girls could maintain a healthy skepticism when we ran into the barriers and punitive shocks that accompany female erotic development. When the frat boys hounded the women walking up Telegraph, when the old letch offered money to Sandy, when Carol Doda's nipple lights blinked, even when the models on the cover of *Seventeen* promised it would all feel so good for us only *if*—enough change had taken place around us for us to be able to say, to ourselves and our friends if not out loud in public, "This can't be it. This can't be all. Maybe sex is—becoming a woman is—something else; something whose meaning I'll have to create for myself as I go along. Here: let me find out by telling it *my* way." And sure enough, the stories the women in this book told me follow the erotic plot lines of neither the old-fashioned, Hugh Hefner version of sexual revolution nor the retrofeminist account. In these stories there are neither sluts nor victims but determined authors of their own biographies, intent—as so many women, I found, had been long before we or our mothers were born—on forging, finally, a new philosophy of desire.

It was actually kind of beautiful, Jeanne had concluded of the male body even after an hour and a half of narrating the most harrowing teenage sexual memories. In a life story such as hers, I found, the heroine refuses to lose sight of what she is determined sex will be for her and mean to her. That is what is impressive about the enterprise of "becoming a woman" in a time as challenging for girls and women as our own. The right to "do it" came from the sexual revolution; the right to "tell it my way" came from the feminist one. Only when the second is fully incorporated into the first—to the discomfort, no doubt, of many contemporary ideologues of both—will a lasting revolution have been achieved.

When, over the course of those years, did we "become women"? Was it when we first put on makeup? With our first kiss? When we discovered our sexual identity? When we first had intercourse? When we earned our own money for the first time? When we graduated from high school? When we first became pregnant, those of us who did? When those of us who did so first got married? No. None of those events turned us into women. I think we in our culture became women when we made the gradual decision that, even if we didn't know what womanhood meant or when we had arrived there for sure, all the markers imposed on us were flawed; and we were somehow going to find a way, through whatever struggle it would take, to determine for ourselves the meaning of "becoming women."

And all of us, to a greater or lesser extent, did indeed find various ways through—not all the way to where we wanted to be, but closer.

I did not sleep much that last night in the city. Early the next morning, as soon as it was light enough, I walked up and down Haight Street. It was Saturday. I saw the high school girls working in the stores and the cafés, unlocking the doors and setting out the tables. They had red-black nails and shag haircuts, or they wore black jeans and T-shirts. In one restaurant, a merry young woman behind a bar poured a cup of coffee for a waiter, and her bicep tensed under a blue tattoo of the earth. In a café, a thin teenager in a patchwork skirt nervously counted out change. I watched the straight and the gay girls work and laugh with the customers, the cute boys and hot girls, the grown women and men. I thought I saw something of our old selves in them: ironic, idealistic, subversive, curious—doing their best with what there was.

Then I walked to the top of Parnassus Street, where the houses meet the bottom of the cloud cover. I looked over the Panhandle and the park and Cole Valley. I remembered how at fourteen we used to ride our bikes over the hills. I thought of how it had felt to be so cold, pushing against gravity; what it felt like to be changing through time and space with every minute. And I recalled our laughing as the wind took the breath out of us, because each of us was trying to go faster than all the others.

Notes

Introduction: First Person Sexual

xv important work: See, for the primary examples of valuable recent con-
tributions to this genre, Lyn Mikel Brown and Carol Gilligan, *Meeting at
the Crossroads: Women's Psychology and Girls' Development* (Cambridge, Mass.,
and London: Harvard University Press, 1992); Mary Pipher, M.D.'s
empathic *Reviving Ophelia: Saving the Selves of Adolescent Girls* (New York:
Ballantine, 1995), especially the chapter "Sex and Violence," 203–32;
and Peggy Orenstein, with the American Association of University
Women, *Schoolgirls: Young Women, Self-Esteem and the Confidence Gap* (New
York: Anchor, 1995), especially the chapter "Fear of Falling: Sluts,"
52–56.

xvii Latin for "promiscuous": *Concise Oxford Dictionary*, 5th ed., H. W. Fowler
and F. G. Fowler, eds.

xix *Our Bodies, Ourselves:* Wendy Sanford and Paula Doress, affiliated with
the Boston Women's Health Book Collective, track the history of censorship efforts targeting *Our Bodies, Ourselves* in their article, "*Our Bodies,
Ourselves* and Censorship," *Library Acquisitions: Practice and Theory* 5
(1981): 133–42. Censorship attempts began in earnest in 1977, peak-
ing with the Reagan administration. The authors list twenty communities that faced banning efforts. Defenders of libraries' right to place the
book on their shelves have included the American Civil Liberties
Union, local NOW chapters, librarians, high school students, and parents. In their explanation of why the collective had compiled the book
initially, Sanford and Doress note, "We discovered . . . that sex was a
painful subject for many of us: we had been taught not to know or trust
our bodies or accept our sexual feelings. The so-called sexual revolution wasn't making things much better; we needed more information,
more equal relationships, and more self-respect." Having explained this
simple goal, the authors point out that "The New Right censors'" most
frequently voiced objection to *Our Bodies, Ourselves* was that "it will mis-

lead young people. The majority of attempts to restrict its use are aimed at keeping it from teenagers." The authors note that Jerry Falwell warned his constituents: "They [secular humanists] realize that we will not endorse free love, free sex, so they are brainwashing our children." The authors summarize the position of those seeking to curtail the distribution of the book: "The fear is that the explicit sections of the book will persuade teens to try sex, lesbianism, abortion, communal living, and other 'perversions.' Would-be censors fail to recognize the blatant sexual messages and pressures bombarding teens in the media every day." A physician's endorsement of *Our Bodies, Ourselves* may suggest the unspoken reasons behind the efforts to ban the book: ". . . there is no other book that even approaches *OBOS* as an honest, medically complete discussion of female sexuality actively discouraging shame and ignorance and instead encouraging responsibility and control" (Sanford and Doress, 136). Note also newspaper headlines collected in unpublished materials provided by the Boston Women's Health Book Collective: "*OBOS* Backlash"; "Eagle Forum Attacks Class on 'Our Bodies' "; "Body Book 'Shocking' "; "Deviate Sex in Plainview"; "Book 'Our Bodies, Ourselves' May Lead to Criminal Violation"; "Textbook is Trash"; "Humanistic Garbage." One minister in Swansville, Maine, Jim Evans, led his crusade against the book by characterizing it as "support[ing] abortion, lesbianism, incest, and bestiality." In a Moral Majority mailing of January 1, 1981, Falwell singles out for opprobrium the chapter "The Anatomy and Physiology of Sexuality and Reproduction." In *The Bellevue American*, a local Bellevue, Washington, newspaper, the PTA president, Mary Cirineo, is quoted as warning that "there are two classes of young girls. For the girls who tend toward promiscuity, the book will make prostitutes out of them, because it gives them the information right off the bat, without them having to go out looking for it." (Claudia Mitchell, "Woman Confident She'll Recruit More Parents in Book-Banning Campaign," *The Bellevue American*, April 10, 1979.) See also American Library Association, *Newsletter on Intellectual Freedom* 32 (March 1983): 55; and Carol E. Iaciofano, "Women Know Thyself [sic]: A Fight Against the Book Banners," *Boston Herald-American*, Aug. 28, 1981.

xx McCarthy: See Mary McCarthy, *Memories of a Catholic Girlhood* (New York: Penguin, 1985 [1957]), 154–56. Her description of sexual initiation of a sort, at fifteen, is a classic manifestation of the distancing voice, the "sexual aphasia" or abdication of self to a dissociative agent such as alcohol, that is expected to descend upon the adolescent girl when she is experiencing and noting the "first person sexual." For a writer of McCarthy's powers of alertness, this descent into passivity of the observing self is all the more striking. "Some hours later, I woke up in a strange room and found there was a man in bed with me . . . I was undressed. I had no recollection of the room or how we had got there. . . . The very first night, the very first man. . . . Nothing had happened, he kept murmuring. . . . This was not all, I was certain; it did not explain what he was doing there, with his arms around me. I decided not to inquire. If there had been a certain amount of necking (which now began to come back to me, hazily) I did not want to hear about it. . . . Had I drawn a blank [her girlfriends] inquired, solicitously. I had to ask the meaning of this expression. Was it different from 'passing out'? Oh, very different, replied Ruth: you walked around and did and said things which you could not remember afterwards. A peculiar smile, reminiscent, flitted across the assembled faces. . . . It was all right, said Ruth, kindly: Betty used to draw blanks too, when she was younger." Contrast the abdicated sexual voice in this nonfiction memoir of adolescence to the graphic scene of sexual self-discovery and pleasure in the fictionalized account of McCarthy's growing up with her peers, *The Group* (San Diego: Harcourt Brace, 1991 [1963]), 39–48. See also Carol Brightman's superb *Writing Dangerously: Mary McCarthy and Her World* (New York: Clarkson Potter, 1992), especially "Coming of Age in Seattle," 34–46 and "Seduction and Betrayal," 151–73.

xx Barrett Browning: Elizabeth Barrett Browning, *Aurora Leigh and Other Poems*, John Robert Glorney Bolton and Julia Bolton Holloway, eds. (London: Penguin, 1995 [1856]), 33: "Came a morn / I stood upon the brink of twenty years / And looked before and after, as I stood / Woman and artist,—either incomplete, / Both credulous of completion. There I held / The whole creation in my little cup / And smiled with thirsty lips before I drank, / . . . The June was in me . . . And roses reddening where the calyx split. / I felt so young, so strong, so sure of God!"

xx de Beauvoir: Simone de Beauvoir, *Memoirs of a Dutiful Daughter*, James Kirkup, trans. (New York: Harper & Row, 1974 [1958]), 289–91. The clear-eyed and scrupulous Simone de Beauvoir, in her coming-of-age memoirs, reveals her early aversion to sexuality, and stresses, in language that suggests she may have been protesting too much, her attraction to intellectual transcendence of carnal feelings: "Where did these resistances and prohibitions stem from? Is it my Catholic upbringing which has left me with such a fixation on purity that the slightest allusion to fleshly things causes me this indescribable distress? I think of Alain Fournier's Colombe, who drowned herself in a lake before she would sully her purity. . . . Obviously I did not hold that one should languish in perpetual virginity. But I was sure that the wedding-night should be a white mass: true love sublimates the physical embrace, and in the arms of her chosen one the pure young girl is briskly changed into a radiant young woman . . . [yet] sometimes I had been momentarily seized by a physical urge: at the Jockey for example, in the arms of certain dancers . . . but I enjoyed these intoxicating sensations which made me feel in tune with my body; it was curiosity and sensuality that made me want to discover the resources and secrets of my body; I waited without apprehension and even without impatience for the moment when I would become a woman. . . ." Nonetheless, the narrator returns from this acknowledgment of a fairly innocent sensuality to reassert: "I was a soul, a pure disembodied spirit; . . . The advent of sexuality destroyed this angelic concept; it suddenly revealed to me, in all their dreadful unity, sexual appetite and sexual violence . . . if men had bodies that were heavy and racked with lust, the world was not the place I had thought it was." Finally, rather shockingly, in the next sentence, having fully distanced herself from this fallen, lustful "male" state, she associates it with "Poverty, crime, oppression, war: I was afforded confused glimpses of perspectives that terrified me."

xx   Lessing: Doris Lessing, *Martha Quest: A Novel* (New York: HarperPerennial, 1995). See 216–17.

xx   Ker Conway: Jill Ker Conway, *The Road from Coorain* (New York: Vintage, 1990).

xx   Smith: Betty Smith, *A Tree Grows in Brooklyn* (New York: HarperPerennial, 1992 [1943]), 217–19: "She [Francie] crossed out the sentence and rewrote it to read: 'I am curious about sex.' "

xx   *Gone With the Wind*: Margaret Mitchell, *Gone With the Wind* (New York: Warner, 1993 [1936]), 298: ". . . [S]he suddenly thought how nice it was to see a man who was whole. . . . His brown face was bland and his mouth, red lipped, clear cut as a woman's frankly sensual, smiled carelessly as he lifted her into the carriage. The muscles of his big body rippled against his well-tailored clothes, as he got in beside her, and, as always, the sense of his great physical power struck her like a blow. She watched the swell of his powerful shoulders against the cloth with a fascination that was disturbing, a little frightening. His body seemed so tough and hard. . . ."

xx   Rousseau: Jean-Jacques Rousseau, *The Confessions*, J. M. Cohen, trans. (London: Penguin, 1953 [1781]), 108–9: "Soon I . . . learned that dangerous means of cheating Nature, which leads in young men of my temperament to various excesses, that eventually imperil their health, their strength, and sometimes their lives. This vice, which shame and timidity find so convenient, has a particular attraction for lively imaginations. It allows them to dispose, so to speak, of the whole female sex at their will, and to make any beauty who tempts them serve their pleasure without the need of first obtaining her consent. . . . Added to my temptations, too, were the circumstances in which I lived, in the house of a pretty woman, fondling her image in my secret heart, . . . surrounded at night by objects to remind me of her, lying in a bed where I knew she had lain. How much to stimulate me!"

xx   Lawrence: D. H. Lawrence, *Sons and Lovers* (London: Penguin, 1992 [1913]), 294: "though still virgin, the sex instinct . . . now grew particularly strong. Often, as he talked to Clara, came that thickening and quickening of his blood, . . . a new self or new center of consciousness, warning him that sooner or later he would have to ask some woman or another." See also 381–83: "The first kiss on her breast made him pant with fear. The great dread, the great humility, and the awful desire, were nearly too much. . . ."

xx   Hemingway: Ernest Hemingway, *For Whom the Bell Tolls* (New York: Scribner, 1995 [1940]), 70: "As she cried he could feel the rounded, firm-pointed breasts touching through the shirt she wore. . . . Now as they lay all that before had been shielded was unshielded. Where there had been roughness of fabric all was smooth with a smoothness and firm rounded pressing and a long warm coolness, cool outside and warm within, long and light and closely holding, closely held, lonely, hollow-making with contours, happy-making, young and loving and now all warmly smooth with a hollowing, chest-aching, tight-held loneliness that was such that Robert Jordan felt he could not stand it. . . ."

xx   Kerouac: Jack Kerouac, *On the Road* (New York: Penguin, 1991 [1957]). See also Ann Charters, ed., *The Portable Beat Reader* (New York: Penguin, 1992), 11, 17, 25.

xx   Salinger: J. D. Salinger, *The Catcher in the Rye* (Boston: Little, Brown, 1991 [1945]). See 93–98, 145–49.

xx   Roth: Philip Roth, *Goodbye Columbus, and Five Short Stories* (New York: Vintage, 1993 [1959]). See 14, 45–46.

xx   Wolff: Tobias Wolff, *This Boy's Life: A Memoir* (New York: Harper & Row, 1990), 44: "As soon as [Annette Funicello] appeared on the show . . . Taylor would start moaning and Silver would lick the screen with his tongue. 'Come here, baby,' he'd say. 'I've got six inches of piping hot flesh just for you.' We all said that—It was a formality."

xxi   Anne Frank: Anne Frank, *The Diary of a Young Girl: The Definitive Edition*, Otto H. Frank and Mirjam Pressler, eds. (New York: Anchor, 1995 [1947]). See vi.

xxi   "Jennifer's sex diary": Mike Pearl and Michael Shain, "Battle Over Jenny's Diary," *New York Post*, Dec. 5, 1986: 9. Beth Fallon, "Chambers' Defense: Tale of a Cowardly Victim," *New York Post*, Dec. 5, 1986: 9. See also Anne Conover Heller, "Jennifer Levin and Robert Chambers: A Walk with Love and Death," *Mademoiselle*, Jan. 1987: 145–47, 175–76. Other headlines include: "Sex Play 'Got Rough' " and " 'She Raped Me' " (cited in Samuel G. Freedman, "Sexual Politics and a Slaying: Anger at Chambers's Defense," *New York Times*, Dec. 4, 1986: A1; this article quotes Elizabeth M. Schneider, a Brooklyn Law School professor with an expertise in women's rights law, as saying, "Nobody would be the least surprised to find Chambers was sexually active. . . . But the fact that Jennifer Levin was young and appears to have been sexually active added a whole new dimension to the case." See also Mike McAlary and Marianne Arneberg, "Suspect: Death Was Accident During Sexual Tryst in Park," *Newsday,* Aug. 29, 1986: 3; and Kirk Johnson, "Levin Diary Is at Center of Raging Legal Debate," *New York Times,* Dec. 26, 1986: B3. According to Pearl and Shain, Jack Litman, Robert Chambers's lawyer, had asked for the diary and suggested that it contained documentation of her sexual activity; he wanted the diaries, he said, to see " 'whether Jennifer Levin was initially the aggressor in Central Park by utilizing . . . unusual sexual activities against Mr. Chambers.' . . . Litman said the diary may contain the names of others who have had sexual relations with Miss Levin and could testify to her sex practices. Litman claimed the diary 'chronicled the sexual activity of Jennifer Levin' during the last year of her life." Arguing against Litman, the Levin family lawyer said it contained no details of the girl's sexual activity. Litman told the court that Miss Levin had no right to privacy anymore."

xxi   Jennifer Levin: "Jenny Killed in Wild Sex," *New York Post,* cited in Maria Laurino, "Prosecuting Jennifer Levin's Killer," *Ms.,* Sept. 1987: 70–113.

xxi   Patricia Bowman: "That meant that she and her friends liked to drive fast cars, go to parties and skip classes, the friend said." Fox Butterfield with Mary B. W. Tabor, "Woman in Florida Rape Inquiry Fought Adversity and Sought Acceptance," *New York Times,* April 17, 1991: A17.

xxi   Kimba Wood: "According to White House Sources, White House Chief Counsel Bernard Nussbaum had learned from Wood late December 4 that she had trained for five days as a Playboy Club waitress, or 'bunny,' as a joke while studying in London in 1966." "Kimba Wood," *Facts on File Yearbook 1993: The Indexed Record of World Events,* vol. 53 (New York: Facts on File, 1994), 80.

xxiii   *Seventeen* magazine: Abigail Wood, "Young Living," *Seventeen,* June 1970: 140.

xxiii   *The Happy Hooker:* Xaviera Hollander, with Robin Moore and Yvonne Dunleavy, *The Happy Hooker* (New York: Dell, 1972).

xxiii   *The Sensuous Woman:* Terry Garrity, *The Sensuous Woman: The First How-To Book for the Female Who Yearns to Be All Woman,* by "J." (New York: Dell, 1969).

xxiii   Nabokov: Vladimir Nabokov, *Lolita* (New York: Vintage, 1989 [1955]).

xxiii   1960s guides: E.g., Evelyn Millis Duvall, *Love and the Facts of Life* (New York: Association Press, 1963); Rabbi Roland B. Gittelsohn, *Consecrated Unto Me: A Jewish View of Love and Marriage* (New York: Union of American Hebrew Congregations, 1965); The Child Study Association of America, *What to Tell Your Children About Sex,* Adie Suehsdorf, ed. (New York: Permabooks, 1958); The Boston Women's Health Book Collective, *Our Bodies, Ourselves* and *The New Our Bodies, Ourselves* (New York: Simon & Schuster, 1976, 1984).

xxiv   seven ethnic groups: Margaret Mead, *Male and Female: A Study of the Sexes in a Changing World* (New York: Dell, 1962 [1949]). One must note that Mead's observations of sex roles, while still considered classics of comparative gender-role analysis, have been both challenged and, more recently, defended within the anthropological community.

xxiv   She must live in a culture: Margaret Mead, as cited in Alice Kahn Ladas et al., *The G Spot and Other Recent Discoveries About Human Sexuality* (New York: Dell, 1982), 10, 11–12.

xxv   Masters and Johnson: Direct laboratory observation of more than 10,000 episodes of sexual activity in 382 women and 312 men first appeared in their landmark work *Human Sexual Response* (New York: Little, Brown, 1966). For a textbook summary of their research, see William H. Masters, Virginia Johnson, and Robert C. Kolodny, *Human Sexuality* (New York: HarperCollins, 1992).

xxv   Kinsey: Alfred C. Kinsey, Wardell B. Pomeroy, Clyde E. Martin, and Paul H. Gebhard, *Sexual Behavior in the Human Female* (Philadelphia: W. B. Saunders and Co., 1953), 510–759.

xxv   ". . . The End": For this approach I was inspired by the opening argument in Michel Foucault, *The History of Sexuality: An Introduction, Part One*, Robert Hurley, trans. (New York: Vintage, 1990). See "The Repressive Hypothesis," 15–50. To make his argument against the received story of Victorian repression, he first sets it out, then sets out to dismantle it.

xxv   *Story of O*: Pauline Reage, *Story of O* (New York: Grove Press, 1978).

xxvi   anatomists and sex educators: See Mary Jane Sherfey, *The Nature and Evolution of Female Sexuality* (New York: Random House, 1972). In human females, she claims, "a potentially . . . inordinately high sexual drive and orgasmic capacity existing in primate females continues to exist in women . . . the suppression by cultural forces of women's inordinately high sexual drive and orgasmic capacity must have been an important prerequisite for the evolution of modern human societies and has continued, of necessity, to be a major preoccupation of practically every civilization" (52). Masters and Johnson's *Human Sexuality* cites a study by Waterman and Chiauzzi (1982) that found that consistent orgasm was more correlated to sexual happiness in women than it was in men (Masters, Johnson, and Kolodny, 83). See also Alice Kahn Ladas et al.

xxvi   women's capacity for pleasure . . .: For discussions of various cultures that hold that women are far more sexual than men, and constrain women accordingly, see Geraldine Brooks, *Nine Parts of Desire: The Hidden World of Islamic Women* (New York: Anchor, 1995); Lynn Bennett, *Dangerous Wives and Sacred Sisters: Social and Symbolic Roles of High-Caste Women in Nepal* (New York: Columbia University Press, 1983), 239–41; and Alice Walker and Pratibha Parmar, *Warrior Marks: Female Genital Mutilation and the Sexual Blinding of Women* (San Diego: Harvest Books, 1996).

xxvi   women's presumed carnality: From Heinrich Kramer and Jakob
        Sprenger, *The Malleus Maleficarum* (New York: Dover, 1971 [1486]),
        cited in Selma R. Williams and Pamela Williams Adelman, *Riding the
        Nightmare: Women and Witchcraft from the Old World to Colonial Salem* (New
        York: HarperPerennial, 1992), 39. See also "From Heresy to Witch-
        craft" in Sarah Dening, *The Mythology of Sex: An Illustrated Exploration of
        Sexual Customs and Practices from Ancient Times to the Present* (New York:
        Macmillian, 1996), 160–69.

xxviii "real toads in imaginary gardens": Marianne Moore, "Poetry" in *Collected
        Poems*, with an Introduction by T. S. Eliot (Franklin Center, Pa.: The
        Franklin Library, 1981), 38.

xxviii "tell all the Truth—but tell it Slant—": Emily Dickinson, "Poem 1129"
        in Richard Ellman and Robert O'Clair, eds., *The Norton Anthology of Mod-
        ern Poetry*, Second Edition (New York: Norton, 1988), 22.

1. *The Time and the Place:* 1968–1971

8   Donner Pass: Harry Hansen, ed., *California: A Guide to the Golden State*,
     American Guide Series (New York: Hastings House, 1967), 564–65.

8   *Golden Hind:* Thomas William Edgar Roche, *The Golden Hind* (New York
     and Washington: Praeger Publishers, 1973), 148.

8   "the Big One": William Bronson, *The Earth Shook, the Sky Burned* (Garden
     City: Doubleday, 1959).

13   post-Victorian sense of childhood: For documentation of the "inven-
     tion" of childhood as a time of innocence, see Ann Douglas, *The Femi-
     nization of American Culture* (New York: Knopf, 1977).

3. *Activity into Passivity: Blanking Out*

27   Carol Gilligan: Lyn Mikel Brown and Carol Gilligan, *Meeting at the Cross-
     roads: Women's Psychology and Girls' Development* (Cambridge, Mass.: Har-
     vard University Press, 1992).

27   Fawn: Lewis Carroll, *Alice in Wonderland and Through the Looking Glass*
     (New York: Quality Paperback Book Club, 1994 [1865, 1871]), 220.

4. *Free Flight to House Arrest: Slowing Down*

30   Maggie Tulliver: George Eliot, *The Mill on the Floss* (Oxford: Oxford
     University Press, 1980 [1880]).

30   Catherine: Emily Bronte, *Wuthering Heights* (Middlesex, U.K.: Penguin,
     1965 [1847]).

33   An extraordinary number: See Alfred C. Kinsey, Wardell B. Pomeroy,
     Clyde E. Martin, and Paul H. Gebhard, *Sexual Behavior in the Human*

Female (Philadelphia: W. B. Saunders, 1953), cited in John Crewdson, *By Silence Betrayed: Sexual Abuse of Children in America* (Boston: Little, Brown, 1988), 25.

5. Nakedness: Pride and Shame

35   "So you see": Kimberly-Clark, "The Miracle of You," The Life Cycle Library (Neehah, Wis.: Life Cycle Center Kotex Products, Kimberly-Clark Corporation, 1968, 1973). This material was in use from the late 1960s to the late 1970s, according to a Kimberly-Clark spokeswoman, Nancy Lee Carter, trademark counsel. "There were not many sources of such information available, and it's likely the older materials were used for many girls during the 1970s," she writes. Most public schools could not afford the new materials coming out, so they made use of the Kimberly-Clark materials, which were provided at no cost or at very low cost to schools. Indeed, this was true of my middle school; I recognized the Life Cycle Library, with its coy illustrations, from my own sex education classes in eighth grade.

35   "feelings of shame": Peggy Orenstein's superb chapter, "Fear of Falling: Sluts," in her book *Schoolgirls: Young Women, Self-Esteem and the Confidence Gap* (New York: Anchor, 1995, 52–66), makes the connection between the fear of being a "slut," the imposition of sexual shame, the absence of a female "discourse of desire" in sex education classes, and faulty protection from pregnancy and STDs.

35   During the 1970s: "Proliferation and Distribution of Sexually Explicit Materials," *Final Report of the Attorney General's Commission on Pornography* (Nashville: Rutledge Hill Press, 1986), 345.

35   Anne Frank: Anne Frank, *The Diary of a Young Girl: The Definitive Edition*, Otto H. Frank and Mirjam Pressler, eds. (New York: Anchor, 1995 [1947]). "Once when Father and I were talking about sex, he said I was too young to understand that kind of desire. But I thought I did understand it, and now I'm sure I do. Nothing is as dear to me now as my darling Peter! . . . Think of me, my dearest Peter!" 166–67.

48   At the turn of the twentieth century: cited in Edward Brecher, *The Sex Researchers* (San Francisco: Specific Press, 1969), 5–6. For a condensed version of Ellis's seven-volume *Studies in the Psychology of Sex*, see Havelock Ellis, *Psychology of Sex: A Manual for Students* (New York: Ray Long and Richard Smith, Inc., 1933).

48   Fifth-century Alexandrian women: Clement of Alexandria in Brecher, 6, citing Ellis.

48   "the sight of complete nakedness": Brecher, 6, citing Ellis.

48   In the early Middle Ages: G. Rattray Taylor, *Sex in History* (New York: Vanguard Press, 1954), 26.

48   One traveler in Ireland: Brecher, 8, citing Ellis.

48 At about the same time in Venice: Brecher, 8.

48 This style so charmed: Brecher, 8, citing Ellis.

6. *Girlfriends*

53 Duvall: Evelyn Millis Duvall, *Love and the Facts of Life* (New York: Association Press, 1963), 34–35.

54 Sappho: Fragment 8, in Diane J. Rayor, trans., *Sappho's Lyre: Archaic Lyric and Women Poets of Ancient Greece* (Berkeley: University of California Press, 1991), 57.

55 *"Whenever I look"*: Raynor, 57.

7. *Sluts*

64 Orenstein: Peggy Orenstein, with the Americam Association of University Women, *Schoolgirls: Young Girls, Self-Esteem and the Confidence Gap* (New York: Anchor, 1995), 51–56.

70 *The Sensuous Woman*: Terry Garrity, *The Sensuous Woman: The First How-To Book for the Female Who Yearns to Be All Woman*, by "J." (New York: Dell, 1969).

73 Some theorists: Riane Eisler, *The Chalice and the Blade: Our History, Our Future* (New York: HarperCollins, 1987), cf. 7, 19, 44; Marija Gimbutas, *The Language of the Goddess* (San Francisco: Harper & Row, 1989), 139.

73 the reign of the Great Mother: Sarah Dening, *The Mythology of Sex: An Illustrated Exploration of Sexual Customs and Practices from Ancient Times to the Present* (New York: Macmillan, 1996), 9.

73 2500 B.C.E.: Dening, 9.

73 the patriarchy: Reay Tannahill, *Sex in History* (Chelsea, Md.: Scarborough House, 1992), 51.

73 "subsidiary to husbands": Tannahill, 54.

73 In Sumer: Dening, 9.

73 Enkidu: David Ferry, trans., *Gilgamesh: A New Rendering in English Verse* (New York: Farrar, Straus and Giroux, 1992), iii–iv, 6–7.

74 Herodotus: See Herodotus, *Book One: The Histories*, Aubrey de Selincourt, trans. (New York: Penguin, 1996 [1954]), 79.

74 Strabo . . . "excised": Tannahill, 68.

74 legacy of joy: Dening, 128.

74 "The usual remedy": Merrill Frederick Unger, *Unger's Bible Dictionary* (Chicago: Moody Press, 1961), 24; for an alternative tradition, which stresses the divine nature of sexual pleasure, female as well as male, within marriage, see *Zohar: Book of Splendor*, Gershom Scholem, ed. (New York: Schocken Books, 1949), 34–37.

75 Male unfaithfulness: Cf. also Unger, 24. For an overview of the origin and development of the Judeo-Christian sexual ethic, see Richard

Lewinsohn, *A History of Sexual Customs*, Alexander Mayce, trans. (New York: Harper & Brothers, 1958), 1–102, 151–72.

75 Rome maintained a cadre: Sarah Pomeroy, *Goddesses, Whores, Wives and Slaves* (New York: Schocken Books, 1995), 210.

76 pool-table rape: Peggy Reeves Sanday, *A Woman Scorned: Acquaintance Rape on Trial* (New York: Doubleday, 1996), 42: "Tommy [a defendant] testified that Angela had to be carried out of the room because she couldn't walk on her own, and others noted that her eyes were rolling back into her head."

76 Nicole Brown Simpson "drank excessively": William Claiborne, "Nicole Simpson's Character Attacked," *Washington Post*, Oct. 25, 1996, A3.

76 "As long as Angela": Sanday, 29, 31, 33.

76 ground for divorce in . . . Rome: Tannahil, 123. Also see Aline Rousselle, "The Family Under the Roman Empire: Signs and Gestures," in *A History of the Family: Volume I: Distant Worlds, Ancient Worlds*, Andre Burguière, Christiane Klapisch-Zuber, Martine Segalen, and Françoise Zonabend, eds., introduction by Claude Lévi-Strauss and Georges Duby (Cambridge, Mass.: Harvard University Press, 1996): "A woman's sexuality was thus under her father's control in the first instance, and then under her husband's. . . . [A]ll other women [than daughters or wives of citizens] . . . were available to [the Roman paterfamilias] without any legal sanctions, that is, without the risk of being accused of adultery or depravity and losing his property if not his life. . . . The paterfamilias could also demand sexual services from his slaves or even his freed slaves. . . . Freedwomen were prevented from making complaints about their patron," 293–94.

76 "perverse and disgusting conduct": Tannahil, 107.

76 Chesler: Phyllis Chesler, *Mothers on Trial: The Battle for Children and Custody* (San Diego: Harvest, 1986).

76 seen as "unfit": Chesler, 82.

77 "Two lesbian mothers": Chesler, 115.

77 female licentiousness: Tannahill, 123. See also Rousselle, 293–94.

77 imperial times: Tannahill, 123.

77 Tacitus: Tacitus, *Annals*. 2. 85, cited in Pomeroy, 212.

77 Simpson: William Claiborne.

77 Roman law: Tannahill, 107; see also, as precursor to the Roman system, the Greek influence on the Roman view of virginity in Giulia Sissa, *Greek Virginity* (Cambridge, Mass.: Harvard University Press, 1990), 105–9. For a full explanation of Roman sexual power relations, see Rousselle, 271–309. See also Pomeroy, 159–60, 210: "Augustus declared adultery a public offense only in women. Consistent with the powers of the paterfamilias, the father of the adulteress was permitted to kill her if she had not been emancipated from his power," Pomeroy, citing Ulpian, *Digest*, 48.5.21 (20). Female slaves in the Roman Empire

did not even have the sanction of this double standard in relation to marriage; until the third century, they could not marry and lived in a state of unregulated promiscuity. See also Paul Veyne, ed., Philippe Ariès and Georges Duby, general eds., *A History of Private Life: From Pagan Rome to Byzantium* (Cambridge, Mass.: Harvard University Press, 1992), 33, 139. However, wealthy widows "enjoyed the best fate Rome had to offer the female sex. Their lovers had to take pains to please them in bed, to the dismay of Seneca and Martial" (76).

78   worship of Bacchus: Tannahill, 125.

78   community at large: Tannahill, 119. See also, Veyne et al., 118; and Dening, 78–80. For more on the salacious reputation of the female-dominated cults, see the satirist Juvenal, cited in Pomeroy, 205: "My god! the sacred mysteries of the special Goddess of Women are no longer secret! Women get all stirred up with wine and wild music; they drive themselves crazy; they shriek and writhe—worshippers of Phallus. And sex. They moan, they quiver with lust; there's a steady stream running down their legs. . . . Their lust can't wait; they drop their pretenses; the temple rings with the cry, 'Bring on the men.' "

78   The early Church: For a detailed discussion of how asceticism and an aversion to female sexuality became aligned with the early Christian tradition, see Uta Ranke-Heinemann, *Eunuchs for the Kingdom of Heaven: Women, Sexuality and the Catholic Church* (New York: Penguin, 1991), 125–45. For elucidation of the Pauline relationship to physicality and its influence on the Western tradition, see Phillipe Ariès, "St. Paul and the Flesh," in *Western Sexuality: Practise and Precept in Past and Present Times*, Philippe Ariès and Andre Bejin, eds. (Oxford: Basil Blackwell, 1987), 36–40; for a discussion of the cultural evolution of the idea of unchastity, see Michel Foucault, "The Battle for Chastity," in Ariès and Bejin, 14–26.

78   Latin term for passion: Michel Rouche, "The Early Middle Ages in the West: Violence and Death" in Veyne et al., 481.

79   Eighth-century penitentials: Rouche, 497.

79   "Women blamed . . .": Rouche, 483. For a more detailed discussion of family life in Europe from the time of the Germanic and Romano-barbarian peoples until the conquest of the Saxons by Charlemagne, see Pierre Guichard and Jean-Pierre Cuvillier, "Barbarian Europe," especially the section, "Germanic and Romano-barbarian Peoples in the Age of the Laws," in Burguière et al., 347–72.

79   "burning with hot desire": Rouche, 481.

79   Merovingians: Rouche, 466, 467.

79   decree of Clotaire II: Rouche, 467.

79   Visigoth Code: Veyne et al., 469. Veyne cites Tacitus (in *Germania*, 19), noting that among first-century Germans, a wife's adultery is punished by her husband driving her, naked and with her hair shorn, in the presence of relatives, out of the house with a whip.

79   "overcome by desire": Rouche, 481.

80   "a corrupted woman had no further value": Rouche, 469.

80   During the early Middle Ages: Rouche, 471. See also Guichard and Cuvillier, "The History and Anthropology of 'Obscure Centuries' of the Family in Western Societies," in Burguière et al., 319.

80   "stench of adultery": Rouche, 471.

80   Among Gallo-Romans: Rouche, 471

82   Fourteen-year-old German girl: Rouche, 472.

9. Second Base: Love and Control

87   "For to him": Jack Kerouac, On the Road (New York: Penguin, 1991 [1957]), 17, 25.

95   Dr. Amy Holtzworth-Munroe: Cited in Daniel Goleman, "Standard Therapies May Help Only Impulsive Spouse Abuse," New York Times, June 22, 1994: C11. In the most definitive study to date of domestic violence in 6,002 households, about 12 percent of couples "will have an incident of at least mild violence by the man, like pushing, shoving or slapping, in any year." In only 3.4 percent is the violence "severely abusive." According to the clinical definition, Ben's violence was slowly intensifying from the former category to the latter.

10. Crash Course: Their Bodies

98   " 'Bend over and take the penis' ": Terry Garrity, The Sensuous Woman: The First How-To Book for the Female Who Yearns to Be All Woman, by "J." (New York: Dell, 1969), 120.

98   " 'Now run your tongue' ": Garrity, 121.

98   " 'Now stretch your mouth' ": Garrity, 120.

11. Third Base: Identity

112   The Demon Lover: Robin Morgan, The Demon Lover: On the Sexuality of Terrorism (New York: Norton, 1990), 55–57. On page 113, Morgan notes that the lineage of the Demon Lover was originally traced by Mario Praz in The Romantic Agony (London: Oxford University Press, 1970). On page 216 she notes, "The combination of promised rewards—from rebellion through respect, charisma, relative freedom and power, requited love, and becoming in his terms nearly human—is one she finds irresistible."

112   Stanley Kowalski: Tenessee Williams, A Streetcar Named Desire (New York: Limited Editions Club, 1982), 185.

113   Susan Griffin and Andrea Dworkin: Susan Griffin, Pornography and Silence: Culture's Revenge Against Nature (New York: Harper & Row, 1981); Andrea Dworkin, Pornography: Men Possessing Women (New York: E.P. Dutton, 1989), and Intercourse (New York: Free Press, 1987).

12. Fourth Base: How to Make a Woman

118   *Edward the Dyke:* Judy Grahn, *Edward the Dyke and Other Poems* (Oakland, Calif.: Women's Press Collective, 1971).

130   Anthropologists: Margaret Mead, *Male and Female: A Study of the Sexes in a Changing World* (New York: Dell, 1973 [1949]), 166; Bronislaw Malinowski, *The Sexual Life of Savages in North-western Melanesia* (Boston: Beacon Press, 1987 [1932]), 53–59; Mircea Eliade, *Rites and Symbols of Initiation: The Mysteries of Birth and Rebirth*, Willard R. Trask, trans. (Woodstock, Conn.: Spring Publications, 1958); M. F. Ashley-Montagu, *Coming Into Being Among the Australian Aborigines: A Study of the Procreative Beliefs of the Native Tribes of Australia* (London: Routledge, 1976 [1937]); Anne Cameron, *Daughters of Copper Woman* (Vancouver, B.C.: Press Gang Publishers, 1981), 101–3.

130   *quinceañera:* Mary D. Lankford, *Quinceañera: A Latina's Journey to Womanhood* (Brookfield, Conn.: Millbrook Press, 1994).

131   initiation rites: Eliade, 25–28.

131   During the time of living separately: Eliade, 25.

131   parts of Africa: See, for instance, Alice Walker and Pratibha Parmar, *Warrior Marks: Female Genital Mutilation and the Sexual Blinding of Women* (San Diego: Harvest Books, 1996), 320–21.

131   northern Australia: Eliade, citing Berndt, 43.

132–33 "[A]nd every day": Cameron, 101–3.

134   de Beauvoir: Simone de Beauvoir, *The Second Sex*, H. M. Parshley, trans. (Middlesex, U.K.: Penguin, 1986 [1949]), 770.

135   Historians and anthropologists: See, for instance, Eva Cantarella, *Pandora's Daughters: The Role and Status of Women in Greek and Roman Antiquity* (Baltimore: Johns Hopkins University Press, 1987), 21. "So-called primitive societies have rites that mark an individual's entrance into a group and determine his or her position in it. . . . The rites represent an essential moment in the life of the individual, the moment that symbolizes and brings about access to the knowledge of the collectivity, the awareness of being part of it, and the corresponding certainty that whoever is not a part of it is different" (21). Cantarella notes that in Spartan female initiation rites girls moved from the protection of Artemis to that of Helen "to whom was entrusted the task of making them into women in her image" (21). In Athens, during the fifth century B.C.E., there were still traces of the ancient girls' initiation rituals that included symbolic death and resurrection and involved participation in "an orgiastic festival," after which they were "finally ready to enter the ranks of adult women."

135–36 One long-term study: Sharon Thompson, "Putting a Big Thing Into a Little Hole: Teenage Girls' Accounts of Sexual Initiation," *Journal of Sex Research* 27, no. 3 (August 1990): 341–61. For another compilation of women's accounts of losing their virginity, see Karen Bouris, *The First*

Time: Women Speak Out About "Losing Their Virginity" (Berkeley: Conari Press, 1993).

136   alcohol is a factor: Brooke A. Masters, "Women Drinking Like Men, College Alcohol Study Finds; Number Intent on Getting Intoxicated Soars," *Washington Post*, June 8, 1994: A1. See also Peggy Reeves Sanday, *A Woman Scorned: Acquaintance Rape on Trial* (New York: Doubleday, 1996), 33.

137   according to . . . the Alan Guttmacher Institute: *Facts in Brief: Teen Sex and Pregnancy* (New York: Alan Guttmacher Institute, 1996), 18. Sources of data: AGI report *Sex and American Teenagers*, citing the Centers for Disease Control and the National Center for Health Statistics, 1994, and *The Journal of Family Planning Perspectives,* 1994.

137   "It ain't easy": Cameron, 101.

13. Skipped Homework: Our Bodies

139   Indeed, today . . . : The Alan Guttmacher Institute, "Teen Sex and Pregnancy," *Trends in Adolescent Sexuality and Fertility* (New York: Alan Guttmacher Institute, 1994), 50–51. Current population surveys, the National Survey of Family Growth, and the Kantner-Zelnick surveys, Forrest (1986) estimates that 43 percent of all adolescent girls, regardless of marital status, will become pregnant at least once before their twentieth birthday (40 percent of white teenagers and 63 percent of black teenagers); 23.9 percent of these will become pregnant by 18 (derived from national surveys, vital statistics, and U.S. Census data).

139   Thanks to *Our Bodies, Ourselves:* The Boston Women's Health Book Collective, *The New Our Bodies, Ourselves: A Book by and for Women* (New York: Simon & Schuster, 1984 [1973]); Terry Garrity, *The Sensuous Woman*, by "J." (New York: Dell, 1969); Shere Hite, *The Hite Report* (New York: Macmillan, 1976).

141   "You have probably discovered": Kimberly-Clark, "Bodies Interest Everyone" in "The Miracle of You," The Life Cycle Library (Neehah, Wis.: Life Cycle Center Kotex Products, Kimberly-Clark Corporation, 1973).

142   "It is important to acknowledge": Kimberly-Clark, "Your Years of Self-discovery."

142   "at the onset of adolescence": Alfred C. Kinsey, Wardell B. Pomeroy, Clyde E. Martin, and Paul H. Gebhard, *Sexual Behavior in the Human Female* (Philadelphia: W. B. Saunders, 1953), 729.

143   "a structure": *From Fiction to Fact: Teacher's Guide* (Tambrands, 1973).

143   "a small organ": Kimberly-Clark, "Your Years of Self-discovery."

143   version now current: Kimberly-Clark, "Julie's Story," The Life Cycle Library (1983).

143–53 Lost and Found: Thomas Laqueur, *Making Sex: Body and Gender from the Greeks to Freud* (Cambridge, Mass.: Harvard University Press, 1990).

143   "preeminently the seat": Renaldus Columbus, *De Re Anatomica* (Venice, 1559), 11.16, 447–896; in Laqueur, 64–66.

144   Jane Sharp: Jane Sharp, *The Midwives Book, Or the Whole Art of Midwifery Discovered Directing Childbearing Women How to Behave Themselves in Their Conception, Breeding, Bearing and Nursing Children* (London, 1671), 40; in Laqueur, 65.

144   Caspar Bartholin: Laqueur, 92.

144   Regner de Graaf: Laqueur, 182.

144   William Cowper: Laqueur, 160.

144   seventeenth-century French obstetrician: Laqueur, 239.

144   Princess Maria Theresa: Laqueur, 150.

145   Albrecht von Haller: Laqueur, 183.

145   Other historians: Linda Gordon, *Woman's Body, Woman's Right: Birth Control in America* (New York: Penguin, 1990), 15, 16.

146   The new ideology: Gordon, 21–22. For additional discussions of the rise of the asexual or less-sexual Victorian ideal of womanhood, see also G. J. Barker-Benfield, *The Horrors of the Half-Known Life: Male Attitudes Toward Women and Sexuality in Nineteenth-Century America* (New York: Harper & Row, 1976), chapter 9, "The Rise of Gynecology," and chapter 10, "Architect of The Vagina"; Ellen K. Rothman, *Hands and Hearts, A History of Courtship in America* (Cambridge, Mass.: Harvard University Press, 1984), 41, 186–89; Michael Mason, *The Making of Victorian Sexuality* (New York: Oxford University Press, 1994); and Anne Martin-Fugier, "Bourgeois Rituals," and Alain Corbin, "Intimate Relations," in *A History of Private Life, Volume IV: From the Fires of Revolution to the Great War*, Michelle Perrot, ed., Arthur Goldhammer, trans., Philippe Ariès and Georges Duby, general eds. (Cambridge, Mass.: Harvard University Press, 1990).

146   As a result: Gordon, 22.

146   "In the sexual evolution": Barker-Benfield, 83.

146   standards for this "purity": Gordon, 22.

147   revisionist historians: Peter Gay, *The Tender Passion*, vol. 2 of *The Bourgeois Experience, Victoria to Freud* (New York: Oxford University Press, 1986), 44–96; Steven Marcus, *The Other Victorians: A Study of Sexuality and Pornography in Mid-Nineteenth-Century England* (New York: Basic Books, 1964, 1974); see also Michel Foucault, *The History of Sexuality, An Introduction* (New York: Random House, 1990 [1978]), 37: ". . . [T]his much is certain. . . . The nineteenth century and our own have been . . . the age of multiplication: a dispersion of sexualities, a strengthening of their disparate forms, a multiple implantation of 'perversions.' Our epoch has initiated sexual heterogeneities."

The revisionists have a great deal of support in the historical record. Frederick Hollick, a physician, committed himself to lecturing on female sexuality to women's groups. For this transgression, in 1860, a group of "Medical Old *Fogies*," as he called them, tried to suppress his marriage guide. Some doctors held that contraception gave women such license with their passions as to give them the mentality of prostitutes, and that such women risked developing "uterine disease" unless they managed to attain "an entire absence of orgasm" (Reay Tannahill, *Sex in History* [Chelsea, Md.: Scarborough House, 1992], 408). Some even saw "fallen women" sympathetically, as having been "respectable women driven by thwarted desire" (Mason, 218). A few instruction guides for girls recognize that even teenage virgins cannot be turned away from "the mighty influence" of their sexual passion (indeed, doctors believed that sexual stimulation brings on female puberty). These guides even sometimes advocated that marriage not be delayed too much beyond those lusting teenage years, so that this "powerful engine" not be treated dangerously casually. Even spiritualized marriage manuals spoke of the "hurry and throb of Man's and Woman's hearts . . . not because of their hurry and throb impure" (Mason, 219). Some medical textbooks asserted that female desire was so intense that it could trigger an orgasm just from the sensation of blood flowing during menstruation, or from hearing a lover's voice, or from a touch to the cervix. Some wondered whether female orgasm was caused by the sensation of being bathed internally by semen. Others still renewed the old discussion of which sex had more pleasure during intercourse. Many commentators held (as did the Taoists) that overindulgence in sexual pleasure was far less harmful to women than it was to men, whereas celibacy was debilitating to women but more salubrious for men.

Fashion gives a hint that women themselves had drawn closer to their own sexuality by the 1880s as a consequence of contraception. For the first time, nightgowns became attractive rather than almost deliberately repellant. The same women who once would have been relieved by their husbands' reliance on prostitutes now found they wished to compete with those prostitutes for their husbands' interest (Tannahill, 411).

In 1892, Clelia Duel Mosher actually decided to ask women about the pleasure they felt, or did not feel. Mores had loosened enough to permit this revolutionary research to take place. What she found is intriguing to modern eyes, for it revealed—at least as far as self-reporting among a select group of women went—that sexual satisfaction actually may have been higher among turn-of-the-century women than it is today: 80 percent of Mosher's respondents said that they had orgasms (Ellen Chesler, *Woman of Valor: Margaret Sanger and the Birth Control Movement in America* [New York: Simon & Schuster, 1992], 37, 71).

But the depressing state of sexual tension that most women of the time would have lived in is evident. Most of these orgasmic women were very ambivalent about having sex and were relieved to be spared their husbands' approaches. From Mosher's work we get a glimpse of the

terrible contradiction in the sexual experience of women before contraception became reliable: a woman would have desire, know pleasure,
and experience gratification—and still fear intercourse, with its risks of
pregnancy and childbirth (Martha Vicinus, ed., *Suffer and Be Still: Women
in the Victorian Age* [Bloomington: Indiana University Press, 1973]).

147   Good wives: Phyllis Rose, *Parallel Lives: Five Victorian Marriages* (New
York: Vintage, 1983), 66.

147   "defined normal sexual intercourse": Gordon, 22–23.

148   Dr. William Acton: Peter Cominos, "Innocent Femina Sensualis in
Unconscious Conflict," in Vincinus, 83. For the rise of moralism about
female sexuality codified within the emerging field of male-dominated
nineteenth-century gynecology, see also Barker-Benfield, 82–90: in this
period, "woman's nervous complaints [were] regarded as the result of
her sexual transgressions."

148   *The Westminster Review:* Cited in E. M. Sigsworth and T. J. Wyke, "A
Study of Victorian Prostitution and Venereal Disease," in Vicinus,
77–99.

148   "Literally every woman": Henry Mayhew, *London Labour and the London
Poor*, IV (London: 1861), 213.

148   Peter Cominos: Peter Cominos, in Vicinus, 164. See also Carl N.
Degler, "What Ought to Be and What Was: Women's Sexuality in the
Nineteenth Century," *American Historical Review* 79, 5 (December 1974):
1467–91.

149   An 1836 Handbook: Laqueur, 189. For more information on contemporary popular literature regarding expectations of female sexual desire
(or the lack of it), see also Michael Gordon, *From an Unfortunate Necessity
to a Cult of Mutual Orgasm: Sex in American Marital Education Literature,
1830–1940* (New York: Jones M. Hensling, 1978), 53–77.

149   Richard von Krafft-Ebing: "If [a woman] is normally developed mentally . . ." Cited in Edward Brecher, *The Sex Researchers* (San Francisco:
Specific Press, 1969), 59.

149   "Every woman has": Henry Havelock Ellis, *Psychology of Sex: A Manual
for Students* (New York: Ray Long and Richard Smith, Inc., 1933), 30.

150   "the unbridled impulse": Cited in Brecher, 149.

150   Sigmund Freud's contribution: *Three Essays on the Theory of Sexuality* (London: Hogarth Press, 1925 [1905]); "Some Psychological Consequences
of the Anatomical Distinction Between the Sexes," in *A General Introduction to Psychoanalysis* (Garden City, N.Y.: Garden City Publishing,
1943); "Formulations Regarding Two Principles in Mental Function-
ing," in *Selected Papers*, 4:13–21 (London: Hogarth Press, 1946); "The
Differentiation Between Men and Women," 287 ff., in *The Freud Reader*,
Peter Gay, ed. (New York: Norton, 1989), 1995.

151   "Few clients": Hannah Stone and Abraham Stone, *Marriage Manual*
(New York: Simon & Schuster, 1935), 219, 269–70. See also Ellen

Chesler, *Woman of Valor: Margaret Sanger and the Birth Control Movement in America* (New York: Simon & Schuster, 1992), 304–5. See also M. J. Exner, *The Sexual Side of Marriage* (New York: Norton, 1932) and T. H. van de Velde, *Ideal Marriage* (Chicago: Pascal Covici, 1931).

151 *Married Love:* Dr. Marie Carmichael Stopes, *Married Love* (New York: Eugenics Publishing Co., 1918, 1927), 54, 55.

151 Almost seventy years later: Sally Tisdale, "Talk Dirty to Me: A Woman's Taste for Pornography," *Harper's*, Feb. 1992: 37–46.

151–52 The supreme law: Stopes, 82–85.

152 Dutch gynecologist: Michael Gordon, in his survey of marital sex literature from the nineteenth to the twentieth centuries, notes that during the first two decades of this century, marital sex manuals showed "an increased emphasis on the woman's right to sexual satisfaction (read: her right to experience orgasm)." He points out that by the 1930s, manuals focused on discussions of sexual techniques directed at pleasing women. He cites Wilfrid Lay, *A Plea for Monogamy* (New York: Boni and Liveright, 1923), 155; Don Cabot McCowwan, *Love and Life* (Chicago: Pascal Covici, 1928), 168; and Thurman B. Rice, *The Age of Romance* (Chicago: American Medical Association, 1933), 35, to this effect, and identifies van de Velde's *Ideal Marriage* as being typical of this genre and characteristic in conveying this message. Then, he demonstrates, "we find in the 1930s a spate of publications (Stone and Stone, Hutton, etc.) which are similarly committed to foreplay and technique" (73).

Michael Gordon's conclusion is that the literature shows that sex went from being "a pariah topic to a virtual preoccupation" in the decades he has studied, and that one sign of this evolution is the heightened attention given to the validity and requirements of female sexuality, a change which he ascribes to women's increased participation in the workforce.

152 "maraichinage": Cited in Brecher 91, 95.

153 "A wife who allows": Helena Wright, *The Sex Factor in Marriage* (New York: Vanguard Press, 1931).

153 "small round body": Wright, 67.

153 "Arrange a good light": Wright (1947 edition), cited in Brecher, 181–83.

154 "Many, many women": Stopes, 54.

154 "Women," she wrote: Hite, 11.

14. More Skipped Homework: Our Pleasure

158 Masters and Johnson: Cited in Mary Jane Sherfey, *The Nature and Evolution of Female Sexuality* (New York: Random House, 1972), 109.

158 "the labia minora": Kinsey et al., 591–92.

158   "The more orgasms": Sherfey, 112; for discussions of the role of tumescence in female desire, see also William H. Masters, Virginia Johnson, and Robert C. Kolodny, *Human Sexuality* (New York: HarperCollins, 1992), 71, and Alfred C. Kinsey, Wardell B. Pomeroy, Clyde E. Martin, and Paul H. Gebhard, *Sexual Behavior in the Human Female* (Philadelphia: W. B. Saunders, 1953), 604.

158   "erotic network": Sherfey, 94.

159   Dr. Sherfey maintains: "The sexuality of primate females shows four characteristics closely related to their androgen responsivity. The first is the remarkable evolution of the clitoral system in conjunction with the evolution of the vagina. Secondly, the evolution of the single pair of pectoral mammae occurred concomitantly with the evolution of diverse skin secondary sexual characteristics and the development of the intense skin erotism. (The biologists do not seem to appreciate that the mutual grooming so important in the evolution of primate social life is based on their skin erotism) . . ." (51). For more evidence from evolutionary biology about the Darwinian importance of female desire, see Mary Batten, *Sexual Strategies: How Females Choose Their Mates* (New York: Putnam, 1992), 21–59. Among the four characteristics of female desire among various species, one constant theme is "selection of males for aesthetic traits" (Batten, 26). Other qualities that females find attractive include aesthetically novel characteristics, protectiveness, and deep voices.

159   Some theorists: Elaine Morgan, *The Descent of Woman* (New York: Bantam, 1972,1979), 119.

159–60 "The human female": Helen E. Fisher, *The Sex Contract: The Evolution of Human Behavior* (New York: William Morrow, 1982), 24, 31.

160   Still another theorist: David Buss, *The Evolution of Desire* (New York: Basic Books, 1994).

160   evolutionary boon: "The hormonal combinations producing the anatomical features which create the strongest, most prolonged sexual drive and highest capacity for sexual pleasure are the same hormonal combinations which produce the greatest fertility, the fewest abortions, the most viable offspring, and the healthiest animals. These are the females most dominant in the female social hierarchy among primates" (Sherfey, 52).

160   Leitenberg and Henning: Harold Leitenberg and Kris Henning, "Sexual Fantasy," *Psychological Bulletin* 117, 3 (1995): 469–96.

161   Ellis and Symons: Cited in Leitenberg and Henning.

161   Knoth et al.: Cited in Leitenberg and Henning.

161   Sue: Cited in Leitenberg and Henning.

161   Cado and Leitenberg: Cited in Leitenberg and Henning.

161   Carlson and Coleman: Cited in Leitenberg and Henning.

161   One 1990 study: J. C. Jones and D. H. Barlow, cited in Leitenberg and Henning.

15. Babies

163   The cost to society: *Kids Having Kids: A Robin Hood Foundation Special Report on the Costs of Adolescent Childbearing*, Rebecca A. Maynard, ed. (New York: The Robin Hood Foundation, 1996), 20.

165   For the belief: Thomas Laqueur, *Making Sex: Body and Gender from the Greeks to Freud* (Cambridge, Mass.: Harvard University Press, 1990), 3.

165   Aristotle knew: Laqueur, 48.

166   Pliny's recipe: Reay Tannahill, *Sex in History* (Chelsea, Md.: Scarborough House, 1992), 128. See also Linda Gordon's list of contraceptives in history, which includes rock salt, oil, tannic acid, tampons of lint soaked with honey and acacia, pessaries made of algae, seaweed, bamboo fiber, wool, linen, sea sponges, and okralike seed pods in Linda Gordon, *Woman's Body, Woman's Right: Birth Control in America* (New York: Penguin, 1990), 42–45.

166   "a specifically sexual itch": Cited in Laqueur, 45.

166   "at their making": Cited in Laqueur, 47. Carl N. Degler ("What Ought to Be and What Was: Women's Sexuality in the Nineteenth Century," *American Historical Review* 79, no. 5 [December 1974]: 1467–91) confirms the prevalence of this belief in the West well into the nineteenth century: "[George H.] Napheys in his popular book of advice for women [*The Physical Life of Woman: or, Advice to Both Sexes* (New York, 1866, 1897)] also alluded to the prevalent idea that conception and pleasure were connected. He said that many people erroneously believed that conception could be known from the 'more than ordinary degree of pleasure' on the part of the woman during the sexual act" (1475). Degler goes on—confirming the dualistic nature of ideologies about female sexuality in the nineteenth century—to comment in a footnote, "This belief, which other writers also speak of, may well have affected some women's attitudes toward orgasm, for if a woman, under this view, could repress pleasure or climax, orgasm could be prevented" (1475).

167   "petting is dynamite": Rabbi Roland B. Gittelsohn, *Consecrated Unto Me: A Jewish View of Love and Marriage* (New York: Union of American Hebrew Congregations, 1965), 174.

167   safe, comfortable level: Gittelsohn, 174.

167   "wide range of activities": Cyril Bibby, *Sex Education: A Guide for Parents, Teachers and Youth Leaders* (New York: Emerson Books, 1946).

167   "petting is nature's preface": Gittelsohn, 174.

168   "how far is enough": Gittelsohn, 174.

168   Another guide: Bibby, 144–45.

168   culture of petting: Ellen K. Rothman, *Hands and Hearts: A History of Courtship in America* (Cambridge, Mass.: Harvard University Press, 1984), 293–96. This is a definitive history of petting in the United States. To see evidence going even further back in the century, see also

Prof. T. W. Shannon, *Ethics of the Unmarried, or Spooning* (Marietta, Ohio: S. A. Mullikin Co., 1913).

This issue of whether teaching petting makes good sense has been addressed in an essay in *The Atlantic Monthly* by Barbara Dafoe Whitehead, "The Failure of Sex Education" (October 1994): 55–77. Whitehead reaches a conclusion opposite to mine. She attacks "Comprehensive Sex Education," a version of sex education, considered radical, which includes "the sexology of masturbation and massage" and stresses "a broad thing called noncoital sex, or, in the argot of advocates, 'sexual expression without risk.' Noncoital sex includes a range of behaviors, from deep kissing to masturbation to mutual masturbation to full body massage" (in other words, petting). She notes that New Jersey parents have shown strong support for this program, which received the "the equivalent of a five-star rating" from SIECUS, the national sex educators' advocacy group. With opprobrium, Whitehead quotes the teaching material on the female genitalia: "Clitoris is a small sensitive part that only girls have, and it sometimes makes you feel good." Whitehead's attack makes note of her view that the sex education program in question is taught in a way that she finds morally relativistic, and she observes that there is no evidence that the "noncoital sex" program teaches kids to postpone intercourse. I would argue that a program promoting petting, taught in combination with a moral framework that stressed responsible choices, may well show a very different outcome than the one she claims.

See also Alain Corbin, on the tolerant attitude toward "petting" of nineteenth-century peasants in France, in "Intimate Relations," in *A History of Private Life, Volume IV: From the Fires of Revolution to the Great War*, Michelle Perrot, ed., Arthur Goldhammer, trans., Philippe Ariès and Georges Duby, general eds. (Cambridge, Mass.: Harvard University Press, 1990), 575: "With approval from their families, young people could then begin to 'make love,' that is, to court. . . . Various means of coping with sexual needs before marriage were employed. Fondling and petting were codified and monitored by the group, in this case not the whole community but the peer group consisting of other youths."

169   "Antioch Rules": See, for instance, Katie Roiphe, *The Morning After: Sex, Fear and Feminism on Campus* (Boston: Little, Brown, 1993), 272. The Antioch rules were unrealistic and excessive in the level of negotiation they required; but it seemed to me that the furor they provoked was about the sense that if sex were made conscious, it would lose its erotic charge.

169   "Every individual in the world": Gittelsohn, 175.

169   "Girls are getting pregnant": Rosann Wisman, Planned Parenthood, during a C-Span abortion panel, held by the Women of Washington, September 1996. The best exploration of girls' reasons for becoming pregnant is Kristin Luker's important *Dubious Conceptions: The Politics of*

Teenage Pregnancy (Cambridge, Mass.: Harvard University Press, 1996), especially the revealing chapter "Why Do They Do It?" (134–74). Luker notes girls' passivity in the face of the "slut's dominion": "In short, the skills a young woman needs in order to use contraception effectively are precisely the skills that society discourages in 'nice girls,' who are expected to be passive, modest, shy, sexually inexperienced (or at least less experienced than their partners) and dedicated to the comfort of others" (148).

170   Solutions from the Right: "How to Help Your Kids Say 'No to Sex' " (Vancouver, B.C.: Focus on the Family, 1994).

16. *Cheap or Precious?*

172   *"This* is the secret": For the Lawrentian manifesto on female desire from the point of view of the woman who was the model for many of Lawrence's observations of feminine eros, see Frieda Lawrence, *Not I, But the Wind* . . . (London: Granada Press, 1983 [1934]).

174   "The Fascination of Decadence": L. Morrow, *Time,* Sept. 10, 1979, 85–86.

180   *"Let us now lock the double door":* Jolan Chang, *The Tao of Love and Sex: The Ancient Chinese Way to Ecstasy* (New York: Penguin, 1991), 15–16. See also Daniel P. Reid, *The Tao of Health, Sex and Longevity* (New York: Fireside, 1989), especially his chapter "Taoist Bedroom Arts." Reid explains that the Taoist rules about sexuality were handed down in China over a period spanning five millennia; "pillow books," he writes, were part of every young marrying couple's trousseau from the third century B.C.E. until 1949, when such texts were prohibited by the communists. The commonplace manuals were called "pillow books" because they were meant to be left open on a pillow while guiding the inexperienced bride and her young husband through the various recommended acts. One of the most revered texts was a dialogue between The Plain Girl and The Yellow Emperor, and subsequently the female literary character was seen by women initiated into new sexual practices as a respected mentor. (The Yellow Emperor, according to *The Classic of the Plain Girl,* a volume that dates from the second or third century B.C.E. but which encodes wisdom that had been part of Chinese lore for over two millennia before it was recorded, was instructed in the Tao of yin and yang by three advisers, all of whom, significantly, were female: the Plain Girl, Su Nu; the Mysterious Girl, Hsuan Nu; and the Rainbow Girl, Tsai Nu [Reid, 2].) Plain Girl's advice includes such wisdom as the following: An "instrument that is wielded roughly and without due consideration for the woman's feelings is not nearly as desirable as one used with careful attention to the woman's responses." Reid notes that "Chinese poets, like Taoist physicians, paid far closer attention to the details of female anatomy than to male, and . . . the focal point of their

attentions was always that mysterious, magical 'one square inch' portal known so fondly as the 'Jade Gate' " (Reid, 315).

181   "passion becomes greatly aroused": Chang, 16.

182   "[sex] was never associated": R. H. van Gulik, *Sexual Life in Ancient China*, rev. ed. (Atlantic Highlands, N.J.: Humanities Press, 1971).

182   "more volatile, more active": Chang, 35.

182   Women's yin essence: Reay Tannahill, *Sex in History* (Chelsea, Md.: Scarborough House, 1992), 170. It must be noted that an unmediated model of Chinese sexual harmony might well be very unappealing to Western men; it involved a form of male continence in which men were encouraged to avoid emission.

183   "the Open Peony Blossom": Tannahill, 171, 175. For more on the woman-valuing rhetoric of the Tao of Loving, see Reid, 313–15: "[C]ervix: inner gate; clitoris: Jade Terrace, Precious Pearl, Seed, Yin Bean; clitoris (frenulum of): Lute Strings; clitoris (prepuce of): Divine Field; cunnilingus: Sipping the Vast Spring; . . . homosexual sex (female): Rubbing Mirrors; labia minor: Wheat Buds, Red Pearls; mons veneris: Sedge Hill; orgasm (female): High Tide, Tide of Yin; . . . urethral orifice (female): Vast Spring; . . . vagina (orifice): Jade Gate, Jade Door, Cinnabar Cave, Child Gate, One Square Inch; vagina (lower vestibule): Little Stream; vagina (middle): Deep Valley, Hidden Place, Path of Yin; vagina (upper): Celestial Palace, Valley of Solitude; vulva (upper): Golden Gulley; vulva (lower): Jade Vein; uterus: Child Palace, Vermilion Chamber." Reid summarizes: "Taoist bedroom arts aim at prolonging as long as possible the 'Ambassador's' visit to the 'Celestial Palace' by teaching the man proper protocol and endowing him with the correct 'credentials' as a lover." See also Gulik; and John Blofield, *Taoism: The Road to Immortality* (Boulder, Colo.: Shambhala, 1978).

183   "once every five days": Tannahill, 184.

183   "(2) He must know how": Chang, 79.

184   Not until the Golden Cleft: Tannahill, 175.

184   "his five organs": Tannahill, 79.

185   "If the man moves": Tannahill, 174.

185   "There are ten indications": Chang, 70–71. For a definition of "The Way," see Lao Tzu, *Tao Te Ching*, D. C. Lau, trans. (London: Penguin, 1963), 5.

186   For the Zuni Indians: Ramon A. Gutierrez, *When Jesus Came, the Corn Mothers Went Away: Marriage, Sexuality, and Power in New Mexico, 1500–1846* (Stanford: Stanford University Press, 1991), 14. It is important to note that these mores were not universal even at this time and in this region. In pre-Conquest Mexico, "Female sexuality . . . was systematically repressed. . . . Woman was considered insatiable, and hence represented a worrying threat to man," writes Carmen Bernand and Serge Gruzinski in "Children of the Apocalypse: The Family in Meso-

America and the Andes," in *A History of the Family, Volume II: The Impact of Modernity*, Andre Burguière, Christiane Klapisch-Zuber, Martine Segalen, and Françoise Zonabend, eds. (Cambridge, Mass.: Harvard University Press, 1996), 161–215; they also note that, while Inca society was more tolerant and female virginity was not especially prized, adultery was punished severely. In the Andes, unmarried girls "took part in collective rites of intoxication accompanied by sexual license." But they caution that the reader must keep in mind that, since the records are based on the reporting of Christianized Indians, the accounts may be blurred either by idealization or by demonization (168–69). For a nuanced discussion of gender roles, sexuality, and the imposition of Hispanic mores on the Americas, see Richard C. Trexler, *Sex and Conquest: Gendered Violence, Political Order, and the European Conquest of the Americas* (Ithaca, N.Y.: Cornell University Press, 1995), 1–38, 82–118.

186   "After feeding": Gutierrez, 17–18.
186   "For a man to enjoy": Gutierrez, 17.
187   Peruvian drinking vessels: Tannahill, 298.
187   According to the colonizers: Gutierrez, 18.
187   The Spanish friars: Gutierrez, 90.
187   "shameful parts": Gutierrez, 210.
187–88 orgiastic fertility rites: Gutierrez, 79.
188   "cloud spirits": Gutierrez, 74.
188   "When the wife is purified": *Zohar: Book of Splendor*, Gershom Scholem, ed. (New York: Schocken, 1949), 35–36.
188   "without it a woman": Geraldine Brooks, *Nine Parts of Desire: The Hidden World of Islamic Women* (New York: Anchor, 1995), 42; see also *The Koran Interpreted*, A. J. Arberry, trans. (New York: Simon & Schuster, 1955, 1996), 60: "Do not retain [women] by force, to transgress; whoever does that has wronged himself."
189   "the lessening of women's sexual pleasure": Brooks, 45.
189   "For Tantra": *Tantra: The Cult of the Feminine* (York Beach, Maine: Andre Van Lysebeth, 1995), 233. See also *Tantra: A Pillow Book*, LOEC (San Francisco and New York: HarperCollins, 1994). This small volume explains clearly for a Western reader the religious philosophy behind the sexual practices of the Tantras: "All Tantras are based on reverence for a dual male-female religious principle. In Hinduism this means the Great Mother goddess and her consort, usually Parvati-Kali and Shiva. The god and goddess are lovers, separate yet ultimately indistinguishable. . . . In their lovemaking, the god and goddess achieve a union that recalls their origin in a single, ineffable oneness which resides outside space and time.

"The goal of the human tantric is to experience that state of primeval oneness. . . . The lover's body is a temple, to be worshipped. It is a sacred place, the home of the spirit. The yoni of the woman is a holy well, fount of life, source of miracles . . ." (Lysebeth, 5).

For the spiritual aspect of sexuality urged upon men as well as women in Tantra, see the prayer *Mantramahodadhi* (1589 C.E.; in Lysebeth, 14): "Up to this moment, whatever was thought, said or done by my mind, tongue, hands, feet and penis, whether in a waking, dreaming or sleeping state, whether pertinent to the spirit, the mind, or the body—I dedicate it utterly and completely to the absolute One." In a world that held this approach to male sexuality, the young woman who was assaulted by the fraternity brothers would surely be safer. For further references to the way Tantra asks men to perceive the Divine within the sexuality of women, see *Mahanirvanatantram* (nineteenth century C.E.; in Lysebeth, 18): "The tantric and his wife should meditate together, seated side by side on their bed. Let him place his left arm about her shoulders and with his right hand invoke the goddess into her body, uttering the appropriate mantras as he touches and blesses her head, her chin, her throat and each of her two breasts. . . ." For Tantra's guidance to men in appreciating women's physical nature, see *Mantramahodadhi* (1589 C.E.; in Lysebeth, 12): "While meditating upon the yoni of a beautiful woman, the adept shall utter the sacred mantra . . . whilst meditating upon the yoni of a woman in her moontime . . . he shall become as captivating as any practitioner of the poetic art"; the Yonitantram teaches, "The devotee who at prayers utters the sacred cry 'yoni, yoni,' is blessed by the goddess and enjoys both pleasure and freedom" (ca. sixteenth century: Lysebeth, 38).

For further readings, see Sunyata Saraswati and Bodhi Avinasha, *Jewel in the Lotus: The Sexual Path to Higher Consciousness* (Taos, N.Mex.: TanTrika International, 1987, 1994); and Philip Rawson, *Tantra: The Indian Cult of Ecstasy* (London: Thames and Hudson, 1993), 16: "Tantra focuses its attention and meditation on the female as the most direct approach to the intuition of truth. It uses many female icons, including lotus-flowers, the strange natural form of the *coco-de-mer* which resembles the female genitals, caves and natural clefts or hollows in stones and trees, downward-pointing triangles, and representational images of the female vulva itself. But most often, it centers it adoration on the image of the Goddess . . . which represents her as a beautiful girl. . . . The Tantrika's mind is continually absorbed in that shining and fascinating image. Every woman appears to him clothed in it. But it is not, for him, the woman who personifies the Goddess, but the Goddess who appears in the woman."

In the *Devimahatmya* (fourth century C.E.; in *Tantra: A Pillow Book*, 46), the story is told of a demon lord who seeks to kidnap and rape a beautiful woman: "So perfect a body, such flawless limbs have never before been seen in this world. Find out who she is and kidnap her, O demon lord." The demon does not realize that the woman in question is in fact the Great Goddess, and he is thwarted. Such stories clearly are parables that include instructions to men never to defile female sexuality because they must never forget that the Divine Feminine inheres in all women.

189–90 "The Tantrist is able": Lysebeth, 245–46.

190 "In Hinduism, sex": Sir Richard Burton and F. F. Arbuthnot, trans., *The Illustrated Kama Sutra, Ananga-Ranga, Perfumed Garden: The Classic Eastern Love Texts* (Rochester, Vt.: Park Street Press, 1987), 10.

190 "A girl forcibly enjoyed": Burton and Arbuthnot, 27.

190 Forcing sex: Tannahill, 213.

190 "Even young maids": Burton and Arbuthnot, 26, 37.

17. Adults

193 " 'There would have been a sultan' ": Vladimir Nabokov, *Lolita* (New York: Vintage, 1989 [1955]), 134.

193 " 'Pubescent Lo swooned' ": Nabokov, 104.

194 girls and adult men . . . apart: Margaret Mead, *Male and Female: A Study of the Sexes in a Changing World* (New York: Dell, 1973 [1949]), 166.

194 two out of three teenage pregnancies: In 1995, the Alan Guttmacher Institute found that two thirds of teen mothers were impregnated by adult males. The legal ramifications are debated in Michelle Oberman and Richard Delgado, "At Issue: Statutory Rape Laws," *American Bar Association Journal* (August 1996) 82: 86–87. Most statutory rape laws only penalize the older partner if there is a two- to five-year age difference involved.

18. A Virus

203 Countee Cullen book: Countee Cullen, *The Lost Zoo* (Englewood Cliffs, N.J.: Silver Burdett Press, 1992).

19. An Hypocrisy

215 "I want to hold you close": Candace Falk, *Love, Anarchy, and Emma Goldman* (New York: Holt, 1984), 217.

216 vulnerable to male sexuality: Phyllis Rose, *Parallel Lives: Five Victorian Marriages* (New York: Vintage, 1983), 124. For a complete exploration of the relationship of first-wave feminism to sexuality, see William Leach, *True Love and Perfect Union: The Feminist Reform of Sex and Society* (Middletown, Conn.: Wesleyan University Press, 1989).

216 "He speaks as if": See Linda Gordon, *Woman's Body, Woman's Right* (New York: Penguin, 1990) for an analysis of first-wave feminist sexual idealism.

217   "weakness in love": Falk, 152, 154. In her famous lecture "Marriage and Love" (1912), Goldman radically linked economic inequality with the issue of female sexual ignorance: "a cause much deeper and by far of greater importance is the complete ignorance on sex matters. It is a conceded fact that woman has been reared as a sex commodity, and yet she is kept in absolute ignorance of the meaning and importance of sex. So long as a girl is not to know how to take care of herself, not to know the function of the most important part of her life, we need not be surprised if she becomes an easy prey to prostitution or any other form of a relationship which degrades her to the position of an object for mere sex gratification" (cited in Falk, 124).

217   Typically enough: Falk, 22.

218   "It is like tearing off my clothes": Falk, xv.

218   "You have opened up the prison gates": Falk, 4.

218   "Do you think that one": Falk, 84.

218   "I was caught": Falk, 68.

218   "the woman, the woman": Falk, 76.

218   "just in the age": Falk, 144.

219   "If ever our correspondence": Falk, 4, 6.

219   "Yes, I am a woman": Falk, 57.

220   "the creative spirit": Falk, 160.

Bibliography

Alan Guttmacher Institute. "Adolescent Sexuality, Pregnancy and Childbearing," *Trends in Adolescent Sexuality and Fertility.* New York: Alan Guttmacher Institute, 1994.

———. *Sex and America's Teenagers.* New York: Alan Guttmacher Institute, 1994.

Allardice, Pamela. *Aphrodisiacs and Love Magic: The Mystic Lure of Love Charms.* New York: Avery Publishing Group, 1989.

Anderson, Elijah. *Sexuality and American Social Policy: Sexuality, Poverty, and the Inner City.* Menlo Park, Calif.: Henry J. Kaiser Family Foundation, 1994.

Arberry, A. J., trans. *The Koran Interpreted.* New York: Simon & Schuster, 1996.

Ariès, Philippe, and Andre Bejin. *Western Sexuality: Practise and Precept in Past and Present Times.* Oxford: Basil Blackwell, Inc., 1987.

Ariès, Philippe, and Georges Duby, general eds. *A History of Private Life.* Vol. 1, *From Pagan Rome to Byzantium.* Edited by Paul Veyne. Vol. 2, *Revelations of the Medieval World.* Edited by Georges Duby. Vol. 3, *Passions of the Renaissance.* Edited by Roger Chartier. Vol. 4, *From the Fires of Revolution to the Great War.* Edited by Michelle Perrot. Cambridge, Mass.: Harvard University Press, 1992.

Aristotle. *The Art of Rhetoric.* Translated by H. C. Lawson-Tancred. London: Penguin, 1991.

Barker-Benfield, G. J. *The Horrors of the Half-Known Life: Male Attitudes Toward Women and Sexuality in Nineteenth-Century America.* New York: Harper & Row, 1976.

Batten, Mary. *Sexual Strategies: How Females Choose Their Mates.* New York: Putnam, 1992.

de Beauvoir, Simone. *The Second Sex.* 1949. Translated by H. M. Parshley. Middlesex, U.K.: Penguin, 1986.

———. *Memoirs of a Dutiful Daughter.* 1958. Translated by James Kirkup. New York: Harper & Row, 1974.

Bennett, Lynn. *Dangerous Wives and Sacred Sisters: Social and Symbolic Ropes of High-Caste Women in Nepal.* New York: Columbia University Press, 1983.

Besserman, Perle, ed. *The Way of the Jewish Mystics.* Boston: Shambhala, 1994.

Bibby, Cyril. *Sex Education: A Guide for Parents, Teachers and Youth Leaders.* New York: Emerson Books, 1946.

Blofeld, John. *Taoism: The Road to Immortality.* Boulder, Colo.: Shambhala, 1978.

Boston Women's Health Book Collective. *Our Bodies, Ourselves.* New York: Simon & Schuster, 1976.

———. *The New Our Bodies, Ourselves.* New York: Simon & Schuster, 1984.

Bouris, Karen. *The First Time: Women Speak Out About "Losing Their Virginity."* Berkeley: Conari Press, 1993.

Brav, Stanley R. *Since Eve: A Sex Ethic Inspired by Hebrew Scripture.* New York: Pagent, 1959.

Brecher, Edward M. *The Sex Researchers.* 1969. Expanded ed. San Francisco: Specific Press, 1979.

Brightman, Carol. *Writing Dangerously: Mary McCarthy and Her World.* New York: Clarkson Potter, 1992.

Bronson, William. *The Earth Shook, the Sky Burned.* Garden City, N.Y.: Doubleday, 1959.

Brontë, Emily. *Wuthering Heights.* 1847. Middlesex, U.K.: Penguin, 1965.

Brooks, Geraldine. *Nine Parts of Desire: The Hidden World of Islamic Women.* New York: Anchor, 1995.

Brown, Lyn Mikel, and Carol Gilligan. *Meeting at the Crossroads: Women's Psychology and Girls' Development.* Cambridge, Mass.: Harvard University Press, 1992.

Browning, Elizabeth Barrett. *Aurora Leigh and Other Poems.* 1856. Edited by John Robert Glorney Bolton and Julia Bolton Hollaway. London: Penguin, 1995.

Burguirère, Andre, Christiane Klapisch-Zuber, Martine Segalen, and Françoise Zonabend, eds. *A History of the Family.* Vol. 1, *Distant Worlds, Ancient Worlds.* Vol. 2, *The Impact of Modernity.* Cambridge, Mass.: Harvard University Press, 1996.

Burton, Sir Richard, trans. *The Illustrated Kama Sutra, Ananga-Ranga, Perfumed Garden: The Classic Eastern Love Texts.* Rochester, Vt.: Park Street Press, 1987.

Butterfield, Fox, and Mary B. W. Tabor. "Woman in Florida Rape Inquiry Fought Adversity and Sought Acceptance," *The New York Times,* April 17, 1991, p. A17.

Cado, S., and H. Leitenberg. "Guilt Reactions to Sexual Fantasy During Intercourse," *Archives of Sexual Behavior,* no. 19, 1990, pp. 49–63.

Cameron, Anne. *Daughters of Copper Woman.* Vancouver, B.C.: Press Gang Publishers, 1981.

Cantarella, Eva. *Pandora's Daughters: The Role and Status of Women in Greek and Roman Antiquity.* Baltimore: Johns Hopkins University Press, 1987.

Carlson, E. R., and C. E. H. Coleman. "Experiential and Motivational Determinants of the Richness of an Induced Sexual Fantasy," *Journal of Personality,* 1977, pp. 528–42.

Carroll, Lewis. *Alice in Wonderland and Through the Looking Glass.* 1865, 1871. New York: Quality Paperback Book Club, 1994.

Chang, Jolan. *The Tao of Love and Sex: The Ancient Chinese Way to Ecstasy.* New York: Penguin, 1991.

Charters, Ann, ed. *The Portable Beat Reader*. New York: Penguin, 1992.

Chen, Constance M. *"The Sex Side of Life": Mary Ware Dennett's Pioneering Battle for Birth Control and Sex Education*. New York: The New Press, 1996.

Chesler, Ellen. *Woman of Valor: Margaret Sanger and the Birth Control Movement in America*. New York: Simon & Schuster, 1992.

Chesler, Phyllis. *Mothers on Trial: The Battle for Children and Custody*. San Diego: Harvest, 1986.

Chopin, Kate. *The Awakening*. 1899. New York: Bantam, 1989.

Claiborne, William. "Nicole Simpson's Character Attacked," *The Washington Post*, October 1996.

Conway, Jill Ker. *The Road from Coorain*. New York: Vintage, 1990.

Crewdson, John. *By Silence Betrayed: Sexual Abuse of Children in America*. Boston: Little, Brown, 1988.

Cullen, Countee. *The Lost Zoo*. Englewood Cliffs, N.J.: Silver Burdett Press, 1992.

Daniélou, Alain. *The Complete Kama Sutra: The First Unabridged Modern Translation of the Classic Indian Text by Vatsyayana*. Rochester, Vt.: Park Street Press, 1994.

Degler, Carl N. "What Ought to Be and What Was: Women's Sexuality in the Nineteenth Century," *American Historical Review* 79, no. 5, December 1974, pp. 1467–91.

Dening, Sarah. *The Mythology of Sex: An Illustrated Exploration of Sexual Customs and Practices from Ancient Times to the Present*. New York: Macmillan, 1996.

Douglas, Ann. *The Feminization of American Culture*. New York: Knopf, 1977.

Douglas, Nik, and Penny Slinger. *The Erotic Sentiment in the Painting of India and Nepal*. Rochester, Vt.: Park Street Press, 1989.

Duras, Marguerite. *The Lover*. Glasgow: William Collins Sons & Co., 1985.

Duvall, Evelyn Millis. *Love and the Facts of Life*. New York: Association Press, 1963.

Dworkin, Andrea. *Intercourse*. New York: Free Press, 1987.

———. *Pornography: Men Possessing Women*. New York: E. P. Dutton, 1989.

Eisenstein, Zillah R. *The Female Body and the Law*. Berkeley: University of California Press, 1988.

Eisler, Riane. *The Chalice and the Blade: Our History, Our Future*. New York: Harper-Collins, 1987.

Eliade, Mircea. *Rites and Symbols of Initiation: The Mysteries of Birth and Rebirth*. 1958. Translated by Willard R. Trask. Woodstock, Conn.: Spring Publications, 1995.

Eliot, George. *Middlemarch*. 1872. Middlesex, U.K.: Penguin, 1984.

———. *The Mill on the Floss*. 1880. Oxford: Oxford University Press, 1980.

Ellis, Henry Havelock. *Psychology of Sex: A Manual for Students*. New York: Ray Long and Richard Smith, Inc., 1933.

Faderman, Lillian. *Odd Girls and Twilight Lovers: A History of Lesbian Life in Twentieth-Century America*. New York: Penguin, 1992.

Falk, Candace. *Love, Anarchy, and Emma Goldman*. New York: Holt, 1984.

Fallon, Beth. "Chambers's Defense: Tale of a Cowardly Victim," *New York Post,* December 5, 1986, p. 9.

Ferry, David, trans. *Gilgamesh: A New Rendering in English Verse.* New York: Farrar, Straus and Giroux, 1992.

Fisher, Helen E. *The Sex Contract: The Evolution of Human Behavior.* New York: Morrow, 1982.

Foucault, Michel. *The History of Sexuality: An Introduction, Volume One.* 1978. Translated by Robert Hurley. New York: Vintage, 1990.

Frank, Anne. *The Diary of a Young Girl: The Definitive Edition.* 1947. Edited by Otto H. Frank and Mirjam Pressler. New York: Anchor, 1995.

Freedman, Samuel G. "Sexual Politics and a Slaying: Anger at Chambers's Defense," *The New York Times,* December 4, 1986, p. A1.

Freud, Sigmund. *Introductory Lectures on Psycho-Analysis.* 1917. Edited by James Strachey. New York: Norton, 1989.

Friday, Nancy. *My Secret Garden: Women's Sexual Fantasies.* 1976. London: Quartet Books, 1985.

————. *Women on Top: How Real Life Has Changed Women's Sexual Fantasies.* New York: Simon & Schuster, 1991, 1993.

Gay, Peter. *The Bourgeois Experience: Victoria to Freud.* Vol. 2, *The Tender Passion.* New York: Oxford University Press, 1986.

Gay, Peter, ed. *The Freud Reader.* New York: Norton, 1989, 1995.

Gimbutas, Marija. *The Language of the Goddess.* San Francisco: Harper & Row, 1989.

Gittelsohn, Rabbi Roland B. *Consecrated Unto Me: A Jewish View of Love and Marriage.* New York: Union of American Hebrew Congregations, 1965.

Goleman, Daniel. "Standard Therapies May Help Only Impulsive Spouse Abuse," *The New York Times,* June 22, 1994, p. C11.

Gordon, Linda. *Woman's Body, Woman's Right: Birth Control in America.* New York: Penguin, 1990.

Gordon, Michael. *From an Unfortunate Necessity to a Cult of Mutual Orgasm: Sex in American Marital Education Literature, 1830–1940.* New York: Jones M. Hensling, 1978.

Grahn, Judy. *Edward the Dyke and Other Poems.* Oakland, Calif.: Women's Press Collective, 1971.

Griffin, Susan. *Pornography and Silence: Culture's Revenge Against Nature.* New York: Harper & Row, 1981.

Gutierrez, Ramon A. *When Jesus Came, the Corn Mothers Went Away: Marriage, Sexuality, and Power in New Mexico, 1500–1846.* Stanford: Stanford University Press, 1992.

Hahn, Emily. *Once Upon a Pedestal.* New York: Meridian, 1975.

Harding, Esther. *The Way of All Women: A Psychological Interpretation.* 1933. New York: Longmans, Green, 1950.

Heller, Anne Conover. "Jennifer Levin and Robert Chambers: A Walk with Love and Death," *Mademoiselle,* January 1987, p. 145.

Hemingway, Ernest. *For Whom the Bell Tolls.* 1940. New York: Scribner, 1995.

Herodotus. *Book One: The Histories.* Translated by Aubrey de Selincourt. London: Penguin (1954 English), 1996.

Hill, Bridget. *Eighteenth Century Women: An Anthology.* London: Allen and Unwin, 1987.

Hite, Shere. *The Hite Report on Female Sexuality.* New York: Macmillan, 1976.

Hollander, Xaviera, with Robin Moore and Yvonne Dunleavy. *The Happy Hooker.* New York: Dell, 1972.

Iaciofano, Carol E. "Women Know Thyself [sic]: A Fight Against the Book Banners," *Boston Herald American,* August 28, 1981.

Isherwood, Christopher. *Christopher and His Kind.* 1976. New York: North Point Press, 1996.

"J" [Terry Garrity]. *The Sensuous Woman: The First How-To Book for the Female Who Yearns to Be All Woman.* New York: Dell, 1969.

Johnson, Kirk. "Levin Diary Is at Center of Raging Legal Debate," *The New York Times,* December 26, 1986, p. B3.

Jones, J. C., and D. H. Barlow. "Self-Reported Frequency of Sexual Urges, Fantasies, and Masturbatory Fantasies in Heterosexual Males and Females," *Archives of Sexual Behavior,* no. 19, 1990, pp. 269–79.

Jong, Erica. *Fear of Flying.* 1973. New York: Signet, 1988.

Joyce, James. *A Portrait of the Artist as a Young Man.* 1916. New York: Bantam, 1992.

Kelsey, Morton, and Barbara Kelsey. *Sacrament of Sexuality.* Rockport, Mass.: Element, 1986, 1991.

Kerouac, Jack. *On the Road.* 1957. New York: Penguin, 1991.

Kimberly-Clark Corporation. The Life Cycle Library. Vol. 1, "The Miracle of You." Vol. 2, "Your Years of Self-discovery." Vol. 3, "You and Your Daughter." Vol. 4, "The Years of Independence." Vol. 5, "Getting Married." Vol. 6, "Your First Pregnancy." Neehah, Wis.: Kimberly-Clark Corporation, 1969, 1970, 1973.

Kinsey, Alfred C., Wardell B. Pomeroy, Clyde E. Martin, and Paul H. Gebhard. *Sexual Behavior in the Human Female.* Philadelphia: W. B. Saunders, 1953.

Klein, Viola. *The Feminine Character: History of an Idealogy.* New York: International Universities Press, 1949.

Krafft-Ebing, Richard von. *Abberations of Sexual Life: The Psychopathia Sexualis.* London: Panther, 1951.

Ladas, Alice Kahn, Beverly Whipple, and John D. Perry. *The G Spot: And Other Recent Discoveries About Human Sexuality.* New York: Dell, 1974.

Lankford, Mary D. *Quinceañera: A Latina's Journey to Womanhood.* Brookfield, Conn.: Millbrook Press, 1994.

Lanval, Marc. *An Inquiry into the Intimate Lives of Women.* New York: Cadillac Publishing, 1950.

Lao Tzu. *Te Tao Ching.* Translated by D. C. Lau. London: Penguin, 1963.

Laqueur, Thomas. *Making Sex: Body and Gender from the Greeks to Freud.* Cambridge, Mass.: Harvard University Press, 1990.

Lauersen, Niels, and Eileen Stukane. *You're in Charge: A Teenage Girl's Guide to Sex and Her Body.* New York: Fawcett Columbine, 1993.

Laurino, Maria. "Prosecuting Jennifer Levin's Killer," *Ms.,* September 1987, pp. 70–113.

Lawrence, D. H. *Sons and Lovers*. 1913. London: Penguin, 1992.

Lawrence, Frieda. *Not I, But the Wind . . .* 1934. London: Granada Press, 1983.

Leach, William. *True Love and Perfect Union: The Feminist Reform of Sex and Society.* Middletown, Conn.: Wesleyan University Press, 1989.

Lenin, V. I. *The Emancipation of Women*. 1934. New York: International Publishers, 1984.

Lessing, Doris. *Martha Quest: A Novel*. 1952. New York: HarperPerennial, 1995.

Lewinsohn, Richard. *A History of Sexual Customs*. Translated by Alexander Mayce. New York: Harper & Brothers, 1958.

Luker, Kristin. *Dubious Conceptions: The Politics of Teenage Pregnancy*. Cambridge, Mass.: Harvard University Press, 1996.

Lysebeth, André Van. *Tantra: The Cult of the Feminine*. York Beach, Maine: Samuel Weiser, 1995.

McAlary, Mike, and Marianne Arneberg. "Suspect: Death Was Accident During Sexual Tryst in Park," *Newsday*, August 29, 1986, p. 3.

McCarthy, Mary. *The Group*. 1963. San Diego: Harcourt Brace, 1991.

————. *Memories of a Catholic Girlhood*. 1957. New York: Penguin, 1985.

Maddox, Brenda. *D. H. Lawrence: The Story of a Marriage*. New York: Simon & Schuster, 1994.

Malinowski, Bronislaw. *The Sexual Life of Savages in North-western Melanesia*. 1929. Boston: Beacon Press, 1987.

Marcus, Steven. *The Other Victorians: A Study of Sexuality and Pornography in Mid-Nineteenth-Century England*. New York: Basic Books, 1974.

Mason, Michael. *The Making of Victorian Sexuality*. New York: Oxford University Press, 1994.

Masters, Brooke A. "Women Drinking Like Men, College Alcohol Study Finds; Number Intent on Getting Intoxicated Soars," *The Washington Post*, June 8, 1991, p. A1.

Masters, William H., and Virginia E. Johnson. *Human Sexual Response*. New York: Little, Brown, 1966.

Masters, William H., Virginia E. Johnson, and Robert C. Kolodny. *Human Sexuality*, 4th ed. New York: HarperCollins, 1992.

Maynard, Rebecca A., ed. *Kids Having Kids: A Robin Hood Foundation Special Report on the Costs of Adolescent Childbearing*, 1996.

Mead, Margaret. *Male and Female: A Study of the Sexes in a Changing World*. 1949. New York: Dell, 1973.

————. *Sex and Temperament in Three Primitive Societies*. 1935. New York: Dell, 1971.

Mernissi, Fatima. *Beyond the Veil: Male-Female Dynamics in Modern Muslim Society*. Bloomington: Indiana University Press, 1987.

Meyers, Carol. *Discovering Eve: Ancient Israelite Women in Context*. New York: Oxford University Press, 1988, 1991.

Mitchell, Claudia. "Woman Confident She'll Recruit More Parents in Book-Banning Campaign," *The Bellevue American*, April 10, 1979.

Mitchell, Margaret. *Gone With the Wind*. 1936. New York: Warner, 1993.

Montagu, Ashley. *Coming into Being Among the Australian Aborigines: A Study of the Procreative Beliefs of the Native Tribes of Australia.* 1937. London: George Routeledge and Sons, 1976.

Morgan, Elaine. *The Descent of Woman.* New York: Bantam, 1972, 1979.

Morgan, Robin. *The Demon Lover: On the Sexuality of Terrorism.* New York: Norton, 1990.

Morrow, L. "The Fascination of Decadence," *Time,* September 10, 1979, pp. 85–86.

Mumford, John. *Ecstasy Through Tantra.* St. Paul, Minn.: Llewellyn Publications, 1995.

Nabokov, Vladimir. *Lolita.* 1955. New York: Vintage, 1989.

Oberman, Michelle, and Richard Delgado. "At Issue: Statutory Rape Laws," *American Bar Association Journal,* August 1996, pp. 86–87.

Orenstein, Peggy. *Schoolgirls: Young Women, Self-Esteem, and the Confidence Gap.* New York: Anchor, 1994.

Pearl, Mike, and Michael Shain. "Battle Over Jenny's Diary," *New York Post,* December 5, 1986, p. 9.

Pipher, Mary. *Reviving Ophelia: Saving the Selves of Adolescent Girls.* New York: Ballantine, 1995.

Plath, Sylvia. *The Bell Jar.* 1971. New York: Bantam, 1981.

Pomeroy, Sarah B. *Goddesses, Whores, Wives and Slaves: Women in Classical Antiquity.* New York: Schocken, 1995.

Ranke-Heinemann, Uta. *Eunuchs for the Kingdom of Heaven: Women, Sexuality, and the Catholic Church.* Translated by Peter Heinegg. New York: Penguin, 1991.

Rawson, Philip. *Tantra: The Indian Cult of Ecstasy.* London: Thames and Hudson, 1993.

Rayor, Diane J., trans. *Sappho's Lyre: Archaic Lyric and Women Poets of Ancient Greece.* Berkeley: University of California Press, 1991.

Reage, Pauline. *Story of O.* New York: Grove Press, 1978.

Reed, Evelyn. *Woman's Evolution from Matriarchal Clan to Patriarchal Family.* New York: Pathfinder Press, 1975.

Reid, Daniel P. *The Tao of Health, Sex and Longevity: A Modern Practical Guide to the Ancient Way.* New York: Fireside, 1989.

Roiphe, Katie. *The Morning After: Sex, Fear and Feminism on Campus.* Boston: Little, Brown, 1993.

Rose, Phyllis. *Parallel Lives: Five Victorian Marriages.* New York: Vintage, 1983.

Roth, Philip. *Goodbye, Columbus, and Five Short Stories.* 1959. New York: Vintage, 1993.

Rothman, Ellen K. *Hands and Hearts: A History of Courtship in America.* Cambridge, Mass.: Harvard University Press, 1984.

Rousseau, Jean-Jacques. *The Confessions.* 1781. Translated by J. M. Cohen. London: Penguin, 1953.

Salinger, J. D. *The Catcher in the Rye.* 1945. Boston: Little, Brown, 1991.

Sanday, Peggy Reeves. *A Woman Scorned: Acquaintance Rape on Trial.* New York: Doubleday, 1996.

Saraswati, Sunyata, and Bodhi Avinasha. *Jewel in the Lotus: The Sexual Path to Higher Consciousness.* Taos, N.Mex.: TanTrika International, 1994.

Scholem, Gershom, ed. *Zohar: Book of Splendor.* New York: Schocken, 1949.

Shannon, T. W. *The Ethics of the Unmarried, or Spooning.* Marietta, Ohio: S. A. Mullikin Company, 1913.

Sherfey, Mary Jane. *The Nature and Evolution of Female Sexuality.* New York: Random House, 1972.

Shostak, Marjorie. *Nisa: The Life and Words of a !Kung Woman.* New York: Random House, 1981, 1983.

Sissa, Giulia. *Greek Virginity.* Cambridge, Mass.: Harvard University Press, 1990.

Smith, Betty. *A Tree Grows in Brooklyn.* 1943. New York: HarperPerennial, 1992.

Stone, Hannah, and Abraham Stone. *A Marriage Manual: A Practical Guide-Book to Sex and Marriage.* New York: Simon & Schuster, 1935.

Stopes, Marie Carmichael. *Married Love or Love in Marriage.* New York: Eugenics Publishing Co., 1918, 1927.

Strain, Frances Bruce. *Sex Guidance in Family Life Education: A Handbook for the Schools.* New York: Macmillan, 1942.

Suehsdorf, Adie, ed., and Child Study Association of America. *What to Tell Your Children About Sex.* New York: Permabooks, 1958.

Tampax Incorporated. *Accent on You: Your Personal Questions Answered About Menstruation.* New York: Tampax, Inc., 1971, 1973.

Tannahill, Reay. *Sex in History.* Chelsea, Md.: Scarborough House, 1992.

Tantra: A Pillow Book. New York: HarperCollins, 1995.

Taylor, Rattray G. *Sex in History.* New York: Vanguard Press, 1954.

Thomas, William I. *The Unadjusted Girl with Cases and Standpoint for Behavior Analysis.* New York: Harper & Row, 1967.

Thompson, Sharon. "Putting a Big Thing Into a Little Hole: Teenage Girls' Accounts of Sexual Initiation," *Journal of Sex Research,* 27, no. 3, August 1990, pp. 341–61.

Trexler, Richard C. *Sex and Conquest: Gendered Violence, Political Order, and the European Conquest of the Americas.* Ithaca, N.Y.: Cornell University Press, 1995.

Trilling, Diana, ed. *The Portable D. H. Lawrence.* 1947. New York: Penguin, 1977.

Vance, Carole S. *Pleasure and Danger: Exploring Female Sexuality.* 1984. London: Pandora Press, 1992.

Vicinus, Martha, ed. *Suffer and Be Still: Women in the Victorian Age.* Bloomington: Indiana University Press, 1973.

Walker, Alice, and Pratibha Parmar. *Warrior Marks: Female Genital Mutilation and the Sexual Blinding of Women.* San Diego: Harvest Books, 1996.

Whitehead, Barbara Dafoe. "The Failure of Sex Education," *The Atlantic Monthly,* October 1994, pp. 55–80.

Williams, Selma R., and Pamela J. Williams. *Riding the Nightmare: Women and Witchcraft from the Old World to Colonial Salem.* New York: HarperPerennial, 1992.

Williams, Tennessee. *A Streetcar Named Desire.* New York: Limited Editions Club, 1982.

Wolfe, Thomas. *Look Homeward, Angel: A Story of the Buried Life.* 1929. New York: Simon & Schuster, 1995.

Wolff, Tobias. *This Boy's Life: A Memoir.* New York: Harper & Row, 1990.

Wood, Abigail. "Young Living," *Seventeen,* June 1970, p. 140.

Wright, Helena. *The Sex Factor in Marriage: A Book for Those Who Are About to Be Married.* New York: Vanguard Press, 1931.

Index

ABOUT THE AUTHOR

NAOMI WOLF lives in Washington, D.C., with her husband and daughter. Her first two books, *The Beauty Myth* and *Fire with Fire*, international bestsellers, were both *New York Times* Notable Books of the Year. Her essays appear regularly in *The New Republic*, *The New York Times*, *The Washington Post*, *Glamour*, *Ms.*, and other publications. She has lectured widely about women's issues, and taught a course on the language of politics at George Washington University, where she is a Visiting Scholar.

ABOUT THE TYPE

This book was set in Weiss, a typeface designed by
German artist Emil Rudolf Weiss (1875–1942). The
designs of the roman and italic were completed in
1928 and 1931, respectively. The Weiss types are rich,
well balanced, and even in color, and they reflect the
subtle skill of a fine calligrapher.